Automatic identification and data collection systems

Automatic identification and data collection systems

Jonathan Cohen

McGRAW-HILL BOOK COMPANY

London · New York · St Louis · San Francisco · Auckland
Bogotá · Caracas · Lisbon · Madrid · Mexico · Milan
Montreal · New Delhi · Panama · Paris · San Juan
São Paulo · Singapore · Sydney · Tokyo · Toronto

Published by
McGRAW-HILL Book Company Europe
Shoppenhangers Road, Maidenhead, Berkshire, SL6 2QL, England
Telephone 0628 23432
Fax 0628 770224

British Library Cataloguing in Publication Data
Cohen, Jonathan
  Automatic Identification and Data
  Collection Systems
  I. Title
  006.4

  ISBN 0-07-707914-0

Library of Congress Cataloging-in-Publication Data
Cohen, Jonathan
  Automatic identification and data collection systems/Jonathan Cohen
    p.   cm.
  Includes bibliographical references and index.
  ISBN 0-07-707914-0
  1. Optical character recognition devices. 2. Automatic data collection
    systems. 3. Computerized instruments.   I. Title.
  TA1640.C64   1994
  006—dc20   93-38078
                                                                     CIP

Copyright © 1994 McGraw-Hill International (UK) Limited. All rights reserved. No part of this publication may be reproduced, stored in a retrieval system, or transmitted, in any form or by any means, electronic, mechanical, photocopying, recording, or otherwise, without the prior permission of McGraw-Hill International (UK) Limited.

12345 CUP 987654
Typeset by Datix International Limited, Bungay, Suffolk
and printed and bound at the University Press, Cambridge

*To my darling parents,
Loretta and Gerald*

Contents

Preface	**xiii**
Acknowledgements	**xvii**

PART ONE AUTOMATIC IDENTIFICATION AND DATA COLLECTION IN INFORMATION SYSTEMS

1 Basic principles of data collection systems — **3**
  1.1 When to automate data collection — 3
  1.2 Basic principles and devices — 7
  1.3 Summary — 13

2 An introduction to automatic identification technologies — **15**
  2.1 The concept and its components — 15
  2.2 Bar code technology — 20
  2.3 Optical character recognition — 22
  2.4 Magnetic ink character recognition — 25
  2.5 Magnetic stripes — 25
  2.6 Smart cards — 29
  2.7 Memory cards — 32
  2.8 Radio frequency tags/transponders — 32
  2.9 Vision systems — 36
  2.10 Voice recognition — 38

3 Interfacing automatic identification and data collection systems — **40**
  3.1 Introduction — 40
  3.2 Interfacing auto-ID readers — 41
  3.3 Interfacing data collection devices — 43
  3.4 Radio frequency data communications — 45
  3.5 Electronic data interchange — 48

PART TWO INTRODUCTION TO BAR CODE TECHNOLOGY

4 Basic terminology — **55**
  4.1 Symbologies and their characteristics — 55
  4.2 Resolution and density — 59
  4.3 Colours and contrast — 61
  4.4 Materials — 61
  4.5 Reliability — 63

5 Principal symbologies — 67
- 5.1 Universal product code (UPC) — 67
- 5.2 European article number (EAN-13) — 69
- 5.3 Code 39 — 69
- 5.4 Interleaved 2 of 5 — 70
- 5.5 Code 128 — 72
- 5.6 Codabar — 73

6 Printing bar codes — 74
- 6.1 On-site versus off-site printing — 74
- 6.2 A framework for analysing printing techniques — 75
- 6.3 The film master — 76
- 6.4 Wet-ink printing methods — 77
- 6.5 Toner printing methods — 78
- 6.6 Photographic composition — 79
- 6.7 Impact dot matrix printers — 80
- 6.8 Direct thermal printing — 80
- 6.9 Thermal transfer printing — 81
- 6.10 Inkjet (non contact) printing — 82

7 Reading devices — 83
- 7.1 An introduction to reading technologies — 83
- 7.2 The light pen and slot reader — 86
- 7.3 CCD — 88
- 7.4 Laser technology — 88
- 7.5 Influences on and the measure of reading success — 91

8 Quality assurance and analysis — 93
- 8.1 Introduction — 93
- 8.2 Quality analysis devices — 94
- 8.3 Quality assurance parameters — 94
- 8.4 Analytical methods — 95
- 8.5 Common production mistakes — 97
- 8.6 Existing standards — 99

PART THREE   DATA COLLECTION DEVICES

9 Programmable controllers — 103
- 9.1 Introduction — 103
- 9.2 The PLC as a data collector — 104
- 9.3 Connecting the PLC to a host system — 109
- 9.4 SCADA – supervisory control and data acquisition — 110

10	**Portable data terminals**	**114**
	10.1 Portable data terminals – a comparative framework	114
	10.2 Auto-ID interfaces	119
	10.3 Software design considerations	119
11	**Computerized time and attendance, access control and shop floor terminals**	**121**
	11.1 Introduction	121
	11.2 Hardware configuration	121
	11.3 Communications interface and application software	123
	11.4 Time and attendance	126
	11.5 Shop floor terminals	128
	11.6 Access control	128
12	**Other data collection devices**	**130**

PART FOUR APPLICATIONS

13	**Military and security related applications**	**135**
	13.1 LOGMARS	135
	13.2 Guard patrols	135
	13.3 Crowd control	137
	13.4 Integrated access control	138
14	**Data collection from the factory floor**	**141**
	14.1 Data collection from the factory floor – an overview	141
	14.2 Production time management and work in progress	143
	14.3 Data collection from automated manufacturing processes	146
	14.4 Quality control	149
	14.5 Warehouse management	153
	14.6 'Just-in-time'	156
15	**Trade and service applications**	**157**
	15.1 Retail	157
	15.2 Marketing systems	159
	15.3 Field service systems	160
	15.4 Parcel and file tracking systems	161
	15.5 Direct mailing	162
	15.6 Automatic identification and data collection in hospitals	164
16	**Specialized applications**	**167**
	16.1 Agriculture	167
	16.2 Transportation	169

	16.3	Aviation	172
	16.4	Libraries	173

PART FIVE   THE PLANNING, DESIGN AND IMPLEMENTATION OF DATA COLLECTION SYSTEMS

17   Initial stages — 177
- 17.1   Gathering information — 177
- 17.2   Site surveys of similar installations — 178
- 17.3   Initial feasibility checks — 181
- 17.4   Convincing others and gaining cooperation — 182
- 17.5   Establishing a budget — 184
- 17.6   Defining system objectives — 185
- 17.7   Economic justification — 185

18   Analysing the existing system — 188
- 18.1   Introduction — 188
- 18.2   Defining system boundaries — 189
- 18.3   Calculating existing throughput — 189
- 18.4   Analysing current working procedures — 190
- 18.5   The existing computerized infrastructure — 191

19   System design and specification — 193
- 19.1   Introduction — 193
- 19.2   Hardware configurations — 193
- 19.3   Software specification and design considerations — 195
- 19.4   Interface design considerations — 198
- 19.5   Data structures — 200
- 19.6   Vendors – request for proposals — 203

20   Implementation — 205
- 20.1   Implementation and integration pitfalls and how to avoid them — 205
- 20.2   Assuring system reliability and backup data collection procedures — 208

21   The design of bar code systems — 211
- 21.1   Symbology, printing and reading interdependence — 211
- 21.2   How to choose your symbology — 214
- 21.3   Bar code label software — 215
- 21.4   Choosing a label — 216
- 21.5   Future uses for your bar code — 217

PART SIX   A LOOK AHEAD

22   Future trends and developments   221
   22.1   Future trends for automatic identification   221
   22.2   Future trends for data collection   223
   22.3   Two-dimensional bar codes   224
   22.4   Signature recognition   227
   22.5   Automatic recognition of fingerprints   228
   22.6   Pen computing   228
   22.7   From hardware to hardwear   231
   22.8   Conclusion   232

Bibliography   233
Index   237

Preface

'GIGO' is a well-known acronym in the computing world, standing for 'Garbage In, Garbage Out'. That is, the quality of one's output depends on the quality of one's input. Although today the awareness of and investment in input devices grow rapidly, many existing information systems are still fed by paper and pen. As information technology progresses so too does the requirement to receive *quality information*: that information that is a product of both timely and accurate data. 'Timely' data is data that is reported soon after particular events have occurred or as they occur. 'Accurate' data means reported data that forms a true representation of events that have taken place. Automatic identification and data collection systems are the means of assuring quality information, and it is for this reason that information technologists, industrial engineers as well as other professionals, are now being required to familiarize themselves with every aspect of these systems. The monopoly of the computer monitor and keyboard over the input of data into information systems has come to an end as the automatic capture of data is rapidly expanding into most areas of our lives.

The traditional form of data collection involves the writing of data onto forms and the temporary storage of those forms in files. Later the data from these forms is typed into a computerized system that processes the necessary information for decision-makers. A computerized system enables the storage of vast amounts of data on magnetic or other special media, and the immediate retrieval and quick process of any part of such stored data. Now, instead of collecting data manually with paper and pen, automatic identification and computerized data collection systems have been implemented in order to automate the Achilles' heel of any information-giving process, its means of input. Such systems are designed to automatically identify and record data about events in a controlled and efficient manner. All aim to significantly reduce, if not to totally eliminate, the human element of the data collection process. Data collection systems greatly simplify the task of reporting events and so allow the end-user to devote more time to skilled tasks and to spend less time involved with the drudgery of clerking.

The goal of this book is to present to the reader the basic principles underlining automatic identification and data collection systems, their place and importance in information systems. Both the existing technologies and the latest developments are discussed. I hope this book will be of great benefit to anyone who is interested in finding out how quality information can be generated automatically in an existing working environment. The information it contains is not merely theoretical; rather, a very strong emphasis has been placed on showing how others have succeeded in implementing and thus benefiting from these systems.

Part One defines what makes up an automatic identification and data collection system and examines its role as part of a wider information-giving process. The basic principles underlying the field are discussed, along with a brief outline of the automatic identification and data collection devices involved. Supplementary and related technologies are also discussed, in order to provide an overall context.

Part Two is devoted entirely to the most commonly implemented automatic identification technology – the bar code – and provides the means to a clear and thorough understanding of this much-misunderstood field. A basic terminology is first defined, then the principal symbologies are explored and their characteristics discussed. Different methods of producing and reading bar codes are presented within a comparative framework. The last chapter in this part deals with the quality assurance of bar codes and discusses some of the existing bar code standards in the industry.

Part Three examines in depth the various data collection devices that exist today, the technology behind them and how they can work in conjunction with the various means of automatic identification. Topics such as hardware, communication and the software configurations of the various devices are examined, as well as some of the variations on these devices that can be found in the market. Part Three also considers the main functional usage of each of the various data collectors.

Part Four presents many detailed examples of well-known and lesser-known applications of the different technologies. In the first part of the book the benefits derived from the implementation of automatic identification and data collection systems are itemized, but this part goes beyond the theoretical material and shows how many areas of trade and industry have implemented such systems, as well as examining the significant advancements achieved by doing so.

Part Five explores how to design and implement a data collection system, from the initial stages of 'selling' the idea to management up to assuring the idea's successful implementation. This part of the book differs from other theoretical texts on the design, implementation and management of information systems in two ways. First, it takes a less theoretical and more practical approach, since the author knows well that some texts in this field present a very comprehensive methodology that cannot always be implemented in its entirety. Second, it considers those known issues of design and implementation that have a special significance for automatic identification and data collection systems. Other, less-known issues unique to these systems are also discussed, as well as how to avoid pitfalls in design and implementation.

Lastly, in Part Six, I address the latest trends and developments in both data collection and automatic identification systems, and examine the directions in which this exciting field is heading.

Acknowledgements

I would like to thank those who helped me during the preparation of the book. A special thanks to Tony Rose, Noam Shuch, Avraham Robinson, M. M., Etzion Cris, Simon Dan, and to Ran Kalush. I would also like to thank my family for putting up with those long hours without me when I was busy at the keyboard.

The pictograms on the cover were produced by courtesy of AIM Europe.

PART ONE
AUTOMATIC IDENTIFICATION AND DATA COLLECTION IN INFORMATION SYSTEMS

1
Basic principles of data collection systems

1.1 When to automate data collection

Before we consider under what circumstances we may wish to automate the task of data collection, let us first define the term 'data collection' itself.

> Data collection is the recording of data items concerning an event or events, at the place where the event occurs and at the time of its occurrence (or thereabouts).

Traditionally the recording of data is either by using paper and pen, or by its direct entry into a computer terminal. In order to clarify the distinction between 'data entry' and 'data collection', let us consider the following example.

A particular information system has as its aim the analysis of failures of a certain product. A field technician records the failure of the product on a form, and reports the following data items: client details, product description, date and time of failure, a description of the problem and how it has been remedied. Later the report is keyed into a computer terminal. Now, when and where were the data collected? Following the above definition of data collection, the *place* at which the collection occurred was the client's address, and the *time*, more or less, at which it occurred was when the failure took place of the particular device concerned. The subsequent typing of the above-mentioned data items from a form into a computerized system is termed *data entry*. Indeed, data entry will always involve the copying of data from one source to another, most commonly from a form to a computer monitor. The actual creation of the original source of data, i.e. the initial report, is *data collection*.

Today most data collection is still performed manually, but there are a number of good reasons to computerize the process, and the major ones now follow.

The importance of the availability of timely data

The time needed to collect data and process it increases with the growth in activity of an organization. In other words greater activity means that larger amounts of data have to be collected. It also means that larger amounts of data have to be processed. The expansion of an organization's activities can and does lead to the upgrading of a computerized system to allow larger storage space for information, to support a larger amount of end-users as well as keeping system response times at an acceptable level. Yet in many instances a bottleneck in a system's information flow is created at its input. An obvious and immediate solution would be to increase the number of personnel involved in the data entry process; it is also the time to consider the automatic capture of data as it is generated.

Sometimes an organization's activity does not increase dramatically, but still the time taken for information production must be decreased substantially to allow the organization to stay ahead in an ever more competitive market. An example of this is the implementation of *just-in-time*, JIT. The introduction of just-in-time would be almost unthinkable without some means of automatically collecting data about events and the immediate reporting of this data to other information consumers in the system. A variation on the theme of just-in-time is *quick response*, a term much used in trade as opposed to manufacturing where JIT originated. In both of these situations different elements act together in the production of a particular service. One element will complete its defined task just at that task's required completion date, eliminating lead times. This is not possible without a smooth flow of information between different elements. Data collection systems are an integral part of the JIT solution. In recent years *electronic data interchange* (EDI: to be discussed in Chapter 3) has played a critical role in JIT.

Total quality management (TQM)

Much has been written about *total quality management* (TQM). This concept, originating in Japan, presents an approach to management based on continual effort to improve quality at every level of a system. In terms of information technology, this means the supply of quality information, as defined in the Preface. An example of this concept in action is *customer order status* (COS). A prime element in the continual effort to improve customer service is not just the reduction of order cycle times but also the provision of prompt and accurate answers to customers' enquiries about the status of their orders. The introduction of a data collection system on a factory floor that has as one of its aims the tracking of the progress of customers' orders is a good example of how progressive information technology fulfils the aims of TQM. A detailed look at COS is taken in Chapter 14.

Data accuracy – closing the loop

Many decisions are based upon estimation, outdated standards and inaccurate data. 'Closing the loop' means incorporating into a system a certain amount of feedback as to the accuracy or effectiveness of decisions made within it. For instance in manufacturing, the actual production cost of a product is based on very many factors including human/machine-hours invested in production, plus raw material costs and energy costs, and also fixed costs such as administration, capital outlay payments, as well as others. Some of these costs are quite dynamic, being dependent on various elements such as which workers were involved in particular production tasks, which machines and so on. Unless data is collected during production tasks, industrial engineers cannot tell how accurate their production and cost planning is. Information concerning actual scrap levels, materials waiting in line for production and actual human/machine-hours invested in production tasks is vital in the fine tuning of production planning. Such data leads not only to more accurate cost accounting, but also to more efficient production. Take the example of the collection of data about percentage rejects per production lot according to machine: it has often been found that while all machines in one production plant can produce all items, percentage rejects are higher for certain items produced on certain machines, only when data is collected on these issues can production efficiency be improved.

Data accuracy – its cost

Some systems cannot tolerate the input of inaccurate data when the price of erroneous data is high or the time required to deal with errors is unacceptable. There are many examples of such systems, the best known being perhaps those where the price of erroneous information may be the loss of a human life. Medical information systems are a good example of this, security systems another. Here data collection systems are implemented in order to greatly reduce the chance of human error by eliminating the need for standard data entry. As I show in the next chapter, auto-ID technologies are instrumental in fulfilling this aim.

The price of erroneous information is also expressed in the time needed to track down the source of error and to verify actual events. Sometimes this task is impossible if events have left no suitable auditing trails. Data collection systems are therefore implemented in order not only to reduce the occurrence of human error, but also to create an audit trail should erroneous data be reported to a system.

Requirements for increasing levels of controls

Today more information systems are required to facilitate greater control mechanisms by supplying more detailed information about events. As a result, increasing amounts of raw data have to be captured when recording such events, making existing processes of data collection lengthier and even infeasible. Data collection systems are introduced to simplify the reporting of data and to reduce the time it takes. Sequential validation (SV), is a case in point. It is basically part and parcel of any good process for tracking the movement of materials round the different areas of an organization. Basically SV demands that information concerning the movement of materials is collected and reported from one station to the next before those materials arrive at that next station. In this way material quantities can be validated at the various stations, an infeasible task for most manual data collection systems.

Capturing data from automated equipment

A common feature in manufacturing is the collection of data concerning the execution of an automated process. More often than not this is achieved by the interfacing of a data collection device, such as a programmable controller, to machinery in order to both monitor and log data in real time as events occur. This would be economically infeasible if it was performed manually.

When tasks are to be performed by unskilled labour

In many different organizations there exists a widespread use of non-professional labour, especially where there is a high turnover of workers. In these situations employees are expected to perform non-skilled or semi-skilled tasks, as well as to record data about the tasks that they perform. Usually actions of the latter kind are the most problematic, especially if workers are unmotivated. In these situations reporting accuracy can be low or even non-existant. Not only this: workers are also required to learn sometimes complicated reporting methods, as well as having to be closely supervised in order to maintain a minimal standard of work. Introducing a data collection system in these circumstances will greatly reduce these burdens. In some instances the introduction of a computerized tool, at first met with some dread, has actually improved the motivation of workers, because placing a data collection device in their hands has been seen as an increase in management's awareness of the workers' relative importance in the system.

Harsh or unusual environmental conditions

Harsh environmental conditions mean that manual data collection is infeasible, and there is no choice except to introduce fully automated data collection systems. Such systems are to be found in hazardous working environments as well as in those with extreme temperatures.

Rate of events

Some events occur at speeds so high that manual data collection is impossible. Thus automatic data collection is essential in, for example, quality control processes on automated production lines.

The need for initial processing in the field

This is a very common reason for computerizing the data collection process. Certain raw data can only be collected after the initial processing of previously collected raw data has occurred. Classic examples are marketing and time study systems. In fact, computerizing the capture of data is worth while whenever the cost of the investment involved is outweighed by the benefits received.

1.2 Basic principles and devices

So far we have defined the concept of data collection and the reasons for computerizing this process. In this section are now presented briefly some of the most common data collection devices. First, though, we must define precisely just what a computerized data collector is.

> A computerized data collector is an independent entity that captures, stores, processes and forwards data to a host computer.

Note that the actual transfer of data can be immediate, for example on-line via radio frequency. It might seem that in such a case the data collector is nothing more than an on-line terminal, but as we see later there exists a distinction between standard on-line terminals and on-line data collectors. In fact there are four basic features of a computerized data collection system:

- means of inputting data
- independent processing capability
- memory capacity for storing data
- data communications to a host system.

It is important at this stage to distinguish carefully between data collection systems and automatic identification systems. Because the systems are complimentary and more often than not integrated together in projects, a tendency has arisen to confuse the two differing technologies and to call one by the name of the other. An automatic identification device is used in data collection or data entry to identify an item without human intervention (apart from, in some cases, the actual operation of the equipment itself). In a sense, auto-ID means giving a computer a pair of eyes or ears. It is important to understand that the actual recording of the data itself is undertaken with a data collection device or data entry terminal.

We can clarify this point by means of an example. A programmable controller (PLC; to be discussed below) can automatically identify items and pass their identity on to a host computer. Yet the PLC itself is the data collector and it can incorporate an automatic identification device such as a bar code reader to perform the task of identification. The PLC then stores this and perhaps other information in its memory and later transmits the required data to a host system. (The full definition and description of an automatic identification system are given in the next chapter.)

There exist three major data collection devices, each with variations. Here each is presented only briefly, pending its detailed discussion later in Chapter 9.

Programmable controller (PLC)

This device (Figure 1.1) is normally found in industrial environments. Its name, however, fails to convey its nature as a collector of data. Indeed the traditional role of the PLC is to monitor and control automatic processes without human intervention. By doing so the PLC communicates with a

Figure 1.1 A programmable controller: Allen Bradley SLC 500 controller. Courtesy Allen Bradley – a Rockwell Company

number of external devices that it is meant to control, receiving the current states of these devices and issuing commands when necessary to control them. To facilitate this the PLC has a number of different types of interface capabilities with a whole range of machinery and other automated equipment. As shown later in Chapter 9, some such interfaces relay the exact or discrete state of a process, for instance operating or not operating, while other types allow the input or output of a range of values, for instance the weight of an item or a reading from a pressure gauge. The PLC comes into its own as a data collecter when it possesses serial communications capability, allowing the reporting of any of the values mentioned above to a host computer for the purpose of process monitoring or, what is more pertinent here, for the logging into a database of various defined events as they happen. In this situation the PLC becomes a part of a *supervisory control and data acquisition system* (SCADA).

The most important characteristic of the PLC in its role as a data collector is its ability to work unattended and to collect data in real time. Yet the extraction of data from the PLC by a host computer can, if so required, be at given time intervals; these may be defined by the user or else *event triggered*, the data being extracted from the PLC following a predefined event. Another unique data collection feature of the PLC is its ability to collect data from numerous inputs, be they sensors, machinery or other PLCs.

In order to understand better the role of a PLC, let us now examine an application of a particular one. Say we have a PLC connected to a personal computer (PC), a weighing scale, a laser bar code scanner, and to a printer. The equipment is located next to a conveyer belt that carries cartons filled with a finished product. On each carton is a small bar code that contains the item number of the product inside the carton. When the carton reaches the laser reader the bar code is read and the decoded item number stored in the PLC's memory. Next the carton passes onto the scale and is weighed. The net weight (the total weight less the weight of the empty carton) is calculated and stored. The PLC then builds a string of data that includes the item number, the net weight, the current date and time, and the product's description. The date and time are extracted from a real-time clock in the PLC, the product description from an item file in the PLC's memory. This data is then sent to the printer, which in turn produces a new label for the carton, as well as to the host computer, which logs the data into a database. This type of use of a PLC and its many variations facilitates the capture of timely information, providing a comprehensive tracking of finished products leaving the production line, as well as the creation and printing of labels for shipment.

The portable data terminal

The portable data terminal (or hand-held terminal) is widely used in the collection of data owing to its portability, which in turn is made possible by its capacity to work from an independent power source. It is used in applications that demand the power and features of a host computer but where environmental circumstances do not permit one to be employed directly. The terminal has an independent processor, RAM, screen, keyboard, data communication ports and the capacity to run programs much like a PC, so much so that the latest generation of these terminals run programs under DOS (a popular PC operating system).

Is then the portable data terminal a data collection device or a small personal computer? Before we answer this question let me confuse you a little further! Another feature of the latest generation of terminals is their ability to work on-line with a host computer via radio frequency. Now we can ask whether the portable data terminal is a small PC or a remote data entry terminal? It is true that as technology advances the distinctions between the various devices become blurred. Yet the portable data terminal is truly a data collection device. Even an advanced DOS-run terminal does not, as a rule, run complete data processing applications, but rather applications that are primarily concerned with the controlled capture of, and initial processing of, data. True, such a device can technically be used as a personal computer, but this is not its usual role. Unlike a typical PC, which has a large memory capacity, a sizeable colour screen and a good-sized keyboard, the portable data terminal has a small memory capacity, a small, narrow, monochrome LCD screen, and an undersized keyboard; it cannot be regarded even as a poor man's laptop computer. Its smallness, though, should not be thought of as a disadvantage, because in order to collect data one does not need a PC, but rather an unobtrusive yet advanced computerized tool, (see Figure 1.2)

As to radio frequency capability, the application program that captures the data is still normally contained in the portable data terminal (unlike a data entry terminal), with data inputted to the portable data terminal being sent on-line to a host system.

To clarify the picture further, here are some distinguishing features between the PLC and the portable data terminal:

– Unlike the portable data terminal, the PLC is a fixed-mount unit normally with no independent power source.
– A PLC can possess analog–digital converters, but a terminal as a rule does not (though see the exception to this rule discussed in Chapter 12).
– A PLC's primary role is to monitor different situations unattended. Terminals are human-operated.
– A PLC can collect data in real time. A portable data terminal works in either batch or on-line modes.

BASIC PRINCIPLES OF DATA COLLECTION SYSTEMS 11

(a)

(b)

Figure 1.2 Portable data terminals from Symbol Technologies: (a) PDT 3300, (b) LDT 3805. Courtesy Symbol Technologies

– A PLC can collect data from a very large amount of sources, sensors and machinery, within a very short period of time. A portable data terminal receives data from its keyboard, its screen or an auto-ID reader.

Computerized time and attendance and shop floor terminals

Like the PLC, the computerized attendance and shop floor terminals are fixed-mount units working from a non-independent power supply (although most have a back-up power supply to sustain them for a limited period of power failure). Unlike the PLC, however, they are operated by an end-user and thus normally do not collect data unattended from automated processes, and this is why they are classified separately. As Chapter 11 shows, these terminals have definite advantages over a regular computer terminal and keyboard or a personal computer in the collection of data from the factory floor. The data collected is normally stored for a period of time in the terminal's memory and only later transmitted to a host computer; in other words these devices operate as batch terminals, (Figure 1.3).

The time and attendance and shop floor terminals share the same hardware and software architecture and yet traditionally are classified separately according to whether their function is collecting time attendance data or other data from the factory floor. When it functions as a computerized time attendance clock the batch terminal normally incorporates a magnetic stripe reader for the identification of an employee's personal identification number or PIN. Once the card is swiped, the clock automatically records the employee ID number plus the date and time of swipe. This information is later uploaded on a periodic basis by a direct connection to a host computer. From here on the data is processed in order to provide attendance reports or even payslips. The same time attendance clock is used in a similar fashion on the factory floor, but here it is called a shop floor terminal. And here the shop floor operator is normally required to enter rather more data than his PIN; data is in fact collected for a wide variety of purposes, such as:

– effective cost accounting through the collection of data concerning actual time invested in production tasks
– monitoring customer order status through the collection of data on which work orders are currently being processed
– maintaining information on materials in progress through the reporting of materials received and consumed
– fault detection
– scrap reporting.

Again in most instances the most important data, such as PINs or work

BASIC PRINCIPLES OF DATA COLLECTION SYSTEMS 13

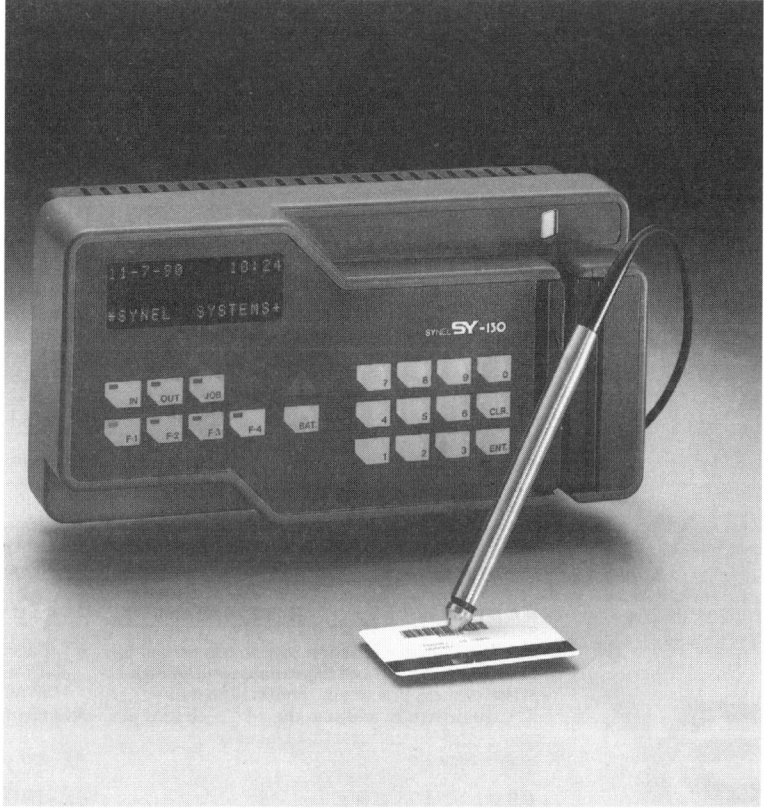

Figure 1.3 Shop floor terminal from Synel Systems. Courtesy Synel Systems, Israel

order numbers, will be encoded into bar codes or magnetic stripes and read into the terminal by a reader, either integral or attached.

Finally, the fixed-mount batch terminals serve two other major purposes, namely access control and logging as well as meal registration. The first of these is also discussed in Chapter 11.

1.3 Summary

Data collection is the initial capture of data about a particular event, at the place and the time of its occurrence. Data collection devices are independent units that collect data in an automatic fashion, with or without human intervention. A data collection device has an independent processing capability, a memory for storing data, and the ability to transmit the data that has been collected to a host system. Such devices are implemented for a host of different reasons; principally, however, it is to allow the automatic, accurate and timely capture of raw data and therefore the drastic reduction in the time needed to produce a credible output. The various forms of data collection devices can be grouped into three general catagories: programmable controllers (PLCs), which are fixed collectors of data that perform their tasks unattended; human-operated portable data terminals which function off an independent power source and therefore can be used in places that regular computers cannot; and time attendance and shop floor terminals. All these devices can, and most usually do, incorporate automatic identification technology, a subject we are about to examine in the next chapter.

2
An introduction to automatic identification technologies

2.1 The concept and its components

Every entity in our daily lives possesses an identity. By giving an entity its identity we achieve two basic goals:

– to distinguish one entity from another
– to provide a certain amount of information that can accurately define the entity itself.

One entity can be distinguished from others either specifically or generically. In the specific case we need to pinpoint an exact object and distinguish it from other similar or even identical ones, and to do this we give it a *personal identification*, a unique code within a defined system, for example an employee number or job order number. In the generic case, on the other hand, one or more objects are identified by their conformity to an *entity type* based their inherent common characteristics, for example a product code.

Sometimes an object is identified by both its entity type and its personal identification code in combination. This leads us to the second goal of identification, that is to provide an entity with an accurate definition. This goal, unlike the first, is not mandatory and is very much dependent on the scope of the system we are working with. In closed systems, where entity identification tasks are performed solely within our own individual working environment, it is not always necessary for an object to be accompanied by entity type indentification, particularly in the case of a system working with one or very few different objects. File tracking is a case in point: in such situations many file storage and tracking systems require files to be identified only with a unique number – in other words, an object's identity has no significance other than in its uniqueness. In systems where a number of different information consumers are present, the type of entity needs to be part of an object's identity, particularly if those information consumers do not have access to a shared database that can provide the entity type after a personal identification has been entered into it. One of the more pertinent issues in all identification systems is: if an object's identification should contain its own definition, how much information is required for the definition? This issue is discussed later on in this chapter.

Whatever the type of identification method chosen, the importance of correctly identifying objects cannot be overemphasized. The identification of an object or event brings with it a series of subsequent actions and decisions, So misidentification can very well lead to the execution of inappropriate actions or the making of incorrect decisions, all of which may well have adverse affects. For instance the incorrect identification of an item at a grocery store may lead that store to overcharge us for that item.

Automatic identification, or 'auto-ID', has three major components:

– encoded data – data that has been transformed to a machine-readable format
– a reader that decodes the encoded data to an analog signal
– a decoder that converts the analog signal to a digital signal and finally to textual characters.

All data that is read by a computer has first to be encoded by a special process, from regular text to a symbol or a unique coding pattern that can be recognized and read by an auto-ID reader. (One exception to this is optical character recognition (OCR), to be discussed later in this chapter; with this technology special characters can already be regarded as an encoded symbol.) This pattern is later decoded by the reader back into readable text characters. Many of these coding patterns are 'for computers only' and illegible to human beings, thus in most cases the patterns are accompanied by a translation that approximates to the pattern itself.

Two major parameters underline all the auto-ID technologies:

– *First read rate* (*FRR*). This is the probability of a successful read (decoding) of the encoded data at the first attempt.
– *Substitution error rate* (*SER*). This is the probability of a misread of the encoded data, or, more specifically, that an encoded character is replaced by an erroneous one.

From these definitions it is clear that any auto-ID technology should have a high FRR with a low SER. Although most auto-ID technologies provide this, a system employing state-of-the-art technology will, if badly planned, lead to poor results for both of these parameters. An understanding of the technology must be clearly backed up by correct procedures of implementation.

As we see in this chapter, there exists a whole host of different auto-ID technologies with a number of variations for most of them. How then, do we choose which technology best suits our needs? Here are some guidelines that are best kept in mind when reviewing the various technologies presented in this chapter.

Industrial standards

Quite a few industrial sectors have already decided upon an industrial standard for the implementation of auto-ID technology. For example, the banking sector has chosen magnetic ink character recognition (MICR) for the automatic identification of cheques, while magnetic stripe technology is used for cash dispenser or ATM financial transactions. In many cases not only has the technology been chosen but a particular standard of that technology has been decided upon. The grocery retail industries not only chose the bar code as the preferred auto-ID method, but decided upon particular bar code standards for labelling products, e.g. UPC in the USA, EAN 13 in Europe. In some cases, the chosen method is not a recommendation but rather a requirement regulated by special industrial committees. There have been occasions where a large commercial body has decided to 'go it alone', as in the case of the US Citibank, which pioneered the 'magic middle card' based on infrared technology for ATM transactions, against the mainstream of magnetic stripes. This failed to gain support from other banks, however, and as a result Citibank today uses those same magnetic stripes that it fought so hard against.

This is not to imply that one should rigidly adhere to pre-chosen solutions; but a careful investigation of existing standards is well advised. Remember that in many cases someone has already done the work for us, and it pays to find out exactly what has been done.

The need to update data

The next major guideline is more technical. Some methods of auto-ID do not facilitate the updating of data once it has been encoded, while others do to a greater or lesser extent. The method of updating, where it is possible, is also a pertinent issue. For instance, a bar code cannot be changed once printed, but printing a bar code is simple and often quick. We see later that the memory card can be updated by data appending, yet its update capability is restricted by its memory capacity; also, while certain forms of *radio frequency* (RF) tags can be updated frequently without any practical limitation, the time updating takes may impose certain constraints on high-speed applications. Thus the three major parameters when considering a technology's ability to update encoded data are:

- the required frequency of updating in a given time period
- the method of updating data
- the time taken to update data.

The amount of data that can be encoded

How much information needs to be encoded in order to identify efficiently a particular event or entity? *Data capacity* and *data density* are two pertinent parameters in this consideration. Data capacity is the maximum amount of data that can be encoded by a particular standard of auto-ID technology, while data density is the maximum amount of data that can be encoded in a given area of media. The usual measurement of the latter of these two parameters is characters per inch (CPI). When we consider which method of auto-ID to implement we have to analyse how much data has to be encoded. Certain methods have severe limitations in this respect, while others, though they are not technically limited, do make reading large amounts of data difficult or expensive. Generally we can classify identification capacity requirements into the following categories:

- 'Licence plate' – a short character string that contains either an entity type code or a personal identification number, or both. In most instances the licence plate acts as a data key or address for a particular record of data in a data file.
- Complete data record of all data items that define a particular entity or event.
- Portable data file – an encoded mobile file containing additional information over and above that needed for identification purposes.

Data security

Is the information to be encoded restricted? Can anyone be allowed to copy it freely? These questions must be answered to choose the right method of auto-ID. Most bar codes can be photocopied and then read. If the bar code is used to encode an item number on the shelf of a supermarket then this limitation has very little importance, but this is not so if the bar code contains a personal identification number that appears on an employee ID card, which in turn is part of a time attendance system.

Most auto-ID technologies provide a greater or lesser degree of data

AN INTRODUCTION TO AUTOMATIC INDENTIFICATION TECHNOLOGIES 19

security. For some methods, data security can be obtained only at a higher price than the standard method of encodation. For instance, there are specially coloured bar codes that cannot be photocopied. However, these bar codes cannot be produced on most printers. Smart cards allow for the encryption of data, yet in these situations data interfacing with a host system becomes a more complex affair.

Some methods of auto-ID do not provide any data security whatsoever. Optical character recognition, where actual printed characters are read, is a case in point (for this reason, special magnetic ink is used to automatically identify cheques – in magnetic ink character recognition).

Data restoration

More advanced auto-ID technologies provide for data restoration or recovery should part of the encoded data become damaged.

Methods of encodation

Among the considerations under this heading are:

– Cost of encodation equipment.
– Technical expertise required to operate the equipment.
– Minimum encodation time required for a given set of data.
– Does the encoded data have to be printed by another method to be human readable? If the encoded data is not printed, then human-interpretable data might later have to be printed onto the media with the encoded data, thus lengthening the production process.

Reading method

The method of decoding data is the acid test of an auto-ID system. For instance, a standard typewriter can be used to produce data that can be read by an optical character reader. The method of encodation is therefore simple and inexpensive, so why use bar codes? The optical character reader can be two, three and more times the price of a bar code reader. However, cost is just one factor in this equation. How is reading performed? Some readers have to actually touch the media on which data is encoded, while others can read data from different distances. Optical auto-ID technologies are all based upon the existence of a line of sight between the encoded data and the reader, but other technologies do not have this limitation. Some auto-ID technologies require the reader to be manually operated for identification to take place, while others also permit an unattended solution whereby items are passed by a reader within a given speed range. Here *access time* is an important parameter, being the miniumum time in which the reader can read and decode the encoded data. The versatility of the method of reading can be the key to a successful auto-ID system. If after implementation a type of reader deemed unsuitable can be changed without changing the method of encodation, then the system is considered to be versatile.

Programmability

Certain auto-ID technologies provide for a degree of programmability. Examples of programmability are:

– The ability to encode data into or read from certain memory storage areas or defined areas of the chosen medium, such as smart cards and magnetic stripes. This feature can be important in keeping data secure or adhering to international data storage and reading standards (such as the three tracks of a magnetic stripe discussed in Section 2.5).
– The ability to manipulate encoded or read data. This is particularly relevant for those technologies that allow encoded data to be updated.

Environmental flexibility

How resilient are the various media and readers to varying environmental conditions? Media can be adversely affected by electromagnetic disturbances, heat, cold, damp and more. Readers also can be affected by these conditions.

2.2 Bar code technology (Figure 2.1)

Part 2 of this book deals entirely with bar code technology, simply because bar codes are clearly the dominant force in auto-ID today. Here, though, bar code technology is compared with other auto-ID technologies. Just why

Figure 2.1 An EAN–13 bar code

the bar code is predominant becomes clear when we look at how it fulfils the considerations presented above.

1. To start with, its substitution error rate is to all intents and purposes zero, and its first read rate above 98 per cent – provided that the system has been correctly planned and its components properly integrated (see Chapter 22).
2. Further, the bar code was the first major auto-ID technology to be widely used. The first bar code type was patented in 1949 in the USA and was later brought into commercial use in the 1960s.
3. In most areas of industry, bar code standards have been established by voluntary industrial committees, which in turn has led to further adoption of the bar code by other bodies and businesses who traditionally follow their industry leaders.
4. However, it is the bar code's production methods and the large selection of reading devices available that have kept it at the forefront. Data can be encoded into bar codes using standard dot matrix and other office printers combined with simple and inexpensive software for on-site production. Bar codes of very high quality can be produced on site at fast print rates using special label printers and bar codes can be printed with standard wet-ink methods off-site. Bar code technology offers a large range of contact and non-contact readers, in either unattended or user-operated working environments.
5. Bar code technology is extremely versatile and easily upgradable.
6. Both numeric and alphanumeric data can be encoded, encodation time is quick, and a good bar code system can be purchased at a very low cost indeed.

On the debit side the bar code's data capacity is greatly limited; in fact, a typical one never extends to more than 20 characters and is usually smaller than this. Theoretically a bar code has no limitation to its length, but one with over 20 characters, even with a high data density, would be very difficult to read. (There is one notable exception to this – the two-dimensional bar code, most bar codes being linear.) Although they can be printed on to most surfaces, bar codes are very susceptible to adverse environmental conditions; there are some unique solutions to the durability problem, but sometimes these are quite expensive. Also, linear bar codes, as opposed to two-dimensional ones, offer no data restoration capability, although as mentioned above there are ways to secure data from being copied. Owing to the widespread availability of bar code readers, the bar code is not recommended as a means of encoding restrictive or sensitive data. Nor is there any way of updating data in a bar code once it is printed.

2.3 Optical character recognition

In recent years there has been an increased use of scanners that transfer printed text to a host computer. This 'computerized photocopying' is not OCR. The read text is stored in the computer and can be retrieved on request, however this data is not stored in the same usable manner as computerized text files. This is because the read text is not composed of ASCII characters (the standard code for many computers); what is produced is a *bit map*, a computerized graphic representation of the printed text. Though the bit map can be pasted into other similar text files, a software package, such as one that checks for spelling mistakes, could make neither head nor tail of such a file. Optical character recognition technology is needed to convert printed textual characters into ASCII characters.

OCR fonts

Optical character recognition is the recognition of printed text by a computer aided by a special OCR reader. However, not all printed text is suitable for OCR readers. Just as each and every one of us has a different form of handwriting, so text can be printed in a vast number of character styles and sizes. The OCR reader has therefore to recognize different character styles, or *fonts*, in order to 'translate' a printed character into an ASCII character. For this purpose, OCR uses a number of well-defined fonts, chiefly OCR-A, comprising of 0 to 9, A to Z and a few special characters, and the more limited OCR-B, consisting of 0 to 9, nine alphanumeric characters and a smaller number of special characters, (Figure 2.2).

OCR character set	
OCR-B1 (MITI)	0 1 2 3 4 5 6 7 8 9 A C E N P S T V X < + > − ¥ . , |
OCR-Multifont — OCR-B1 — 12L/12F — 1403-OCR-A1 — 407-1	¥ 0 1 2 3 4 5 6 7 8 9 > < + #
OCR-B1 Standard	0 1 2 3 4 5 6 7 8 9 C E N S T V X + > < . , |
OCR-A1 (alphanumeric)	0 1 2 3 4 5 6 7 8 9 A B C D E F G H I J K L M N O P Q R S T U V W X Y Z > $ / − + # . ⌐
OCR-A1 Standard	0 1 2 3 4 5 6 7 8 9 A C D M N P R U X Y + / > $. ⌐ |
OCR-A1 NRMA-Eurobanking	0 1 2 3 4 5 6 7 8 9 A C D M N P R U X Y > $ / + # . ⌐ ♪ ¥ ⊣
OCR-A1 Eurobanking	0 1 2 3 4 5 6 7 8 9 C P R U X Z + # / | . ⌐ * ♪ ¥ ⊣

Figure 2.2 OCR fonts

OCR readers

Optical character recognition technology employs a number of different types of readers, each for a different purpose.

PAGE READER

This first appeared in the mid-sixties and was designed to read complete pages of text. It was hoped that the page reader would, in many situations, replace the keyboard in the creation of text files. Today, its principal function is to transfer text between incompatible word processors. It has not caught on, not only because of its high cost, but also because of its high substitution error rate (SER). Thus after a page is read and decoded by OCR software or firmware, postprocessing editing of the translated text is often required to correct mistakes or to determine unrecognized characters.

STUB OR COUPON READER

This more widely used reader is used to read a line of OCR text from a fixed position on paper. This characteristic makes the unit suitable for reading data from utility bills, such as gas and electricity. An example of such an application would be the reading of the client account number and amount payable from a paid bill. The reading is performed by manually passing the document through the reader. There do exist automatic readers that load, read and store bills without human assistance, though as one can imagine they are significantly more expensive.

WAND OR DATA CAPTURE DEVICE

A wand is a rather fat pen that emits light, and is passed manually over the line of text by the user. This device is the least expensive form of OCR reader and the most prevalent. It is found in retail stores as a substitute for a bar code reader.

CCD ARRAY OR LINE CAMERA

Though sometimes classified as an OCR reader this actually falls under the category of machine vision for identification. Therefore it is discussed later on, under vision systems (Section 2.9).

Inks and media

When implementing OCR technology we have to consider a number of very important factors:

- Ink has to be the right colour to give enough contrast between the text and the medium it is printed on. (see Chapter 4).
- If paper is the chosen medium then it is best to use a matt, opaque and flawless sheet at least 0.08 mm thick.
- The printed text should ideally have a data density of 10 characters per inch.

Basic approaches

There are three basic approaches to decoding OCR fonts into ASCII characters:

- *Decision theoretic.* Here the decoder compares the individually read characters to a stored list of characters in its memory, identifying the read character by finding its closest match in the stored list.
- *Syntactic decoding.* This decoding method is based upon a decision tree with each node or decision branch being a comparison of a particular characteristic of the read character against predefined criteria. An example of a node might be the number of holes in the body of the character.
- *Neural network.* This is based upon the mathmatical discipline of neural networks.

Comparison with bar codes

At face value it would seem that OCR is generally a preferable auto-ID technology to that of the bar code. Production does not necessarily require any special software since a lot of printers and even typewriters are able to print OCR fonts. There is little waste of space because, unlike bar codes, OCR data is printed only once whereas bar-coded data is normally printed twice, once in bar code form and again under the bar code in human-readable characters. This feature can be important when a large amount of data has to be printed in a very small space. Unlike OCR fonts, bar codes, if printed with a standard dot matrix printer, wear heavily on the printer head, and printing a bar code normally takes significantly longer than printing an OCR font on the same printer.

Optical character recognition has a more limited use in the market because its substitution error rate (SER) is much higher than that of the bar code. Page readers can in fact reach such high SERs, leading to such extensive data integrity checks after the initial decoding that the response time is increased for each successful read, while the first read rate is reduced. The same is true, to a lesser extent, for the other forms of OCR readers.

These factors, combined with the bar code's strong foothold in the auto-ID world, have held back the spread of OCR technology. OCR, like bar codes, cannot be updated, is highly sensitive to damage and possesses no method of data restoration. This technology has no inherent data security characteristics. Data capacity is equivalent to standard data capacity for written texts, that is from a single character string up to a full page of text.

2.4 Magnetic ink character recognition

Magnetic ink character recognition is a variant of OCR, though here characters are printed with special magnetic ink and are read with magnetic readers as opposed to light pens. Because of this, the reader has to come into contact with the medium being read, so unlike OCR MICR has very few types of reader to offer, the commonest being the stub or coupon reader. Because of the high cost of the readers and the specialized nature of printing with magnetic ink, MICR has very few practical applications other than the automatic identification of bank cheques.

2.5 Magnetic stripes

Magnetic stripe technology is part of our every-day lives, the commonest example being the credit or charge card. With this method of auto-ID data is encoded onto a magnetic stripe that is part of a plastic card or paper ticket.

Encodation

The method of encodation is quite interesting. A magnetic stripe is composed of tiny magnetic particles. Before encodation these particles are in their natural state, with opposite poles adjacent to each other. When exposed to a magnetic flux they reverse their polarity by flipping over, as a north pole becomes south and vice versa. The result, termed *flux reversal*, is that like poles are adjacent to one another. The flux reversal is created by a special form of magnet, a *solenoid*, which is actually a coil of copper wire through which an electric current is passed. The current creates a magnetic field that flips the magnetic particles. The direction of the current in the copper wire determines the polarity of the solenoid, hence the direction of the flip, and therefore their final polarity.

The encodation process of the magnetic stripe involves bringing a solenoid into contact with a magnetic stripe. The magnetic field created by the solenoid is concentrated at a particular point or gap in the wire. This gap is tiny, less than a thousand of an inch, but even so it manages to flip groups of twenty or more particles at a time. The resulting series of flux reversals is a permanent or almost permanent state (see Figure 2.3).

26 AUTOMATIC IDENTIFICATION AND DATA COLLECTION SYSTEMS

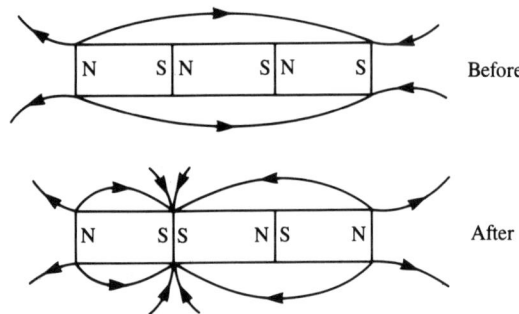

Figure 2.3 Magnetic stripe encoding by flux reversals

Reading

In order to understand the reading or decoding process we need to define a few more terms. The flux reversals are created at constant distances along the magnetic stripe. The distance from one flux reversal to another is known as a *bit cell* (the data density of a magnetic stripe being measured in bits per inch – BPI). A flux reversal at the bit boundary is recognized as a binary 0. However, flux reversals also occur at twice the data density, i.e half way inside a bit cell. These flux reversals receive a binary value of 1. Now we can create a series of 1s and 0s at recognized intervals, allowing us to decode the flux reversals into text characters. This technique is known as *biphase encodation* (Figure 2.4).

In order to read the magnetic stripe another copper coil, this time wrapped round a magnet, is passed over it. The magnetic field produced by the like poles at the bit and half-bit positions causes an electric current to be produced in the copper coil. This affect is the opposite of that in the encodation process and thus is termed as *electromagnetic reciprocity*. The flux reversals cause a current in a particular direction, depending on the

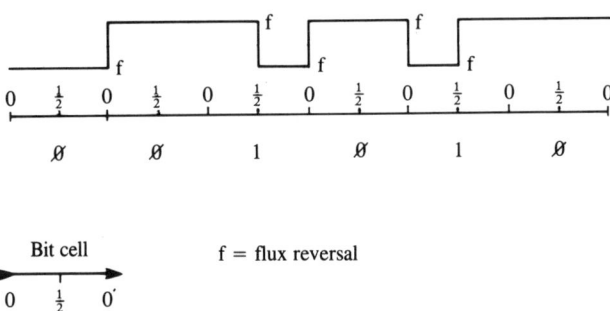

Figure 2.4 Biphase encodation

AN INTRODUCTION TO AUTOMATIC INDENTIFICATION TECHNOLOGIES

polarity of the flux reversal. Inside the reader a circuit detects the peaks in the current as well as its direction. All that is left is to convert the analog signal into a digital binary stream and this, in turn, into text.

The commonest type of conversion of a binary stream to characters is ANSI/ISO BCD. This is no more than a table that contains entries of unique binary streams and the characters that they represent. Within the magnetic stripe there are three tracks within which data can be encoded. The American National Standards Institute have defined the characteristics, functional usage and relative position of these three tracks within the magnetic stripe. Characteristics such as the place within the track where actual encoded data starts, the type of data (numeric or alphanumeric), and data capacity and densities are defined so as to facilitate magnetic stripe cards to be used in open systems. This is similar to the standardization of certain bar codes for certain industries. For instance, track one allows up to 79 characters at a density of 210 BPI. The decoding format for this track is ALPHA 7-BIT, whereas for the other tracks a 5-bit BCD format is used. Track two allows for up to 40 characters to be encoded and track three up to 107 (see Figure 2.5).

Drawbacks

There are inherent problems in the use of magnetic stripe technology, which should be understood before choosing an encoding device or reader.

DURABILITY

Magnetic stripes can be damaged by exposure to foreign magnetic fields, from electric currents or magnetized objects, even a bunch of keys. The ability of the stripe to withstand corruption by other magnetic fields is known as *coercivity*. Both the magnetic medium chosen and the encoder

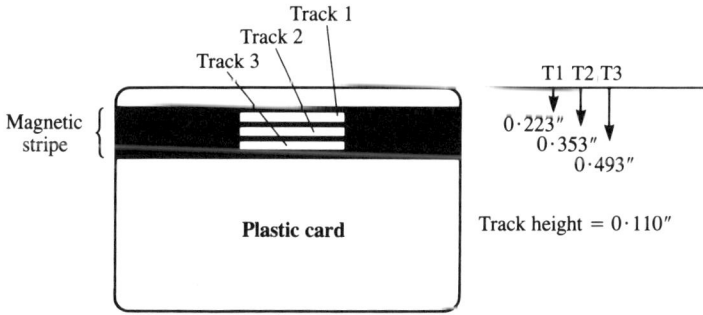

Figure 2.5 Magnetic stripe track locations

used should have a high coercivity if problems are expected in this area. If the magnetic stripe is part of an employee's ID card, which is stored by a time attendance clock and swiped by the worker when entering or leaving the premises, then a high coercivity is not required. But if the card is carried home by the worker and is thus subject to every possible environmental condition then a high-coercivity card (4000 oersteds), should be considered. Another factor that affects the card's durability is the type of read/write head used to read or encode it. Certain non-all-metal heads tend to wear away at the magnetic stripe. These heads are cheaper and thus more commonly used. Pressure against the card is needed to ensure continual good reads. If the life of a magnetic card needs to be long then it is worth investing in all-metal read/write heads.

RELIABILITY OF ENCODATION AND READING

Both encodation and reading are physical processes of passing a read/write head at a given speed over a magnetic stripe. The speed can vary, and this normally can be compensated for automatically, but where a 'jitter' occurs – a sudden and tiny variation in speed, too minute to be caused by the human hand – the result can be a bad encode or misread. There are, however, a number of compensating techniques for this problem, and a reader should be chosen that compensates for jitters at different reading speeds. Always remember that jitters are caused during encodation so it makes no difference whether the reader is a manual or an automatic one.

There are other common mechanical problems that are associated with encoders and readers, which are beyond the scope of this study. A general rule of thumb is a reference from a client. Among the subjects of enquiry are:

– the percentage of bad encodation or misreads
– physical problems that occur while encoding or reading
– the life of the read/write head
– the average life of the card.

Types of reader

The basic reader types for magnetic stripes are:

– Swipers, where the user manually swipes the card through a slot.
– Manual insertion and withdrawal readers.
– Sidewinders, where the card is stationary and the reading head moves.
– Motorized readers, where the card is manually inserted part of the way,

after which the reader draws it in, reads it, and then pushes it a little way out to be withdrawn by the user.

Materials for stripe cards

Magnetic stripe cards are normally composed of one of three types of base materials: paper, polyester or PVC. The first of these is normally used for tickets, for instance train tickets, or for any application not requiring a long-life magnetic stripe card. Paper is also the least expensive of the three base materials. Polyester is normally used for employee ID badges, as this is the most durable of the three materials. PVC is the material used for all credit or charge cards.

Other points

There exist industrial standards for different types of magnetic card applications, which state both the data format and track number to be used. Magnetic stripes are updatable and provide a good level of data security. Encoded data can be, and often is, encrypted within the card. Data can only be copied with an encoder (unlike a bar code, which can be photocopied). Magnetic stripe technology does not provide for any data recovery in the event of a damaged stripe, and as stated earlier, stripes are sensitive to strong magnetic fields as well as to scratches from other objects. By the very nature of the technology, readers require contact with the actual medium and normally require operation by a user. This technology has a certain degree of programmability, because data can be formatted in different ways and located on different tracks.

2.6 Smart cards

A smart card, or IC (integrated circuit) card, is a portable device that is not only used for automatically identifying items, transactions or events, but also can become an integral part of an event by interacting with it. Here we look at *contact* cards, those cards that receive and transmit data by physical contact with a special reader; a variation on the smart card is the RF tag, or *transponder*, which performs basically the same task but receives and transmits data via radio frequency, and this is dealt with in Section 2.8.

The basic smart card

Although termed 'smart cards', these devices can come in many shapes and sizes, not neccessarily as cards. They have the same basic components, however, namely a memory for storage of data, an additional memory for programs, a processor or CPU, and a read/write interface. The smart card's memory is divided into three area types, each of which determines the access to the data stored within. The first memory area allows a reader to freely access its data, the second allows access once a correct password or personal indentification number (PIN) has been verified, and the last area denies access once programmed. This last area normally contains the algorithm to verify PINs. The smart card reading device can come in various forms: an external interface to a host computer, an independent work station, or integrated into another device such as a cash register. (Figure 2.6).

Keyboard and screen versions

A more advanced version of the basic smart card possesses both a keyboard and screen. The keyboard allows the user access to a whole host of additional possibilities including the following:

– The display of data accessed from the smart card's memory.
– The ability to verify a PIN without the need to access a host system.
– The ability to activate a series of functions via function keys on the smart card's keyboard.

Advantages of the smart card

What exactly can a smart card give that other auto-ID technologies either cannot, or can but in a limited fashion?

– *Data capacity*. The smart card can store as little as a few bytes of data up to a portable database of a number of kilobytes.
– *Update ability*. Some versions of the card allow their memories to be updated in real time, either before or after being read.
– *Security*. Smart cards are very hard to counterfeit, and can encrypt data as well as allowing an audit trail to be left.
– *Environmental considerations*. The smart card can read, store, and write data in extreme temperatures and harsh conditions.

From the above we can see that the smart card not only gives out an identity, but also takes on the extra dimension of a data processor. The smart card will not replace conventional auto-ID technologies such as the bar code, since smart card production is a complex affair and is more expensive than that of bar codes. The smart card's market is for applications that demand the automatic identification of data combined with either simple data processing or the retrieval and updating of larger amounts of information than other auto-ID technologies can handle. For this reason the smart card is likely to replace the magnetic stripe in many applications,

AN INTRODUCTION TO AUTOMATIC INDENTIFICATION TECHNOLOGIES 31

(a)

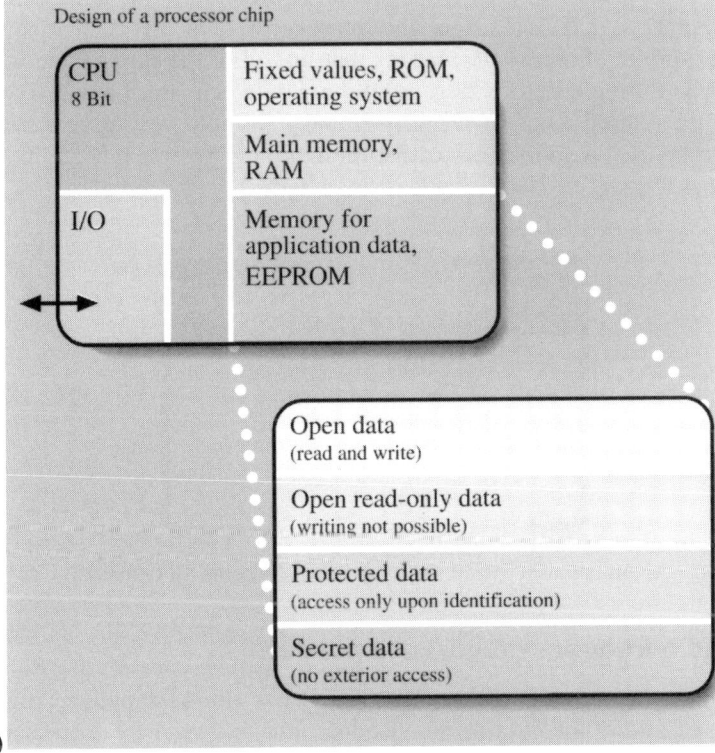
(b)

Figure 2.6 (a) Smart card, (b) Structure of a smart card. Courtesy Glesecke and Devrient

as well as permitting certain uses that until now have proved infeasible with the more conventional forms of auto-ID. The main market for this device is likely to be the financial sector, especially ATMs (automatic telling machines). In France the smart card is already in widespread use with public telephones. One very interesting application of smart cards, in parking control, is presented in Chapter 16.

2.7 Memory cards

A variation on the smart card, the *memory card* (Figure 2.7) was introduced in the early eighties. It is functionally more like the magnetic stripe card than the smart card, as it possesses no data processing capabilities. Yet like the smart card, it can store very large amounts of data and therefore can be referred to as a portable data file. The card's interior is a layer of suspended silver particles; these are burnt by a laser when the card is being written into, so that minute dents are left in the silver layer. Much as with a bar code, data is read by light reflectance (the dents do not reflect light beamed onto them by a laser beam). While memory cards cannot be updated in the same manner as magnetic stripes and smart cards, their vast capacity to hold data (a number of megabytes) means that not all of the card's memory will be utilized during initial writing. Additional data can later be added to and read from unused areas of memory. Finally infrared writing and reading can also be used with memory cards, though these possess inferior memory capacities.

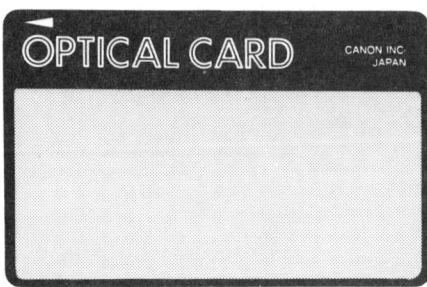

Figure 2.7 Memory card (optical card). Courtesy Cannon, Optical Card Dept

2.8 Radio frequency tags/transponders

This particular auto-ID technology, which has spread rapidly in the last few years, allows for data to be encoded onto and read from special tags via radio frequency (RF). There exist many variations on the theme, but all have the same basic components. First there is the *tag* itself, or *transponder*,

AN INTRODUCTION TO AUTOMATIC INDENTIFICATION TECHNOLOGIES 33

which contains the encoded information. The tag is composed of one or more chips (integrated circuits), which contain the encoded data, and two antennas, one to receive incoming transmissions and one to transmit. The *interrogator*, or reader, is the unit that sends out a signal to as well as receives an incoming transmission from the tag. The interrogator consists basically of two antennas, plus a *radio-frequency unit* (RFU), which both generate a signal as well as decoding the incoming signal from the tag into data. The interrogator also contains a processor that transfers the decoded data to a host system according to a set format, as well as performing the task of the validation of the incoming data (see Figure 2.8).

Encoding

A tag can be encoded in two ways, either within or outside the framework of an application. *Read-only tags* are encoded by the transmittal of a signal at a very short range, up to 1cm. This is done either by the tag vendor or on-site by the customer. More advance tags allow data to be encoded in real time, in which case the tag transmits a signal that is picked up by an interrogator.

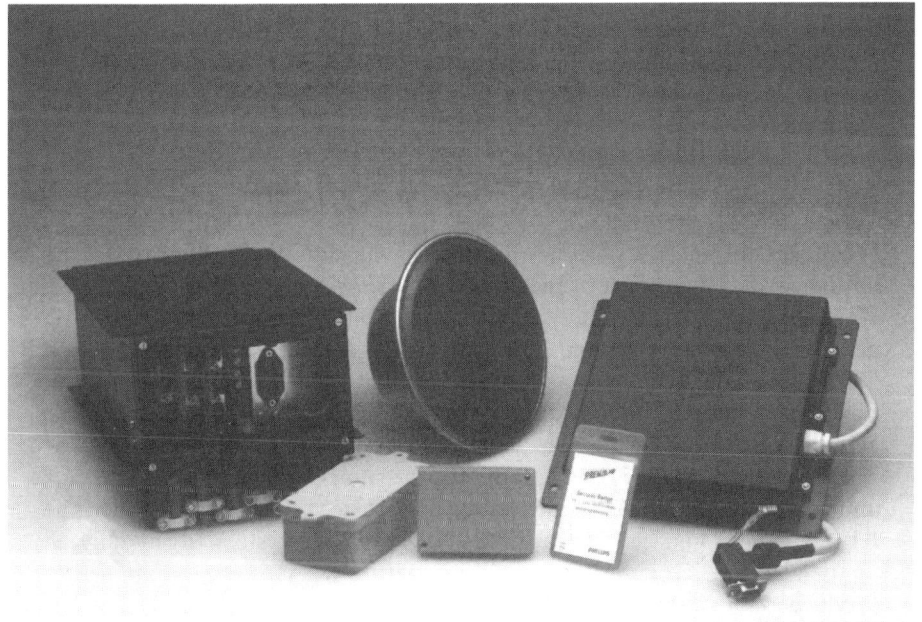

Figure 2.8 Components of an RF tag system: Premid system. Courtesy Saab Automation AB

After the signal is received another signal is sent from the interrogator which results in the encodation of new data in the tag itself. These tags are known as read/write tags.

Active and passive tags

The two main types of RF tags in use today are *active* and *passive*. Once a passive tag is encoded it is applied to an item or person. As soon as the tag enters the transmission or receiving field of the interrogator it receives a signal sent from the interrogator that powers it up. The signal says 'OK, I'm listening, what do you have to say?' At this point the tag sends all or part of the data that has been encoded. As it leaves the transmission field it returns to a dormant state. Meanwhile, the signal that has been sent is decoded into characters and transferred to the host computer by the decoder.

'Active' tags carry their own independent power source, normally a long-life lithium battery. This enables the 'active' tag to receive and store data in real time as opposed to just sending out a fixed signal. It also means that the signal range can be much greater. Unlike with most other forms of auto-ID, the distance between the encoded data and the reader can be quite large. Indeed, RF tag systems that operate on ultra-high frequency (UHF) can reach distances of a few metres (RF tag systems that work on low frequency (LF) rarely exceed a metre).

Implementation

When should such technology be used? The equipment involved is by nature costlier than most of the other auto-ID systems mentioned so far, so RF tag systems are normally implemented where other forms of auto-ID are infeasible or to be found at a great disadvantage. Because information is read by radio frequency, as opposed to light or magnetic fields, physical objects such as cement, wood, mud, asphalt, etc., present no barrier to the actual transmission of the data. Indeed an interrogator can read a tag that is a whole floor above it. Next, most tags are immune to harsh enviroments and can be operable in extreme heat or cold. Also, as mentioned earlier, the RF tag can be updated in real time and an RF tag system is generally an unattended one. Obviously by their very nature RF tags are not applied to products on a supermarket shelf, but rather to items of high intrinsic value, for instance cars on a production line, people or animals. If we look at how an attendance system employing RF tags compares with a similar one based on magnetic stripes, we can see at once that the former system enables 'hands-free' operation: instead of having to swipe a card through a reader a person with an RF tag pinned to his jacket just passes an interrogator and hey presto! he has clocked in. If this may seem an unjustified luxury in many cases, it is by no means so in high-security environments or for identifying lifestock – cows being, as yet, unable to clock on with a magnetic stripe card!

Choice of system

The data capacity of the RF tag can be extremely high indeed, if need be. Again, whether it is so depends on the application. The data capacity requirements of RF tags can range from two or three characters up to a number of kilobytes, making the tags portable databases. Such requirements fall into four general categories:

- *Presence-sensing*: 'Hi I'm here!'
- *Identification*: 'Hi, item number "123456" has just gone by.'
- *Transaction*: a data record containing a number of fields. Normally such tags are updatable.
- *Database*: 'Listen to what I have to tell you,' e.g instructions for automatic machinery.

Let us say that we have decided to implement an RF tag system; what considerations do we have to take into account?

- *Data capacity*. The amount of data needed to fulfil application requirements, i.e. the data capacity required for our tag.
- *Does data have to be updated in real time*? If so we might rule out a non-battery-powered (passive) tag.
- *Range: How far will the interrogator be from the items to be read*? This will help decide both signal strength and signal frequency. (LF or UHF). Active tags can have a stronger signal than 'passive' ones.
- *Access time: how quickly will items pass through the field of transmission*? To know this we have to know how much data is to be sent during a transmission session, the throughput of tags in the system for any given time period as well as the distance between tag and interrogator.
- *Environmental conditions*. RF technology is susceptible to interference ('noise'). Choosing the right frequency is critical here. UHF will give a better performance in this category. However, UHF is more sensitive to other environmental conditions such as the presence of moisture, metals and other common materials.
- *Approval*. RF is state-regulated, so before implementing a system government approval has to be proved by the vendor.

This particular auto-ID technology, unlike the others, requires a great deal of technical expertise to guarantee successful implementation. Though more complex by their very nature, RF tag systems can provide extremely efficient solutions in areas where more conventional forms of auto-ID fail.

Finally, we should note that there exist other methods of transmission for transponders. These are microwave and inductive systems. Microwave tags can provide transmission ranges of up to several metres, have superior *spacial directivity*, that is their read/write area is very well defined, and are resilient to electromagnetic interference. These tags can transmit at very fast rates. The disadvantage of microwave tags is their high cost compared with the other transponder types. Inductive tags work in a range of under a metre, have inferior spacial directivity and lower communication rates. These tags have very little resistance to electromagnetic interference. However, they are relatively inexpensive and work well in harsh environmental conditions.

2.9 Vision systems

Vision systems are another technology aimed at problems that more conventional forms of auto-ID cannot cope with. Here, the system does not involve a unique form of data encodation, but rather can utilize a number of varying methods, some of them already described. For instance, vision systems can read special bar codes or OCR characters. How then does such a system differ from other technologies?

Firstly, the term 'vision system', though a common term, is far too broad for our needs. There are different types of vision systems or machine vision that have very little to do with automatic identification, for example those used in inspection (for instance in quality control), in gauging (for automatic measuring) and in guidance (for navigating, e.g. missiles). Thus in *this* text 'vision systems' refers to those systems that incorporate machine vision for the purpose of *identification*, the reading and decoding data of an identifying mark. This mark, as already mentioned, can vary from system to system and, therefore, while it characterizes a particular vision system, it does not in any way characterize the technology as a whole. A vision system consists of a *CCD array* or *line camera* that captures pictures rather like a regular camera, however, not on film but rather by sending them first to a special decoder, known as a *digitizer*, and then on to a host system. The host system does not receive a conventional picture, rather a decoded string of data (Figure 2.9).

The type of camera used depends much upon the way an item is passed in front of it. A *CCD camera* takes a general 'snapshot' of the item, including its identifying mark. Later this mark is extracted from the general picture by a *feature extractor*. A *line camera* is used when the position of the identifying mark is static, in other words the item is passed in front of the camera in a controlled fashion. In more advanced systems a number of

AN INTRODUCTION TO AUTOMATIC INDENTIFICATION TECHNOLOGIES

Figure 2.9 Vision system: Allen Bradley CVIM system. Courtesy Allen Bradley

cameras can work in unison with a *camera multiplexer* and hence with only a single decoder. An *image buffer* allows the temporary storage of images to facilitate reading and processing simultaneously.

The identifying mark having been extracted, has to be recognized. The method used depends on the type of identifying mark and item to be read, and an example of an OCR approach was given earlier (p. 23). In all cases, however, the picture to be analysed is composed of *pixels*, i.e. dots of light. Some pixels are darker than others, and it is this contrast between the dark and light pixels that enables the digitizer to decode the picture into a binary stream, light pixels receiving a value of 1, dark pixels 0. This binary stream can then be translated into text characters.

Of course, if things were so simple then it would be hard to see what added value vision systems provide us, for what has just been described is not all that different from bar code technology. In fact, vision systems fit in where bar codes or other identifying marks or symbols lack the contrast required for them to be read by a conventional reader. The optical equipment involved in such a system, with its special lenses and filters, can read virtually any symbol with minimal contrast. As we shall see later, in order to be read, a bar code has to have a significant contrast between its bars and spaces, which normally are black on white. Anything that detracts from the required contrast, say dirty smudges on the white bar, will make it unreadable. In the visual process mentioned above, a light threshold is decided upon under which any pixel is considered dark and those above bright. For trickier situations a more advanced and complex decode process can be utilized, where up to 256 different shades of grey can be defined, each being translated into a unique 8-bit binary stream or 'word'. Better decoding can also be attained if a camera's *resolution*, the number of pixels in the picture, is high. 512×512 pixels is considered a good resolution.

Another major advantage of some vision systems is their ability to upgrade decoding dynamically. During the decoding process the actual algorithm is updated or 'fined-tuned' automatically until a stable decoding process is attained. Thus a system has to pass a period of time until it is in tune with its environment.

It is this last point that is worthy of further discussion. Vision systems are sensitive to their environment, and can only truly function in somewhat controlled surroundings.

– *Ambient light*. The Achilles' heel of this technology is that the ambient light, i.e. the light that is not an integral part of the light source used to read the symbol, has to be stable. Shadowing, sunlight and glares adversely affect the working of a vision system. Even fluorescent light that tends to flicker is not recommended.
– The object to be identified must also possess an element of stability, that is it must remain always in the field of view of the camera while being read, and of course in focus. This is referred to as *item positioning*.
– *Mark consistency*. The identifying mark, if not consistent, will possibly lead to non–recognition. For instance, if letters are the identifying mark, then a defined font or fonts should be used and letters should be printed with a stable contrast.

Most environmental problems can be overcome, but the solutions can be expensive in terms of complicated decoding algorithms that allow for certain environmental and indentifying mark tolerance.

2.10 Voice recognition

Voice recognition systems translate the spoken word into ASCII characters. Whereas a vision system provides the computer with eyes, voice recognition is its ears. In most voice recognition systems the end-user is prompted by a synthesized voice, produced by a *voice unit*. This unit can be programmed with a series of spoken questions that prompt the user as to which information to collect. The user's answer is then recognized and transferred to the host computer or stored in a data collection device for later transmission. The recognition process is performed by one of a number of techniques. One is the creation of a *digital voice template*, whereby each

AN INTRODUCTION TO AUTOMATIC INDENTIFICATION TECHNOLOGIES

user is first required to speak each word in the system's vocabulary. In this way the computer is taught to recognize each user's voice patterns and thus builds a personal digital voice pattern for each word in its vocabulary for each user. After the user speaks his answer to the computer, that answer is converted into a digital voice pattern and searched for among a table of patterns for that particular user. When a match is made the answer is translated into ASCII characters. In more advanced systems the user's answer can consist of more than one word, and this is known as *continuous recognition*, as opposed to the single-word *discrete recognition*. Another voice recognition technique allows for a *speaker-independent solution*, whereby recognition takes place regardless of the speaker and without having to 'teach' the system each user's voice. Speaker-independent technology is usually characterized by smaller vocabularies.

Voice recognition technologies are sensitive to environmental noise, and in some industrial situations the use of headphones with attached microphones are necessary. Because a user can make an error when answering a prompted question a good voice system will allow the last entry to be erased by a spoken command such as 'erase'. Also, *echoing* the user's reply not only enables users to check themselves but also actually to validate the recognition process. With such validation voice recognition has become almost an error-free auto-ID technology.

3
Interfacing automatic identification and data collection systems

3.1 Introduction

All auto-ID technologies and most data collectors need some connection with a host device (some data collectors are configured as standalone systems providing information only to printers). In this chapter we look at the most widely used ways to connect up or *interface* to a host system. Throughout the text the term *host system* refers to any computerized device that is the *initial* destination of the data collected in the data collector. In many instances a data collector might interface with a personal computer, which in turn is connected to a larger, mainframe computer. If the PC processes the collected data before passing it on to another system, then the PC will be regarded as the host and not the processed data's final destination. However, if the PC acts merely as a data communications bridge between the data collector and a larger computer, then the larger computer will be regarded as the host. An example of this is in computerized integrated manufacturing (CIM), where a variety of hardware platforms at different levels of the system receive and process data. Data collection systems are normally found at the second level of the CIM hierarchy and interface to the next level up, for example shop floor management or logistic system (Figure 3.1).

While technically the type of interface chosen for auto-ID and for data collection systems might well be identical, they are in most cases functionally dissimilar. This is due to the quantity of data that each one transmits. Auto-ID readers will normally send a single character string or at most a single record of data items in any one transmission (exceptions to this are large-capacity smart cards or RF tags as well as two-dimensional bar codes), whereas data collectors will send one or many transactions or one or more complete data files.

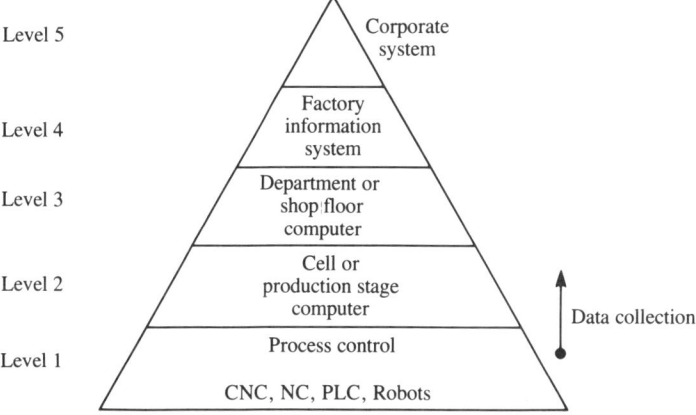

Figure 3.1 CIM hierarchy

3.2 Interfacing auto-ID readers

There are three commonly used ways to interface an auto-ID reader:

- keyboard emulation
- serial communications
- radio frequency data communication.

Keyboard emulation is perhaps the simplest way to transfer read data to a host. The device that enables this to be done is known as a *wedge*. Keyboard emulation means that as far as the host computer is concerned the decoded data has been received from the keyboard; it does not know of the existence of the attached auto-ID reader. This is made possible by disconnecting the keyboard from one of the host's terminals and connecting it to small box or special cable, the wedge (Figure 3.2). The reader is also connected to the wedge and the wedge in turn is connected to the keyboard socket of the terminal. For personal computers an internal wedge, in the form of a printed circuit board, can be slotted into the computer itself. No special software is needed and the end-user can type on the keyboard or read encoded data freely. The wedge will pass on the keystrokes (in the case of the keyboard), or decode the read data and then translate each character the data to its appropriate key signal for the terminal. Some wedges are of the type that allows a measure of programming to enable the wedge to send additional characters other than the decoded data. Additional characters sent before the decoded data are known as *preamble*, those sent after as *postamble*. A postamble might well be a character that affects the operation of the terminal screen, for example a *tab* character which might

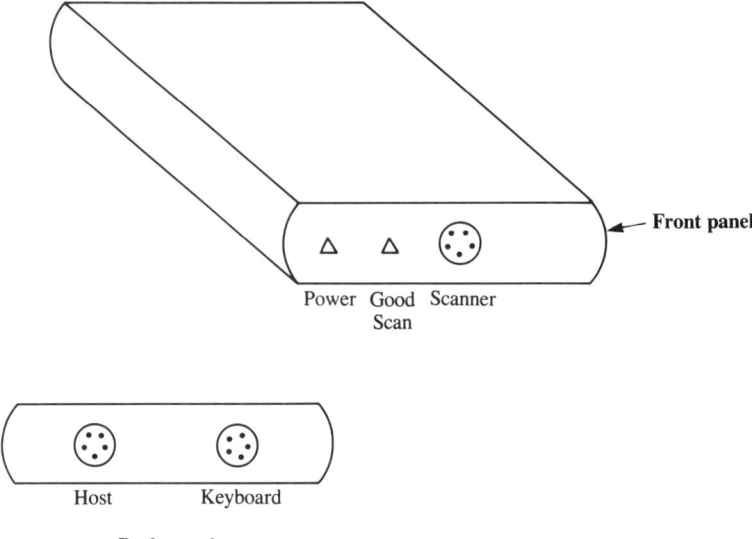

Figure 3.2 A keyboard wedge

instruct the cursor on the screen to skip the next input field or the terminal's *enter* command. Wedges also allow for the manipulation of the decoded data. For instance they can be programmed to truncate a particular data item by a given number of characters. Sophisticated wedges can interface more than one auto-ID reader to a terminal, for instance both a bar code and a magnetic stripe reader. Not all wedges can interface with all keyboard types. If keyboard emulation is a system requirement, it is vital to ensure that the the wedge is suitable for the chosen terminal's keyboard. A list of possible keyboard types should be provided by the vendor. The matching up of a wedge to a particular keyboard type can normally be programmed by the end-user.

We now consider the serial communication interface that connects an auto-ID reader to a terminal of the host computer. Some computers do not have this capability, but personal computers and most computer terminals are supplied with an auxiliary RS232 port (the outlet that is used, for instance, to connect a modem). An RS232 interface is normally used where keyboard emulation cannot be implemented, either because the auto-ID device itself does not permit this or because there exists no wedge suitable for a particular terminal. When serial communication is used the host application program that inputs the decoded data must address the RS232 port in order to capture that data. Alternatively a special TSR or memory resident program, sometimes referred to as *software wedge*, can be run in order to simulate keyboard emulation. This means that the application program will not have to address the relevant port. In short, keyboard emulation comprises of hardware only, whereas RS232 communication is a combined hardware/software solution. The third interface form is radio frequency, which will be discussed in Section 3.4.

3.3 Interfacing data collection devices

Data collection devices can interface functionally to a host system in one of three ways:

1. A batch data collector first stores a number of transactions or events in data files within its memory. Periodically these data files are sent to the host. The data collector can receive data files from the host in the same way.
2. On-line. Each recorded transaction or event is sent separately to the host computer. The host then logically validates the received data before allowing the next transaction to be sent. The communications session between the data collector and the host is therefore an *interactive* process.
3. Real time. Real time data collectors will collect and immediately send data to a host computer without waiting for *logical* validation of the sent data by the host.

The non-functional interface possibilities are similar to auto-ID readers. Keyboard emulation is rarely chosen for data collection devices, as this form of data communications is essentially one-way; that is, the host computer is unable to tell the data collector that it has received the transmission before the next set of data is sent. This data communication process is therefore semi-automated as it requires the end-user to 'mediate' between host and data collection device. The end-user waits for the host computer to give confirmation that the data has been inputted and then instructs the data collection device to send the next data set. Keyboard emulation for the transmission of data from data collectors can be suitable if an on-line solution is a requirement and the use of RF has been ruled out. Keyboard emulation is not advisable in situations where large amounts of data are sent to a host computer.

The vast majority of data collection systems incorporate serial communication interfaces, either RS232, RS422 or RS485; the latter two standards provide for the interfacing of a number of data collectors onto a single line over a wide area. There are a number of possibilities to configure the serial connection, briefly as follows (Figure 3.3):

- The direct connection of a single data collector to a host computer via a single cable.
- The connection of a number of data collectors to a single serial port via a

44 AUTOMATIC IDENTIFICATION AND DATA COLLECTION SYSTEMS

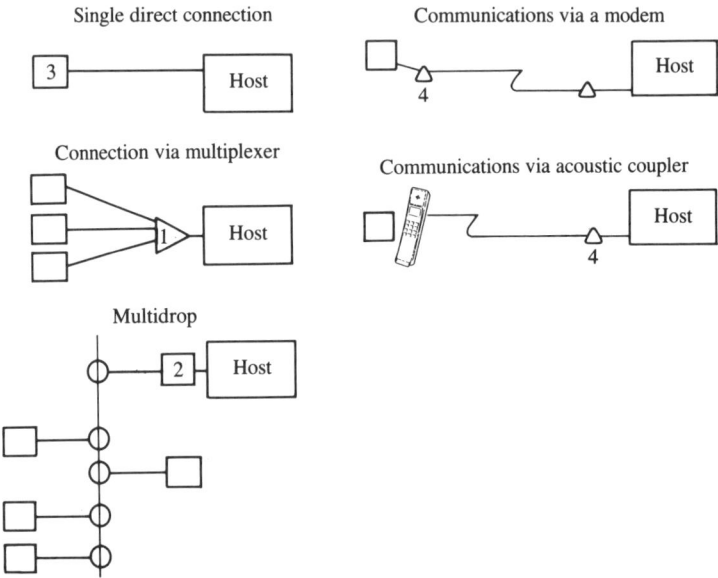

Figure 3.3 Some data communications configuration possibilities: 1, multiplexer; 2, RS 422 to RS 232 converter; 3, data collection device; 4, modem.

multiplexer. Each data collector is connected to the multiplexer by its own cable.
- A multidrop solution, whereby a number of data collection devices are connected to one host computer via a common cable to a single communication port in the host computer.
- The use of a modem to send data over a public telephone line.
- Acoustic coupling, the direct hookup of a data collection device to a telephone line without the use of a modem.

For virtually every working environment there exists an optimal data communications solution. Guidelines on choosing the appropriate solution according to specific needs appear in Chapter 19 on system design. Also, Chapters 9 to 11 on the major data collection devices present a detailed look at the more common interface configurations for each of the various devices. Most vendors of data collection devices are, however, fully responsible for the linkup of their device to the customer's system.

As mentioned in the Preface, accuracy is one of the key goals in any data collection system. Data that is sent or received has to be without error. All data communications within a data collection system include built-in mechanisms to maintain the highest level of data integrity. These mechanisms are part of the definition of the system's *communication protocol*, which can be either a proprietary protocol, specific to a particular data collector or one of the standard protocols on the market today. Among the elements in the protocol, apart from error detection and correction, are to be found:

- Initial synchronization or startup of the communication session between the data collector and host computer. This is commonly referred to as *handshaking*. Here data is sent only after both sides have verified that they both understand the 'language' of the other and are free for a data communication session. The session controller is known as the master, the responder as the slave.
- A common language comprised of agreed *control characters*, for example a request to send or receive the next set of data.

Another pertinent factor in data communications is speed (measured by *baud rate*), i.e. how much data can be transferred within a given time period. As speed increases so does the probability of error. Extensive data validation checks slow down the performance of any system, as does a poor-quality line, if a reasonable level of accuracy is to be maintained (a direct connection is of far superior quality, that is, with less disturbances than with the use of public telephone lines).

The final form of interfacing a data collector to a host system, by radio, is discussed in the next section.

3.4 Radio frequency data communications

Radio frequency data collection means the following:

- Systems are updated on-line as events occur; all new information is immediately brought to the attention of the host system.
- Less data is stored in the data collection device, so these devices will require a smaller memory capacity as opposed to batch terminals.
- This in turn means that there exists a smaller chance of data being lost because of equipment failure.
- Data files, such as lookup tables, will not have to be downloaded to data collection devices at regular intervals.

A radio frequency system generally comprises of the following components.

Base station

This consists of a *radio frequency unit* which houses both transmitter and receiver and a *network controller* that 'manages' the communications between the host system and the various data collection devices. Such management includes buffering data and routeing data to different terminals via an RF communication protocol (see below). A base station receives its transmissions from the various data collection devices, and demodulates the received signal so that it can be sent via a standard RS 232 or 422 interface to the host. Similarly the same base station receives data from the host and modulates this into a signal at a certain frequency recognized by the various data collection devices. The transmitter and receiver may also be housed outside the base station; there are a number of possible configurations, some of which are discussed later.

Data collection device with RF capability

In many cases existing data collection devices are adapted for this purpose by the addition of an external or internal receiver/transmitter.

RF communications protocol

A data collection system utilizing RF communications is usually characterized by a single base station in any one area which transmits and receives data from a number of data collection devices. Thus there is always the possibility that two or more devices will try and send or receive at the same time, a problem that is overcome by the RF communication protocol, which brings 'order' into the system. There are two major categories of protocol, 'polling' and 'carrier sensing', the latter by means of *carrier sense multiple access* (CSMA). In polling the network controller polls each data collector in turn and asks to receive its data. With CSMA each termnial listens to its environment and, if no one is on the air, sends its data. Of course the possibility exists of 'collision' if two or more data collectors attempt to send data simultaneously, so this protocol incorporates a collision rectification mechanism. The CSMA is not suitable for systems with a high data traffic, as response times in these situations can be undeterminable. This is because either a certain terminal can 'hog' air time or repeated collisions can cause the system to slow down. Polling, on the other hand, though less efficient than CSMA for small-scale systems, allows for stable response times in a high-traffic environment.

As with RF identification systems, a data collection device can work on different frequencies. Lower frequencies or narrow bands mean in practice slower rates of transmission as well as shorter ranges than with higher frequencies or wider bands. In the USA *spread spectrum transmission* (SST) is an RF technology that allows for high-speed transmission without compromising performance. With SST the transmission is spread over a wide range of frequencies and then re-collected by the receiver. Another major advantage of this method of transmission is its inherent resilience to high levels of interference. Radio frequency is a complex field with many parameters, affecting in significant ways, the performance of any particular system. The following comprises a competent system:

- *Throughput*. The system should enable the required amount of data to be transmitted in a given period of time.
- *Speed of transmission*. This supports the required throughput.
- *Response time*. Apart from considerations of throughput, the end-user's patience must not be tried. A wait of a few seconds for the completion of each transaction might mean the data collection device is thrown out by the user, who thereupon reverts to pen and paper.
- *Accuracy*. This means very low probability of erroneous data.
- *Insulation*. The system should possess a high threshold of immunity against enviromental disturbances, caused by other electronic equipment, weather conditions, etc.
- *Range*. The system must be able to transmit within the required range equally well at any point and in the most cost-effective way.

An acceptable throughput is achieved by a fast response time. This in turn is achieved by a quick system *turn around time*. The system's turn around time is defined as the time taken for the base station or data collection device to change from a receive state to a transmit one and vice versa. There can be significant differences in turn around times for different types of radio. Only when the amount of data transmitted greatly increases does the relative weight of this factor on throughput fall. In such situations transmission speed will have a greater significance on a system's performance.

Throughput is also affected considerably by the *system configuration*. This can be defined as the layout of both transmitters and receivers in the system, as well as the chain of hardware through which each transmission passes. There are many possible configurations and to examine them all would be beyond the scope of this study, so here are some of the major ones:

- A high-powered base station that contains a single transmitter and is linked to a number of remote receivers via an RS 422 interface.
- Multiple base stations linked together via an RS 422 interface. Each station contains both a transmitter and receiver.
- Multiple radio frequency units (not base stations) linked to a common base station. In order to allow for transmission, the power sent out from the base station is distributed to the various transmitters/receivers via a power splitter. This configuration is also known as *microcells*. The radio frequency units are sometimes referred to as *repeaters*. Some repeaters can also be linked to a common base station via radio frequency, as opposed to being physically linked by a cable.

Each configuration will have its own advantages and disadvantages. Before investing in any proposed system it is vital to examine the vendor's recommended configuration for optimal results.

Finally the use of RF requires permission from the authorities that govern this field. This means that the frequency used by any system *must* be approved for use as well as potential 'gatecrashing' into other reserved frequencies.

3.5 Electronic data interchange

So far in this chapter we have seen how both auto-ID readers and data collection devices can interface to a host computer. In order to complete an overall picture we now look briefly at how data collection devices and automatic identification can conceptually interface into a current revolution in the business world – electronic data interchange.

Electronic data interchange (EDI) is the transfer of commercial documents by means of data communications. EDI can take place within an organization, however it is normally implemented, and most beneficial, when it is the main form of intercourse between two or more independent commercial bodies. There are two functional uses of EDI:

– *quick response* (QS), which is found in retail and service industries
– as part of *just-in-time* (JIT) in manufacturing industry.

The environments may differ, but the goal is the same, namely the elimination of lengthy manual processing ('paper shuffling') by the transfer of documents in a standardized file form from one system to another. This not only greatly speeds up many otherwise cumbersome processes but also increases accuracy; obviously EDI has similarities to auto-ID and data collection systems, in fact in many ways they complement each other.

Before we look at the major components of EDI, we should examine an example of a typical EDI system, (Figure 3.4). Two companies have long been trading partners: Threads Plc is a major supplier of fashion wear and has been using EDI for some time, while Upbeat Ltd is a chain of fashion stores that is an old customer of Threads but has only just jumped onto the EDI bandwagon.

Upbeat places an order with Threads for its latest autumn collection of men's wear, but not all the items are readily available. The order is created in Upbeat's computer system and sent in an EDI format via data communications to the computer at Threads. Once it is received the Threads computer goes to work checking off each ordered item against the stock files, seeing what can and cannot be delivered. The result of this is a preliminary delivery note which, once created, is sent back to Upbeat's system. The preliminary delivery note is checked off against the original order, again by

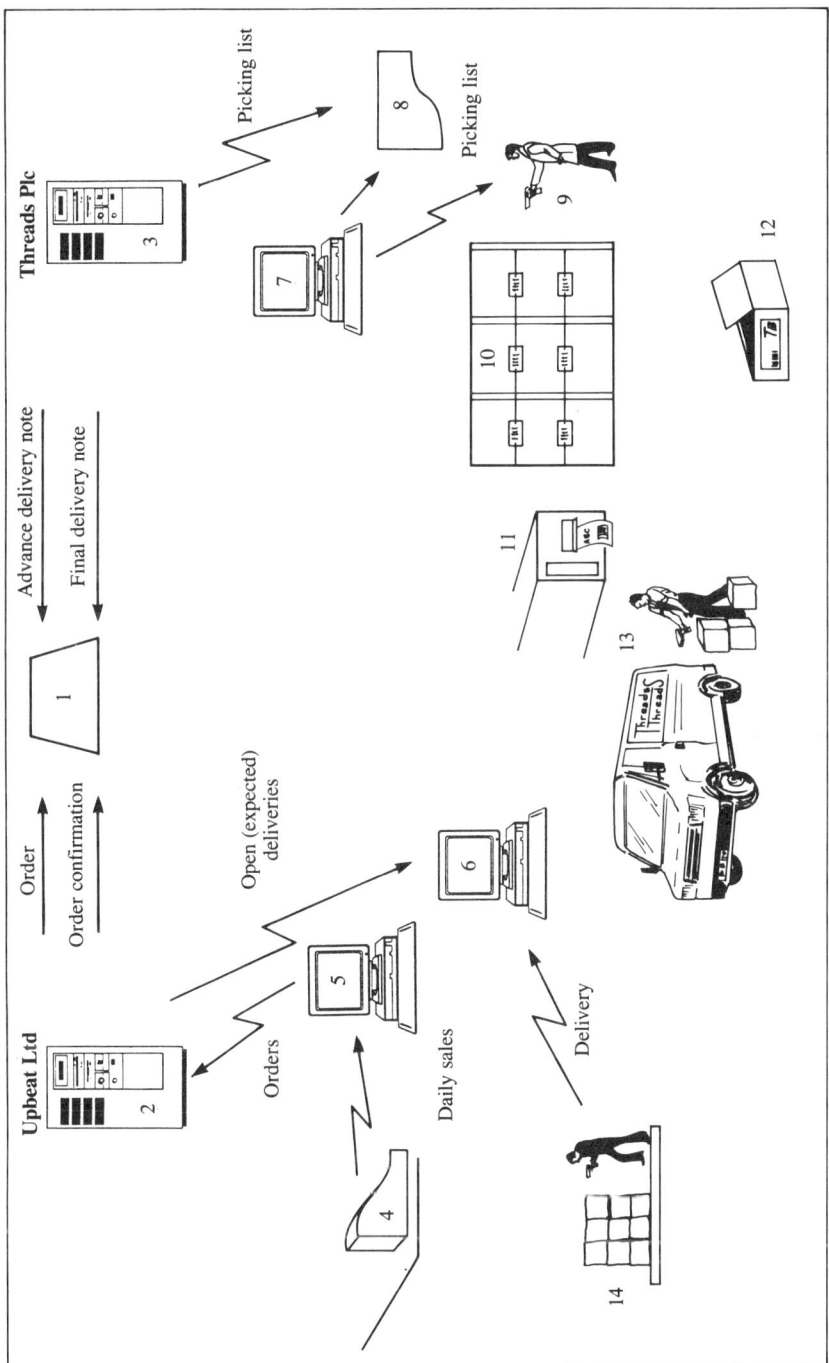

Figure 3.4 Data collection and EDI flow at Threads Plc and Upbeats Ltd: 1, EDI clearing house (VAN); 2, Upbeat central computer; 3, Threads central computer; 4, Upbeat point of sale; 5, Upbeat store back-office computer; 6, Upbeat warehouse computer; 7, Threads warehouse computer; 8, picking list; 9, portable terminal with picking list; 10, Threads warehouse; 11, bar code label printer; 12, bar-coded carton; 13, shipment verification by Threads; 14, delivery verification by Upbeat.

the computer, and discrepancies are reported to Upbeat's sales manager. The order is OK'd and final approval sent by one computer to the other. Next, the Threads' computer prints out a picking list to the warehouse manager, who prepares the order. Once this is done the warehouse reports that the order has been made up. A final delivery note is then sent directly back via EDI to Upbeat and their computer informs their warehouse manager who prepares the warehouse in anticipation of the order.

The whole procedure is fast, accurate and efficient. And to make this picture even more appealing let us add a data collection device and some auto-ID. The first delivery is a big success: the fashions are being sold. In every Upbeat store there is a point of sale with a bar code scanner connected to it. All items bear a price ticket on which the item number is bar-coded; after this is read it is transmitted to a backroom computer which builds a file of daily sales. At the end of each day a file is sent from every store to Upbeat's main computer. All sold items are then automatically reordered (except items that are sold in quantities below a given amount per week), and an EDI order is sent to the Threads' computer.

Once the order is received, processed and finally confirmed, a picking list is then downloaded directly into the Threads' warehouse manager's portable data terminal. This terminal tells the warehouse manager which items to take, from where and in what quantities. It also verifies that the correct item is picked by reading a bar code on the shelf where the item is stored. At the same time special labels are printed out for the cartons that contain the delivered goods. The goods are packed and the correct labels are applied. Each label contains a number of bar codes which encode such information as customer number, the item numbers within the carton, the quantity of items within the carton, delivery note number and order number. The portable data terminal reads the cartons as they are loaded on the truck for delivery. The terminal checks to make sure that all cartons being loaded belong only to the intended customer. The delivery information is then uploaded from the terminal to the main system at Threads once the truck has left.

The same bar code labels are read on delivery at Upbeat's delivery depot. Here, too, a portable data terminal, with the downloaded advance delivery notes in its memory, checks to see that the delivery is complete. All the warehouse manager has to do is read the bar code label on each carton. Once the initial verification is complete, the information from the portable data terminal is uploaded to the host system and as a result Upbeat's stock levels are automatically updated.

The above is a good example of how EDI in conjunction with auto-ID and data collection devices can create a smooth and very efficient operation. How does it work? EDI is an advanced form of data communication involving two or more bodies. It has to have four basic elements:

1. *A communication connection* between the bodies involved. This can take any form, from the use of direct communications with telephone lines via a modem to the use of *EDI clearing houses* whereby different organizations connect up to one central body that passes each document on to its destination, rather like a sorting room in a post office. The advantages of this latter approach is that it relieves much of the technical burden from the trading partners involved. These clearing houses are commonly referred to as *value added networks* (VANs)
2. *A communications protocol* used by all EDI partners such as X 425, based upon the electronic mail protocol X 400.
3. *Standard data formats.* These are the heart and *raison d'être* of EDI. Every document that is sent is sent in a standard format. This means that a common delivery note, a common invoice and so on are used by all concerned. This may not necessarily be a disadvantage, as a carefully designed document answers more than the basic needs of all the partners. Today there exist a number of standards in the world, but the two dominant ones are EDIFACT internationally, and ANSI-X12 for the USA. Of these it seems that EDIFACT will become the world standard. A standard accurately defines the data to be included in the document, the order of the data, and its structure (for instance how many characters are allowed for each piece of data). Standards are flexible and allow a certain degree of customization for particular trading partners or industrial groups.
4. *Translation software.* Standard documentation does not neccessarily mean that your organization has to change its existing system in a drastic way. Rather, existing documentation can be translated into the relevant EDI format. EDI formats that are received are translated to suit a particular proprietary system. The software that performs this task is known as a *message translator.*

Electronic data interchange, when implemented, provides a host of advantages for its users. Cumbersome manual tasks are automated, response time of a commercial body to its environment is drastically increased, and above all EDI is a cost cutter.

The need to come up with a sales forecast in order to plan production or ordering is almost eliminated. 'Quick response' or 'just-in-time' is just that. Companies begin to react faster to customer needs. The automation of ordering, supplying and delivery means that not only do things move quicker, but also an accurate picture is gained of what is going on. More specifically:

– For retailers, when EDI, auto-ID and data collection technologies are integrated, stock levels can be kept lower because the cycle time needed from order to delivery is reduced significantly. Lower stock levels mean better cash flow and more storage space, while the chance of being out of stock of a particular item is greatly reduced.

- Less personnel are required to perform the daily ordering and follow-up activities. All information as to what is to be ordered and what is to be delivered is handled by our friend the computer. The only human intervention required is at the decision-making level.
- Preparation is improved. For better organized companies, where optimization of storage space is undertaken on a daily basis, advance notice of what and how much will be delivered and on what day means that an advance storage plan can be made up ahead of time. Thus stock can be moved in order to make room for the new arrivals and therefore reduce picking times.
- Costs associated with manual processes, such as postal and telephone charges, are reduced.
- There is increased customer satisfaction. The advantages listed above mean that customers have a better chance of finding what they want when they want it and at a better price with a company that uses EDI than with a company that does not.

These advantages hold true for manufacturers. Timely and accurate information is captured as to what is being sold and what is not. Scheduling of production becomes more accurate and costs are reduced. In short, it is clear that a commercial body that implements EDI will find it easier to hold its place in a more competitive market.

PART TWO
INTRODUCTION TO BAR CODE TECHNOLOGY

4
Basic terminology

4.1 Symbologies and their characteristics

Bar code technology is clearly at the forefront of automatic identification systems and is likely to stay there for a long time. Many data collection devices are supplied with built-in interface capability for bar code scanners, and more and more areas of trade and industry around the world are adopting the bar code as their principal means of identifying items automatically. The bar code is seen every day on the packaging of consumer durables sold in retail stores, as well as in other areas of trade and in industry. Different kinds of bar code exist, each with its own characteristics. A particular type is known as a *symbology*, and there are many different symbologies in use today. In order to be able to describe these and to distinguish between them, we need to define some basic terminology.

X dimension

Common to all symbologies is the fact that a bar code is made up of a series of contiguous bars. There are two kinds of these, a dark bar and a light bar, or *space*. The first characteristic of a bar code is the width of the bars themselves. The widths of the bars vary in every bar code, but they are all multiples of the width of the narrowest bar, which is called the *X dimension*. This is the basic unit of measure for all symbologies and is of cardinal importance in the understanding of bar code technology. The number of bar widths in a bar code is another key factor. Some symbologies are based on just two varying widths, wide and narrow, while others have up to four different bar widths, each a multiple of the X dimension. The X dimension is normally measured either in 'mils' (thousandths of an inch) or in millimetres (Figure 4.1).

Character set

A symbology is in fact a language with its own rules of syntax. However, all symbologies translate to the one common computer language of ASCII characters (see Chapter 2). Some symbologies are fully alphanumeric and

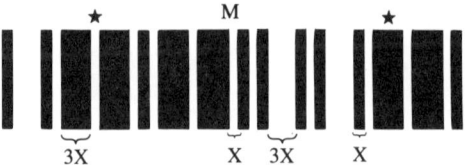

Figure 4.1 The X dimension in a bar code. The symbology is Code 39, with a wide/narrow ratio of 3:1

are known as *full ASCII* symbologies, others are limited to certain alphanumeric characters, while yet others can contain only numeric digits. The list of different characters that one can encode for a particular symbology is known as that symbology's *character set* (Figure 4.2).

Discrete vs continuous symbologies

Each character in the character set is represented in the bar code by a unique combination of bars and spaces. This combination differs from one symbology to the next. There are two basic combination forms used in bar code technology, namely *discrete*, in which a light bar or space of constant width (the *intercharacter gap*) separates each character, and *continuous*, where a character always begins with a dark bar and ends with a light one, and there is no space between characters. Each has its advantages: a continuous bar code takes up less space, while in a discrete one the intercharacter gaps provide a further means of ensuring data integrity.

Fixed vs variable length symbologies

Certain symbologies can be printed only with a fixed number of characters. Both EAN 13 and UPC–A symbologies (discussed in the next chapter) are a case in point: the former always encodes 13 digits, the latter 12.

Symbology definition

A *module* is another name for the X dimension, the narrowest bar in the symbology. Continuous symbologies are generally defined by the quantity of modules and bars that make up a character. This is known as the (n, k) code, where n is the number of modules per character and k is the number of bars (light and dark) for that same character. For instance EAN 13 is a continuous $(7, 2)$ code: 7 modules make up 2 light bars and 2 dark bars for each character. Discrete bar codes use a different definition regime, which can vary. For instance the symbology known as Code 39 is so called because each character is composed of 9 bars, 3 of which are wide.

BASIC TERMINOLOGY 57

Encoded character	Binary representation (B S B S B S B S B)
1	1 0 0 1 0 0 0 0 1
2	0 0 1 1 0 0 0 0 1
3	1 0 1 1 0 0 0 0 0
4	0 0 0 1 1 0 0 0 1
5	1 0 0 1 1 0 0 0 0
6	0 0 1 1 1 0 0 0 0
7	0 0 0 1 0 0 1 0 1
8	1 0 0 1 0 0 1 0 0
9	0 0 1 1 0 0 1 0 0
0	0 0 0 1 1 0 1 0 0
A	1 0 0 0 0 1 0 0 1
B	0 0 1 0 0 1 0 0 1
C	1 0 1 0 0 1 0 0 0
D	0 0 0 0 1 1 0 0 1
E	1 0 0 0 1 1 0 0 0
F	0 0 1 0 1 1 0 0 0
G	0 0 0 0 1 1 1 0 1
H	1 0 0 0 0 1 1 0 0
I	0 0 1 0 0 1 1 0 0
J	0 0 0 0 1 1 1 0 0
K	1 0 0 0 0 0 0 1 1
L	0 0 1 0 0 0 0 1 1
M	1 0 1 0 0 0 0 1 0
N	0 0 0 0 1 0 0 1 1
O	1 0 0 0 1 0 0 1 0
P	0 0 1 0 1 0 0 1 0
Q	0 0 0 0 0 0 1 1 1
R	1 0 0 0 0 0 1 1 0
S	0 0 1 0 0 0 1 1 0
T	0 0 0 0 1 0 1 1 0
U	1 1 0 0 0 0 0 0 1
V	0 1 1 0 0 0 0 0 1
W	1 1 1 0 0 0 0 0 0
X	0 1 0 0 1 0 0 0 1
Y	1 1 0 0 1 0 0 0 0
Z	0 1 1 0 1 0 0 0 0
—	0 1 0 0 0 0 1 0 1
.	1 1 0 0 0 0 1 0 0
Space	0 1 1 0 0 0 1 0 0
*	0 1 0 0 1 0 1 0 0
$	0 1 0 1 0 1 0 0 0
/	0 1 0 1 0 0 0 1 0
+	0 1 0 0 0 1 0 1 0
%	0 0 0 1 0 1 0 1 0

Figure 4.2 Symbology character set (Code 39; an asterisk denotes the start/stop code character). Courtesy AIM Europe

58 AUTOMATIC IDENTIFICATION AND DATA COLLECTION SYSTEMS

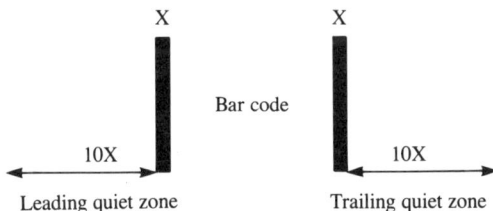

Figure 4.3 The quiet zones of a bar code

Quiet zone

The *quiet zone* is the minimum light space needed before and after the symbology to enable a successful read. It is determined by a multiple of the X dimension. Bar code reading is based on contrast, a subject explored later in this chapter (see Section 4.3). Yet how does a bar code reader define what is light and what is dark? It uses the reference provided by the quiet zone, a given area of light space over which it has to be passed to enable it to recognize a light bar. The size of the quiet zone differs from symbology to symbology (Figure 4.3).

Control characters

A bar code does not consist entirely of significant data; rather, as in data communications, the significant data is enveloped by a group of *control characters*. These include *start*, *stop* and *parity* characters, *shift* and *guard bars* (the latter for UPC and EAN symbologies only). A symbology begins with a start character and ends with a stop character, to enable the bar code to be read in both directions. If the stop character is read first the decoder will simply reverse the data read. Guard bars are start/stop characters for each segment of a bar code encoded using UPC or EAN symbologies. They are examined fully in Sections 5.1 and 5.2 which also deal with parity characters, that guarantee data integrity during the decoding of the bar code.

Control characters have a further function in facilitating the transition between character subsets. Certain symbologies contain more than one character set, i.e. a number of *subsets*, and allow the decoder to jump from one subset to another via a *shift* character.

Basic symbology structure

A bar code has the following basic structure (Figure 4.4):

– leading quiet zone

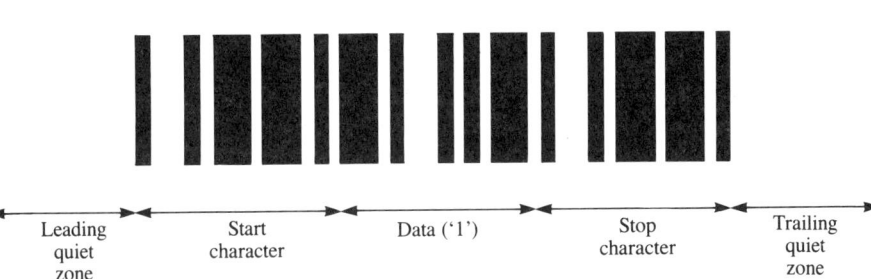

Figure 4.4 Bar code basic structure (Code 39; characters include intercharacter gap)

– start character
– data
– stop character
– trailing quiet zone.

Other symbologies have a more complex structure that incorporates additional control characters. These are discussed in the next chapter.

4.2 Resolution and density

Let us assume for a moment that we wish to encode a six-digit number, for example 123456. Using a number of different symbologies, we receive a variety of bar codes of differing lengths, even though the encoded data is identical. There are a number of reasons for this. First, different symbologies possess a varying number of redundant control characters. Second, the character width of a particular symbology significantly influences its efficiency, that is the amount of bars needed to encode a given data item. The more characters in a set, the more possible bar combinations have to be allowed for and thus the more bars are needed per character. For instance, Code 39 has 9 bars per character as well as an intercharacter gap, and each character can contain up to 15 modules. (For Code 39 there are 2 different bar widths, narrow and wide. Every character has 3 wide bars, giving 9 modules, and 6 narrow bars, which provide another 6 modules, or 15 modules in all. This assumes that the ratio between the narrow and the wide bar is 3 to 1.) Figure 4.5 provides a table that compares the efficiencies of some of the better-known symbologies.

Sometimes we can print a bar code that is too wide for our needs; for example, it might extend past the border of the label on which we wish to print it. We can resolve this problem by altering the *density* of the bar code,

60 AUTOMATIC IDENTIFICATION AND DATA COLLECTION SYSTEMS

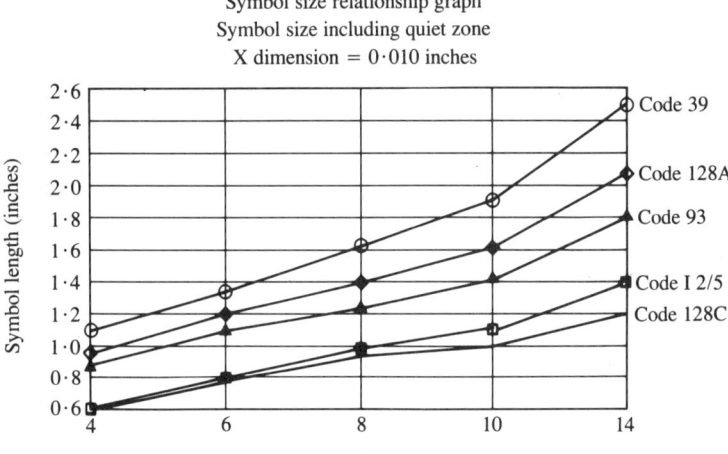

Figure 4.5 Bar code efficiency by symbology. Courtesy Bushnell Consultancy Group

i.e. the number of characters that can be encoded within a given area (normally an inch, so that density is measured in characters per inch, or CPI). Density is determined by two parameters, the width of the X dimension and, in the case of two-width symbologies, the *wide/narrow ratio* (the ratio between the wide bar and the X dimension) as well as the number of control characters used by the symbology. We can calculate in advance the length of a bar code if we know these two parameters and the symbology to be used. Thus to calculate the length of 123456 for Code 39, the symbol length, L, is defined as follows:

$$L = I(1 + C) + (C + 2)(6X + 3NX) + 2Q$$

where I = the width of the intercharacter gap
C = the number of data characters, including the check digit if used
X = the width of the narrow element
N = the wide/narrow ratio
Q = the width of the quiet zone

Note that each symbology specifies both a minimum and a maximum X dimension.

Resolution is often confused with *density* because the two terms are so closely related. Resolution, like density, is based upon the X dimension, but it is based upon this parameter alone, whereas density is also a factor of the number of redundant control characters used by a particular symbology. (It is only because of this confusion that resolution is mentioned here; it really belongs in a discussion of bar code reading rather than in one of symbologies.)

4.3 Colours and contrast

Many bar codes we see are black and white, yet they do not have to be so. The only requirement is that there should be enough contrast between dark and light bars. Coloured bar codes are normally printed to make the packaging of an item more attractive, or even for security reasons. For instance, black bars printed on a red label cannot normally be photocopied. One must be aware that not every combination of colours provides the contrast needed between the light and dark bars. For example, among the following combinations those on the left are permissible while those on the right are not. (This is not a complete list; before a particular colour combination is adopted, testing should be undertaken by an expert.)

Yes	No
Black on white	Yellow on white
Blue on white	Blue on green
Black on orange	Red on green
Blue on orange	Red on orange
Green on white	Red on white
Brown on yellow	Black on blue
Green on yellow	Black on brown
Black on red	Red on gold
Brown on white	Gold on white
Dark brown on orange	Red on blue

(The above assumes that a red light source is emitted by the reader.)

A bar code without the right amount of contrast will be unreadable. Exactly how we define, assure and check for this is examined in Chapter 8.

4.4 Materials

Bar codes can be printed on an extensive number of media and materials. Before we examine some examples, though, the importance of the material on which the bar code is to be printed cannot be overemphasized. Indeed it does not matter how much one has invested in state-of-the-art bar code technology; choosing an unsuitable medium to print the bar code on can bring about the complete failure of a whole bar code project. (Chapter 21 on bar code system design explores this subject in more depth.) Principally, though, a medium is chosen for operating in particular environmental conditions.

The vast majority of bar code media formats outside the retail industry, as well as many in retail, are labels. A label is normally applied to an item and accompanies that item during its complete life span. A label can have three major components (Figure 4.6):

1. *The substrate* or *facestock*. This provides an opaque surface upon which the bar code is actually printed.

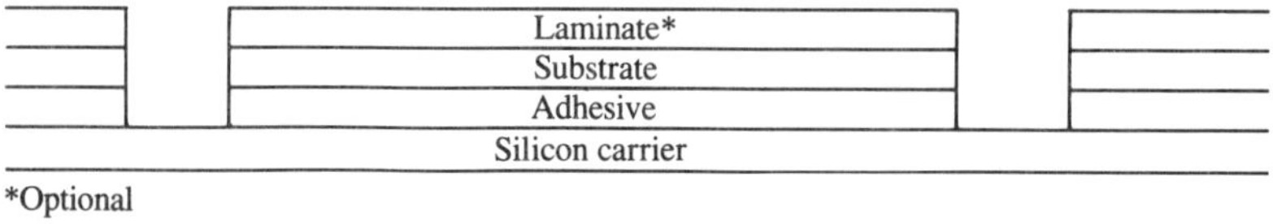

	Laminate*	
	Substrate	
	Adhesive	
Silicon carrier			

*Optional

Figure 4.6 Structure of a label; the laminate is optional

2. *The adhesive.* This bonds the label to a surface.
3. *The laminate* or *surface coating.* This is a special layer above the substrate that provides an extra degree of durability to the label itself, for instance against abrasion.

Substrates

Let us take a brief look at some of the more popular substrates and examine their common uses.

For applications that do not require from a label any special resistance or operational features, a paper substrate is normally used. This can come in different thicknesses as well as in different qualities. In every case it should be of a good quality; that is, it should not contain ash or impurities that might affect contrast. The best paper labels have a matt finish; high-gloss papers should be avoided where possible, because in certain lighting conditions they can adversely affect reading performance.

When a label is required to withstand harsh environmental conditions a paper substrate does not always fit the bill; it can be coated with a laminate, but this is not always within the means of the end-user and may require the expertise of a bar code label vendor. Polyester substrates are a good solution for harsh environments. Like the laminated paper label the polyester label can be wiped clean if it becomes dirty, without any detrimental effect to the label itself. These labels do not tear easily and can be printed on using conventional bar code printing methods such as thermal transfer. While these labels tend to be glossy, they are widely used in a variety of applications. Polyester labels are significantly more expensive than paper labels, however.

One of the most durable substrates is aluminium. Labels made from it possess a great resistance to a variety of chemical agents and are particularly effective in resisting abrasion. The most common use of aluminium labels is for outdoor bar codes, where the label has to be able to withstand different climatic conditions, especially rain. The life span of an aluminium label can exceed twenty years. Aluminium cannot be printed on using regular printing methods and is no doubt the most expensive form of substrate. Should the cost of an aluminium label proved to be too high, a polyester substrate with a polyester laminate has proved to be a good alternative for outdoor bar codes. From the nature of both types it is clear that they are best suited to labelling assets with a high intrinsic value.

Bar codes can be printed on almost any medium that will allow a suitable contrast, including fabric, plastics and mylar. Fabric labels are normally made of a woven polyester material, which, uniquely, allows the label to be washed repeatedly and still remain readable because the label will not fade or absorb colours from other items of clothing. The life span of a fabric label is not unlimited, though, and should be verified with the vendor. Plastics of varying kinds are printed on for a wide range of applications, notably to mark containers sold in supermarkets that hold perishable products such as soft cheese.

Finally a very popular need for bar coding is the marking of printed circuit boards, an application that demands a very small label that can withstand the high temperatures of soldering processes. Here the key is not so much in the substrate but rather in the topcoat. Both paper and polyester bases can be used, but it is essential to consult with an expert who can advise on the correct topcoat for the particular soldering process to be used.

Adhesives

Once a label is chosen and applied to an item, it may, with time, begin to peel away or even drop; this is not such an uncommon occurrence. Thus the choice of adhesive is of the utmost importance. Not only must it be suitable for the chosen substrate and the surface to which it has to bond; it must also have no adverse reactions to any possible extremes of temperature. Basically, adhesives fall into three main categories, *permanent*, *removable* and *reappliable*. As its name implies, the permanent adhesive ensures that the label will stick fast to the surface onto which it is applied and can only be removed with great force (though the bonding process may take some time). This kind of adhesive is used where the price of a peeling label is very high. One common requirement for permanent labels is that if they are removed then the substrate will be destroyed with peeling. This is a great help in security-related applications. Reappliable adhesives, on the other hand, permit the label to be repositioned a number of times within a limited time period, with little or no adhesive left on the surface after each removal, provided the label is removed in time. Removable labels have the same characteristic, but over a far larger time period.

4.5 Reliabilty

The basis for all auto-ID technologies is accuracy. In this respect, bar code technology is seen today as the most reliable of all the auto-ID technologies, that is, the one with the lowest substitution error rate. Not every symbology is deemed to be as reliable as all the others, however, and indeed some require the user to implement measures to ensure a misread does not occur. In this respect symbologies fall broadly into two types, *self-checking* and *non-self-checking* (which are discussed in the next chapter when we review the more widely used symbologies). If a non-self-checking symbology is chosen it may be as well to add a means of assuring the integrity of the data that is decoded, using one of the following techniques.

Check digits

When a check digit is used, immediately after a bar code is read and decoded, the characters in the bar code are passed through an algorithm. The result should be equal to the check digit, which is usually the final character of the bar code. This can be done by a decoder (see Chapter 7). The algorithm is an arithmetic process, which implies that this method is only suitable for numeric bar codes, but with alphanumeric bar codes too it is possibe to use this method by incorporating a table that assigns a numeric value to every character in the symbology's character set. An example of this is the Modulo 43 check digit algorithm for Code 39. The character set for this symbology contains 43 characters, each of which is assigned a unique value, from 0 to 42. After the bar code is decoded the sum of the representative values is calculated and the result divided by 43. The remainder of this calculation is then translated back via the translation table and the character received is the check digit, or in this case the check character. The use of a check digit means that the reading process is not necessarily software-independent; while certain wedges (see Chapter 7) provide built-in algorithms, others do not. With the latter, application software has to determine whether there was a misread. The use of a check digit also has implications for the printing process, and the bar code produced will of course have to contain the check digit as part of the encoded data. The printing routine will therefore have to know how to calculate the correct check digit.

Borders

Interleaved 2 of 5 is a symbology that can accidentally be only partially read: if the scanner passes over only part of the bar code there is a chance that only that part will be decoded. To overcome this problem border bars are printed immediately above and below the bar code, thus creating a misread should the scanner pass over the border. The border has therefore to be wider than the widest bar in the bar code, thereby eliminating the perceived quiet zone (Figure 4.7).

BASIC TERMINOLOGY 65

0 1 2 3

Figure 4.7 Interleaved 2 of 5 with borders

Figure 4.8 Bar code label with data identifiers

Data identifiers

A data identifier is one or more characters that are prefixed to a bar code in order to represent the logical significance of the encoded data. For example, two bar codes in the same label contain the data '123' and '234'. The first bar code represents a part number and the second a serial number of that part. We might add a 'P' before '123' and an 'S' before '234' so as to identify to the application program receiving the data the significance of the data received. The use of data identifiers provides a minimal level of data integrity as is normally implemented to ensure that data is entered into the correct input field (Figure 4.8).

Fixed lengths

This solution is quite commonly used for an Interleaved 2 of 5 symbology. Here the decoder or application program is programmed to accept a data item of a predefined length. A good read containing less than the required number of digits is therefore rejected.

5
Principal symbologies

The following symbologies have the most widespread use in the market today.

5.1 Universal product code (UPC)

This is one of the oldest symbologies and is primarily used for the identification of grocery and other retail items in the USA and Canada. There are two varieties of this code: UPC–A, a 12 digit code, and the half sized, 6-digit UPC-E (Figure 5.1). This shortened version is used when the area on which the bar code is to be printed is too small to allow for all 12 digits. If a UPC bar code is used to identify a grocery item, a manufacturer's or vendor's number must first be obtained from a *numbering association* (this is so for the EAN symbology (Section 5.2)). The reason for this is to ensure the unambiguity of the encoded data in the market. The 10 middle digits of the bar code are composed of the manufacturer's number and the product's number, and when combined represent a numeric combination that uniquely identifies a product's particular. Normally a manufacturer will purchase the right to use a range of numbers. One might think that 10 digits are not enough in order to uniquely identify every product available in the grocery industry, especially when 5 of them represent the different suppliers or manufacturers. For this reason the first digit of this symbology classifies the following 10 digits into *systems*, with each system a product group. The final digit, the twelfth, is a check digit that is automatically printed when UPC is defined, and automatically checked when decoded. UPC-E is the UPC–A symbology with the zeros squeezed out, and is referred to as a *zero-suppressed symbology*. There are a number of suppression methods, and the last digit of this symbology represents the particular method used. This is important, because when the bar code is read the decoder is required to return the zeros to their original positions.

68 AUTOMATIC IDENTIFICATION AND DATA COLLECTION SYSTEMS

Figure 5.1 UPC-A and UPC-E. Courtesy Bushnell Consultancy Group

Parities

Universal product code, like the vast majority of existing symblogies, is a *one-dimensional*, or *linear* bar code. That is, only the width of the bars themselves have any relevance for the decoding algorithm, the height of the bar being redundant. Yet both UPC and EAN symbologies have bars of two differing heights. The taller bars are known as *guard bars*, and are found at the leading and trailing ends of the code, as well as in the middle. These are no more than start/stop characters to indicate the start or end of any particular half of the code. This is important because each half has a different *parity*; the left half uses an odd parity, the right an even one. The parity of the symbology segment is defined as the sum of the dark modules in any character. For instance the number '1' is made up of 2 light modules, 2 dark modules, another single light module and another single dark module, on the left side. Altogether there are 3 dark modules – an odd parity. The same '1' on the right side is made up of 2 dark modules, 2 light modules, another 2 dark modules and 1 light module. The sum of the dark modules this time is 4 – an even parity (Figure 5.2).

If you were observant you would have noticed that UPC characters are comprised of 7 modules. Each bar can be of 4 differing widths, each a multiple of the X dimension (from 1X to 4X). Every character for this symbology contains 2 dark modules and 2 light bar groupings. For this reason UPC is defined as a (7, 2) code. UPC–E sticks to the same parity regime, except that here each half is made of 3 characters instead of 6. A parity regime has two major purposes. First it is a built-in way of checking the integrity of the decoded data and thus reduces the likelihood of character substitution. The combination of this parity regime plus the check digit means that UPC is a self-checking symbology. The parity regime also tells the decoder which half of the bar code is being read, thus providing for *bi–directional* reading.

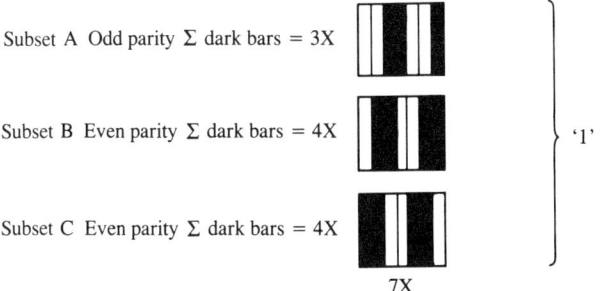

Figure 5.2 The character '1', as encoded with UPC (subsets A, B and C)

5.2 European article number (EAN-13)

This symbology is a superset of UPC and is commonly used in Europe and other countries in the grocery trade. EAN-13 is a 13-digit symbology, which is encoded in the same fashion as UPC (Figure 5.3). The data structure of EAN-13 differs from that of UPC primarily because it is a standard in so many countries. For this reason the first two digits of the symbology identify the country of origin in which the manufacturer's number was allocated. These digits are known as the *country code* or *flag*. The final digit is a check digit, while the remaining digits are divided up between the manufacturer and the product number. It is interesting to note that both UPC and EAN-13 have the same number of bars even though the latter has an extra digit. This is achieved by the existence of a mixed parity in the left-hand side of the EAN symbology; 3 out of the 6 characters on this half have an even parity, and the other 3 an odd one. The various possible combinations provide us with a means of encoding the additional character.

Like UPC, EAN has a short form, called EAN-8 (it has 8 digits). Finally, there is a little bar code tagged onto the right end of an EAN or UPC symbology which is known as a *supplementary code*, which can be either 2 or 5 digits in length. It is printed to encode additional data in the bar code such as price, date of issue, etc.

5.3 Code 39

Code 39 was developed in 1975 in order to allow a greater range of characters to be encoded in a bar code. This symbology has a character set of 43 numeric, alphanumeric and special characters, such as '-', '$', '.', etc. Code 39 is a discrete symbology with a space of fixed length between one character and the next – the *intercharacter gap*. There are two permitted

70 AUTOMATIC IDENTIFICATION AND DATA COLLECTION SYSTEMS

Figure 5.3 EAN-13 and EAN-8. Courtesy Bushnell Consultancy Group

module widths, the relationship between which is defined by the wide-to-narrow ratio, which ranges between 2.25:1 and 3:1, depending on the required density. Unlike the symbologies already examined, Code 39 can be of variable length. Each character is composed of up to 15 modules, clustered into 9 separate bars (4 light and 5 dark). Out of these, 3 of the bars or spaces are wide, hence its name (Figure 5.4). The combination of the intercharacter gap and its start and stop characters means that this symbology is self-checking and bi-directional. There exists also an extended character set of 128 characters, which is accessed by the use of shift control characters (the special characters already mentioned), themselves encoded in the symbology. Code 39's great flexibility has led to it being widely adopted in a whole host of different industries, and especially in the defence establishment. This symbology, however, tends to use more space than is sometimes desired. A newer symbology, Code 128, was developed to solve this problem, which is examined later (Section 5.5).

5.4 Interleaved 2 of 5

This symbology has an interesting geometry. Interleaved 2 of 5 is a numeric-only symbology which permits data compression, whereby two digits are encoded in one character grouping. The character set for Interleaved 2 of 5 therefore begins with '00' and ends with '99'. The digit pairing is facilitated by the first digit being encoded only in the dark bars, the second in the light bars. Because of this feature, Interleaved 2 of 5 is classified as a continuous symbology. Interleaved 2 of 5 derives its name from the fact that in each digit there exist 2 wide bars out of a total of 5 bars altogether (Figure 5.5). Note that this is true for both dark and light bars. Like Code 39, this symbology has a bar width ratio range from 2.25:1 up to 3:1. Because of

PRINCIPAL SYMBOLOGIES 71

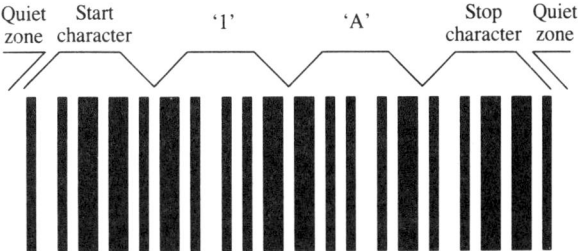

Figure 5.4 Code 39. Courtesy AIM Europe

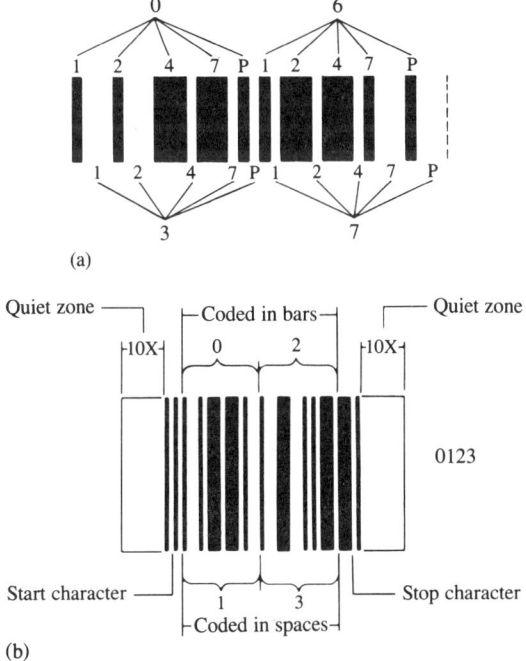

Figure 5.5 Interleaved 2 of 5. (a) Interleaving technique (b) Structure. Courtesy AIM Europe.

Interleaved 2 of 5's unique pairing of digits, only an even length of digits can be encoded using this symbology. If we were to encode '12345', a leading zero would be automatically added, resulting in '012345'. Interleaved 2 of 5 is a variable-length bar code.

The start and stop characters for Interleaved 2 of 5 are very simply constructed, which perhaps accounts for this symbology's most difficult problem area, namely data integrity. Should a bar code reader read only part of the bar code, a partial read can result. In such a case a bar code containing '123456' might be decoded as '12345'. To overcome this problem a check digit is normally incorporated in the bar code. Another common solution is the printing of dark bars directly above and below the bar code. The width of these bars should be over 3X, so that if the bar code reader is not passed over the full length of the bar code a non-read will result. This symbology has been commonly used where a large amount of variable numeric data needs to be encoded in a little space.

5.5 Code 128

Code 128 was introduced in the early eighties to improve further the possibilities offered by an alphanumeric symbology. Unique to this symbology is the fact that it contains three distinct character sets, each of which can be accessed in a single bar code. The first two character sets are alphanumeric and contain 128 different characters each; they are known as 'A' and 'B'. Character set A contains upper-case characters as well as ASCII control characters. Set B has both upper- and lower-case characters. Finally, character set 'C' is very similar to Interleaved 2 of 5, because each character is actually a pair of digits. In addition, all three sets contain special function and shift control characters that facilitate the transfer from one character set to the next in the same bar code. As can be imagined, each set has its own unique start character.

Code 128 is defined as an (11, 3) symbology, of variable length. It is a continuous self-checking code (with different parities for dark and light bars and the use of a check digit). There are four differing bar widths, ranging from 1X to 4X. A special feature of this symbology is its ability to concatenate two or more messages together, by use of a function character. Finally, if we take a ruler and divide a Code 128 symbology into separate characters by counting every 11 modules, we will notice a discrepancy at the end: there is an additional black bar two modules wide at the end of the stop character. (Figure 5.6)

Figure 5.6 Code 128: symbol encoding AIM. Courtesy AIM Europe

Figure 5.7 USS Codabar symbol encoding 'A37859B'. Courtesy AIM Europe

5.6 Codabar

The symbologies examined so far represent the most commonly used symbologies in the market today. *Codabar*, while still widely used, is not often incorporated in new applications. First implemented in 1972, Codabar offers a 16-character set of 0 to 9 and special characters. Basically this symbology uses two differing module widths, although it can work with a staggering 18 differing module widths (not multiples of the X dimension). This special feature was incorporated to allow the symbology to be reproduced by many different printing techniques. *Rationalized Codabar* is a version of this symbology that incorporates only two bar widths. Codabar is a discrete, self-checking symbology, each character being comprised of 7 bars (3 light and 4 dark). Codabar has four separate start/stop characters, A to D, which provides it with built-in *data identifiers* to identify a particular data item. These start and stop characters have also been used to concatenate bar codes. This symbology has been adopted mostly by blood banks, libraries and mail delivery services, because it is a variable-length, numeric code with some special features. Compared to Code 128, however, it is quite outdated (Figure 5.7).

6
Printing bar codes

6.1 On-site versus off-site printing

Any organization considering the implementation of a bar code system will have to decide where the bar codes will be printed. There are two alternatives, either on the premises of that organization, i.e. in-house or on-site, or by a professional printer or bar code label vendor, i.e. off-site. In the latter case the bar code label vendor might well use on-site printing methods, whereas a professional printing company will use printing methods that require a great deal of expertise, such as only it can offer. In this chapter we examine the various bar code printing methods both on- and off-site. First, though, let us look at the considerations involved in making the decision about where to print.

Data

If the data to be encoded in the bar code is non-variable, for example a single product number, and labels can be prepared in advance, then it might be cost-effective to send the work to an outside contractor. Even if the data is variable, but of a serial nature (a defined range of numbers), the same probably still applies. An example might be the requirement for bar code labels that provide files with a unique identification number, for instance for an insurance company. The company might order 50 000 unique bar code labels at a time, requiring only that each contains a unique number not printed before. A bar code label vendor might be chosen to do this work, whereas in the former example, of the single product number, a print shop that already prints the packaging of a company's products will print the required bar code as part of that packaging.

Manpower and expertise

Some companies simply do not want to be bothered with printing bar codes. Even if the data to be encoded varies, provided it is known ahead of time, such a company can provide the contractor with a file on a magnetic medium that contains the data to be printed. One reason for not wanting to be bothered with printing bar codes is the need for someone to assure the quality of the bar codes printed (see Chapter 8) which can be quite a complex task. Bar codes received from bar code vendors are normally of the highest quality.

High and low volumes

Using an outside contractor might be preferable if the required volume of labels is low, for example 10 000 a year. Then buying a bar code label printer may be dearer than paying a small yearly premium for a stock of very fine labels. Conversely, if a very high volume of stock is required very quickly, and the data can be provided ahead of time, printshops are capable of printing at speeds way above those of any regular on-site printer.

Specialized labels

If the label substrate is very specialized, e.g. aluminium, or if a special topcoat is required, regular on-site printers will normally not be able to provide a suitable solution.

We now examine the most popular off-site techniques, but first, so as to be able to evaluate the various printing methods, we need a framework of analysis by which to compare them.

6.2 A framework for analysing printing techniques

The framework of items presented here holds true for both on- and off-site printing; it is analysed in more depth in Chapter 21 on bar code system design.

X dimension

If a high density bar code is required, i.e. one with a small X dimension (under 10 mils, or 0.01 in), we have to make sure that the printing method chosen is capable of printing at the required print resolution with very little variation, i.e. with very small growth or loss of bar width. Thus for the chosen method the minimum X dimension attainable by the printer should be known.

Cost

This includes not only the initial investment but also any operating costs involved in the day-to-day printing of bar codes, the possible replacement cost of working parts such as print heads, and the cost of materials consumed by the printer, such as ribbons, toner, etc.

Substrate possibilities

How flexible is the chosen printing method? Today we may print on a paper substrate, tomorrow on carton. Not all printers print on all substrates.

Bar code life span

Some printing methods print bar codes with a limited life span, which might fade over a period of time.

Speed

This can be a vital factor, especially when high volumes are needed and/or printing is 'on demand'.

Variable data

All on-site printers can print variable data, while some off-site printing devices cannot.

Quality

This varies drastically from method to method. Even off-site devices vary in quality.

Discrete vs continuous symbologies

Some off-site devices cannot print continuous symbologies.

6.3 The film master

In order to print a bar code by traditional printing methods, ('wet-ink' printing), the print shop first requires a *film master* of the bar code to be printed. This item is the basis from which the plate used in wet-ink or offset printing is created, by means of a computer-controlled photographic process. In such a process a moving beam of light conveys the bar code image through a series of lenses onto a photographic medium. The light movement is controlled by a computer, which instructs the beam to move in a path according to a series of coordinates produced by the encoding algorithm of the chosen symbology based on the data to be encoded.

The bar code this process produces does not have bar widths of exactly the same size as those of the printed bar code, because the dark bars printed with wet ink are normally wider than those on the original plate. Ink tends to spread when applied to most substrates, and moreover certain plates also tend to react to pressure (as in the case of flexography; see Section 6.4). This is known as *bar width growth* (BWG), and occurs with most printers and printing methods, particularly wet-ink ones. To compensate for it the film master is normally created with bars that are actually narrower than those in the final printed bar code. The amount of reduction is the *bar width reduction*, and varies from printer to printer.

Finally the film master can be obtained from a bar code vendor, who will then supply that master to the printer designated by the customer. A film master can be produced in very little time and is an inexpensive product.

6.4 Wet-ink printing methods

The common denominator for all wet-ink printing methods is the use of a printing plate that contains the printed image. Wet-ink is applied to the plate and the plate applied to the substrate. The most common wet-ink methods are, offset lithography, rotogravure, flexography and letterpress (Figure 6.1). *Offset lithography* uses a thin metal plate mounted upon a

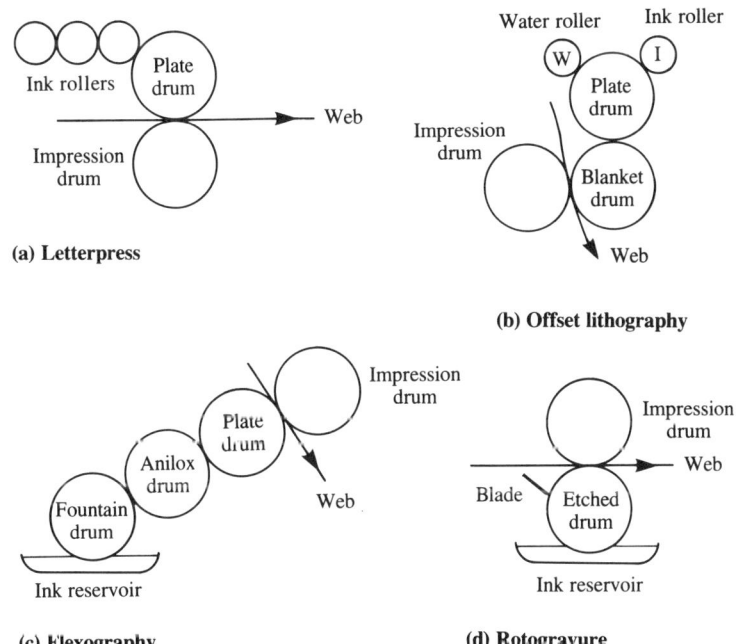

Figure 6.1 Wet-ink printing methods

drum; the image etched on the plate contains oil-receptive and water-repellent areas, the bars, while the spaces have the opposite characteristics. The drum comes into contact with two sets of rollers, a water-dampened set for cleaning the plate, and an oil-based ink set for inking the oil receptive areas of the image. The image is then transferred to an intermediate or 'blanket' drum, which in turn prints the image onto the substrate. The substrate passes between the blanket drum and a third, 'impression' drum.

Rotogravure is a simpler process incorporating only two drums. The first contains the etched image which is composed of minute indentations or cells below the surface of the drum. The drum is rolled through a bed of ink that is taken up by the cells and any excess ink outside them is removed by a *doctor blade*. The substrate is passed between the image drum and an impression drum, which transfers the ink from the cells to the substrate itself under pressure.

Flexography is similar to offset, but the image plate is made of a flexible rubber that is attached to the plate drum. Ink is applied to the plate by two other drums: a *fountain drum* with attached doctor blade revolves in a bed of ink, and an intermediate *anilox drum* transfers the ink to the plate. Here, too, the substrate passes under pressure between the plate drum and impression drum.

Finally, the oldest of these methods is *letterpress*, which uses a plate of raised areas which are spread with a rather thick pasty ink.

For serial data and bar codes a numbering wheel can be used, which turns, forming a unique combination of different patterns according to a predetermined series.

All these traditional printshop methods print good-quality bar codes at rapid speeds at traditional printshop costs. These methods are normally used for high-volume printing of non-variable encoded data. Letterpress is normally limited to discrete symbologies only.

6.5 Toner printing methods

Common to all these techniques is the use of powdered ink or *toner* to produce the final image. A single drum is charged either electrically or magnetically with an image. This charge attracts the toner, which is transferred onto the substrate and then fused by heat and/or pressure to that substrate. The printing technologies employing this technique are xerographic or laser, ion-deposition and magnetographic (Figure 6.2). They can be either off-site or on-site, because printer costs have rapidly fallen in the last few years. The basic difference between these technologies is in the way that the image is created on the plate or image drum.

In *xerographic printers* a light source creates an optical image on a photo-sensitive semiconducting drum. This drum has been electrically pre-charged

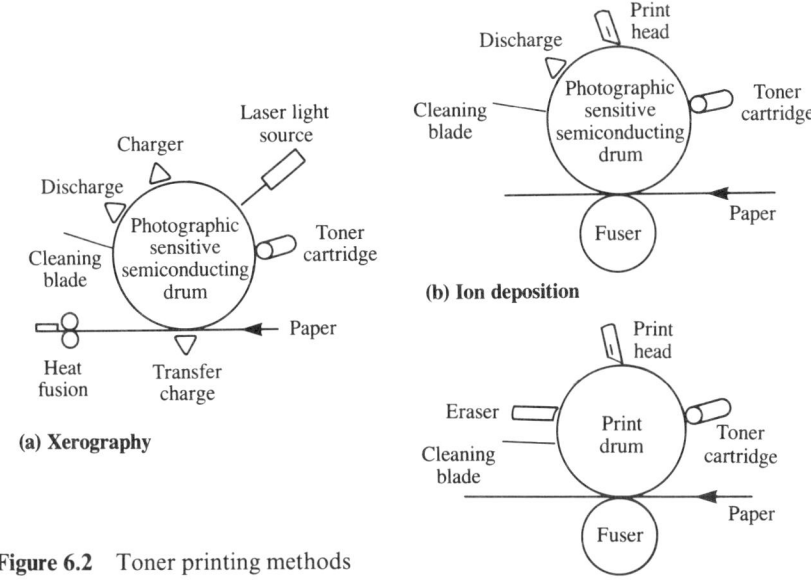

Figure 6.2 Toner printing methods

and its exposure to a modulating light source, normally a laser, which is scanned across the width of the drum, creates an electrostatic image. This image attracts the toner, which is transferred to the substrate by a further charge from the back of the substrate. The drum is then discharged, cleaned and finally recharged.

Ion deposition printers use a printhead of electrodes to create an image on a print drum, while *magnetographic* printers create a magnetic image instead of an electrostatic one. Because of this the toner used is composed of magnetic particles.

These printers can print high-density bar codes of good quality. Ion deposition printers can reach particularly high speeds but are costly and thus are normally considered an off-site solution. Costs of laser printers have fallen rapidly, and these can now print on fan-fold paper, whereas previously they would accept only single sheets of labels. One major advantage of a laser printer for on-site production is that, unlike some other label printers, they can be used for purposes other than label printing. Their substrate range is somewhat limited, however, and is normally confined to paper.

6.6 Photographic composition

Without doubt this technology produces the best-quality bar codes, including extremely high-density ones with an X dimension as small as 3 mils (0.003 in), should they be required, and should the bar code reader be able to handle such densities. Photographic composition is essentially an off-site method, and its first stage uses basically the same process as that employed to produce film masters: a computer-controlled light source is passed through a series of lenses onto a photosensitive substrate. After this the substrate is developed and is made into labels to which the correct adhesive is applied. The method is normally chosen for the production of very durable labels with a required high life expectancy, such as might be used for the marking of assets. Not only is the finished result very durable, as the bars are a photographic image within the substrate itself; it is also very versatile, because bar codes can be printed on a very wide range of substrates, including metals.

6.7 Impact dot matrix printers

Impact dot matrix printers are the simple office printers found in so many places and especially in the home. They come in two main varieties, serial (or character) printers and line printers. 'Dot matrix' describes the design of the printhead, which in a *serial printer* contains a number of tiny hammers or pins which when activated will strike an ink ribbon that lies between it and the substrate, rather like a conventional typewriter. The width of the pin and the number of pins in the printhead determines the quality of the image. Serial printers have normally 9 or 24 pins that make the dot matrix. The pins are 'fired' at the command of a controller inside the printer. The controller, in turn, receives its commands from a computer via a printer interface (cable). *Line printers* are so termed because they will print a line at a time (in serial printers the printhead moves along the width of the page printing a single character at a time). The bar code is produced by a series of printed contiguous joined dots, which affects its quality in a number of ways.

While most impact dot matrix printers produce low-to-medium-density bar codes of only reasonable quality, this may be entirely suitable for in–house, low-volume label production. Serial impact dot matrix printers are normally used for bar code production in order to exploit existing printing resources within a company, while line printers are considered a professional solution for higher-volume bar code production.

6.8 Direct thermal printing

Thermal printing is based on the reproduction of an image by the transfer of ink onto a substrate by heat. In direct thermal printing the substrate contains a special topcoat of clear film that reacts to heat, normally turning black. There are two types of topcoat, *organic* and *inorganic*, composed of different elements. The latter performs better in harsher environments and has a longer lifespan. The printhead in a direct thermal printer contains an array of heating elements that are selectively activated by a controller. The controller also controls the movement of the substrate that is passed under it. There are variations to this configuration. Another type of fixed printhead contains a single bar element for bar codes and a number of single heating elements for human-readable characters. The single bar element is overlapped to form bars of variable width. Lastly, there exists a moving printhead consisting of a small number of heating elements which transverse across the substrate much like the printhead in a serial dot matrix printer.

Direct thermal printers are normally smaller than their thermal transfer cousins (see Section 6.9) and are sometimes used to provide a portable solution for bar code printing. While good-quality, high-density bar codes can be printed relatively inexpensively, the labels are very sensitive to climatic factors and have a low life span. As non-carbon-based ink is used, thermal labels cannot be read by infrared scanners.

6.9 Thermal transfer printing

The basic principles of thermal printing apply to thermal transfer; however, here, regular label stock is used (without the special topcoat), as ink is transferred to the substrate from a special ribbon (Figure 6.3). Normally the ribbon is advanced simultaneously with the substrate on a one-to-one basis, even if parts of the substrate are not printed on. For this reason some printers are supplied with a special ribbon-saver device that will only advance the ribbon once the current section has been used. Ribbons cannot be reused.

Thermal transfer printing has extensively replaced direct thermal printing as the standard on-site method for the high-volume production of quality labels. It does not require thermal labels, so labels printed by it are significantly more durable.

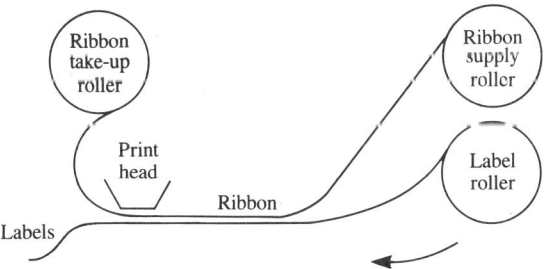

Figure 6.3 Printing by thermal transfer

6.10 Inkjet (non-contact) printing

Inkjet technology stands out on its own in so far as the printhead does not come into direct contact with the substrate; instead, it directs a jet of ink in a controlled fashion onto a particular surface. There are a number of variations on the main theme, but they are all based upon a controlled flow of droplets of special ink being deflected by an electric charge onto a substrate. In the *continuous deflected* version ink is released from a nozzle under pressure. The continuous stream is broken into droplets by an ultrasonic vibration. The ink is then charged and deflected in a controlled fashion in one of eight possible directions for single-nozzle systems; or in a multiple nozzle array system the charge can deflect the ink away from the substrate (Figure 6.4).

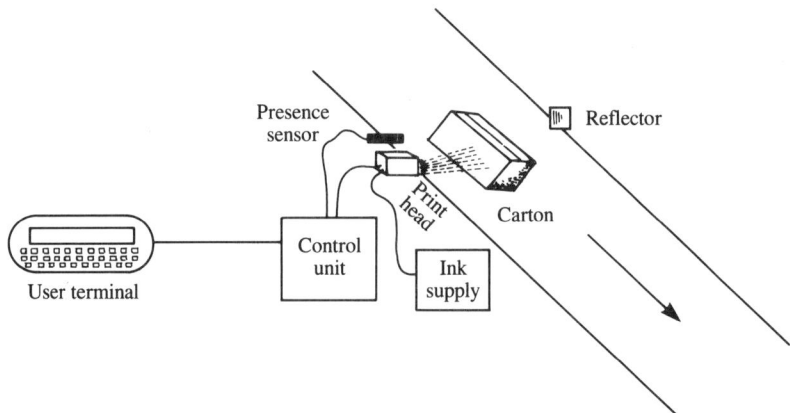

Figure 6.4 Typical inkjet printing configuration. The role of the presence sensor is to detect the presence of the item before printing begins

7
Reading devices

7.1 An introduction to reading technologies

Bar codes are read by a combination of two processes, firstly an optical-electrical process converts reflected light into an electric current, then the current is translated into a bitstream and finally ASCII characters. The first process is done by the bar code reader, the latter by a decoder, which may or may not be an integral part of the reader itself. The reader emits a light source onto the bar code and the dark bars absorb this light while the spaces reflect it. Inside the bar code reader photodiodes convert the reflected light into a very small electric current. The current produced is proportional to the amount of light reflected, and because the strength of the reflected light from both bars and spaces may well vary, a range of reflectance is defined for each.

In order to decode the bar code successfully the decoder needs to know not only the strength of reflected light but also the time period in which that light is reflected at any given strength, in other words the widths of both bars and spaces. This is critical because the varying widths of the bars and spaces determine the unique patterns that make up the character set for any one symbology type. The *spot*, a given area of emitted light, (Figure 7.1),

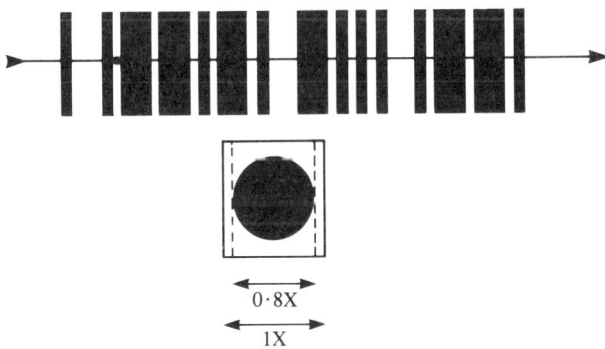

Figure 7.1 A spot passing through a bar code

is used by the reader to determine the width of the various bars and spaces of the bar code. This is calculated by the time taken for the spot to pass from one bar type or bar combination to the next (see below). The width of the spot is termed as the reader's *resolution*, and, as we soon see, matching a reader with the correct print resolution for a bar code is of the upmost importance.

The spot resolution should, in ideal circumstances, be approximately 80 per cent of the X dimension. As the spot passes over a bar code it can determine the transition from a bar to a space and vice versa, or even a bar's absolute width. The first method is known as *edge to similar edge*, and is used to decode continuous bar codes (Figure 7.2). Here is created a framework known as the *t distance*, that is the distance between similar edges of the bar code, whereby each character in the character set can be determined by unique t distances measured in mils. Otherwise the bars and spaces are measured, and these different widths are quantified to provide the unique character.

Once the varying strengths of the reflective light have been translated into electric current by photodiodes, the current has first to be amplified in order to be measured. After amplification the analog signal is transformed into a digital one by a circuit called a *waveshaper*. The principle involved is quite simple: the analog signal will vary, and this varying signal has to be

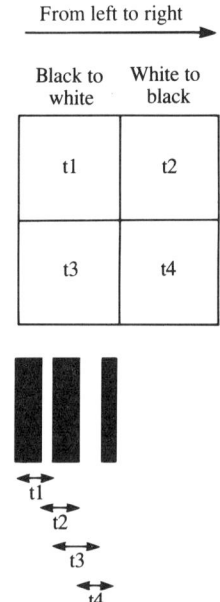

Figure 7.2 t distances – edge to similar edge

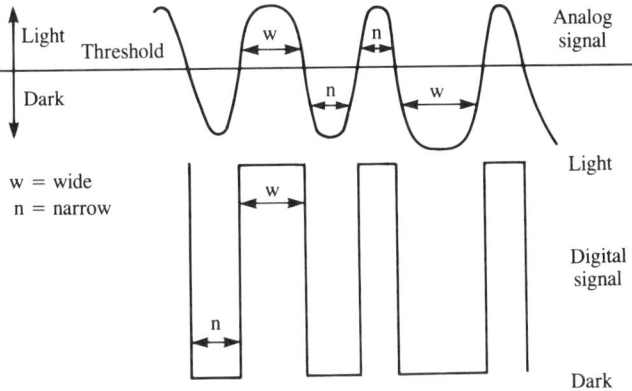

Figure 7.3 Analog and digital signals

formed into a sharp 'yes/no' or '0/1' binary stream according to the predetermined reflected light thresholds for the bars and spaces. Once the digital signal has been formed the symbology's decoding algorithm does the rest (Figure 7.3).

In order to validate the bar code the decoder uses a series of algorithms. It determines the width of each bar and space, identifies the read symbology, uses that symbology's character set to decode data, and then assembles and validates the decoded data.

As bar code technology is based upon reflected light, the light's *wavelength*, measured in nanometers (nm), is of particular importance. Different inks can absorb and reflect light sources within a given range of wavelengths. For example, scanning with a reader that emits infrared light is possible only with high-carbon-based ink used to print the dark bars (non-carbon-based ink will not absorb light at the infrared range). For this reason infrared readers are particularly handy in security-related applications where we can print a bar code that cannot be photocopied. This is done by combining black carbon-based ink dark bars on a non-carbon black label.

The emitted light is operative over a given distance. A concept which is of importance is *depth of field* (Figure 7.4). The working range of the scanner, i.e. the shortest and furthest distances it can read from. This parameter is influenced by a bar code's X dimension: the wider the X dimension, the greater the distance the reader can read from.

Now let us look at the various types of reader on the market today. Bear in mind that in most cases the reader will require a wedge or some other form of interface to the host computer or computer terminal, the decoder is normally part of this interface.

86 AUTOMATIC IDENTIFICATION AND DATA COLLECTION SYSTEMS

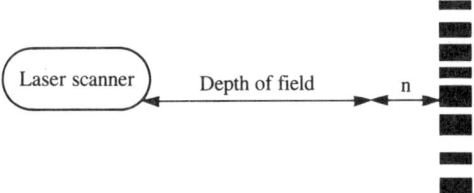

Figure 7.4 Depth of field. The bar code is unreadable if scanner is brought into area 'n'

7.2 The light pen and slot reader

The light pen, or *wand*, is the simplest as well as the least expensive of all bar code readers. Shaped like a fat pen, it is passed by the user over the entire length of the bar code, (Figure 7.5). This form of bar code reading is known as *contact scanning* because the wand comes into physical contact with the bar code itself; that is, its depth of field is zero. The light source is a light-emitting-diode (LED). Some infrared wands are available for special applications.

The rules to be observed when operating a wand are as follows:

- The wand must be held at an angle to the bar code itself, normally between 45 and 90°.
- To ensure a successful read the wand must be passed over the bar code at an even speed.
- Quiet zones: the pass or scan must begin before the leading quiet zone and end after the trailing one. (This is perhaps the most common mistake in reading bar codes with the light pen: people not used to bar code reading tend to remove the pen from the bar code before the trailing quiet zone has been entirely covered.)

A light pen may come with one of a number of resolutions and therefore the resolution should be carefully checked before purchase in order to make sure that it is suitable to that of the printed bar code.

Another version of contact scanning is the *slot reader*; here, instead of the reader being passed over the bar code, the bar code is passed through the reader. The slot reader looks rather like a magnetic stripe reader and is suitable for applications such as reading ID cards. Finally, a close relative of the light pen is the *fixed beam scanner*, for which the light source is normally an LED. This reader allows for a moving bar code to be read at a distance, that is, it has a greater depth of field than that of the light pen.

READING DEVICES 87

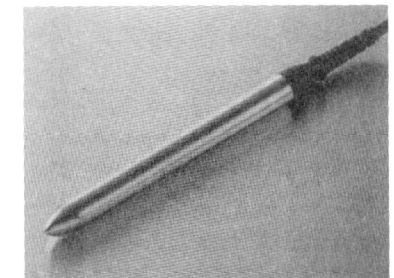

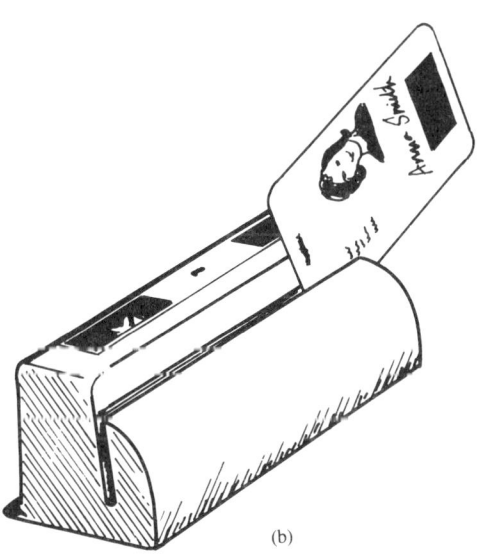

Figure 7.5 (a) Wand and (b) slot readers

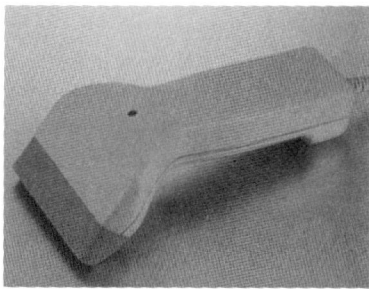

Figure 7.6 CCD scanner

7.3 CCD

'CCD' stands for *charged coupled device*, and describes the technology used for the input configuration of this scanner. Resembling somewhat an electric razor, the reader has the great advantage of scanning the bar code automatically so that the user need not pass it over the full length of the bar code (Figure 7.6). The CCD illuminates the whole bar code and an array of photodiodes in it receive back the reflected light. For each narrow bar in the bar code there are normally between two and four photodiodes. The relative bar widths are determined by the sampling of the state of each diode in turn, which produces a waveform. In order to obtain a snapshot of a bar code, the light emitted from the CCD is normally pulsed. For each pulse the CCD's circuitry will sample one or more times the state of each diode. This type of device is known as a *near-contact reader* because it typically has a small depth of field from contact up to about 1 cm from the bar code itself; recently, however, a new generation of long-range CCD readers have been introduced into the market. As mentioned earlier, the CCD is easier to use than the light pen, but it has one major drawback: it cannot read all bar codes, as any bar code wider than the photodiode array cannot be decoded, so care must be taken to ensure such use is not attempted.

7.4 Laser technology

Laser technology is the most advanced way of reading bar codes, and the most expensive. It has become the industry standard and no doubt once this technology falls below a certain threshold in price it will replace the use of light pens; it has already started to replace the CCD. Laser readers can be divided into a number of categories, as follows (Figure 7.7):

– reader type – hand-held or fixed-mount
– laser light source type
– beam pattern.

READING DEVICES 89

(a)

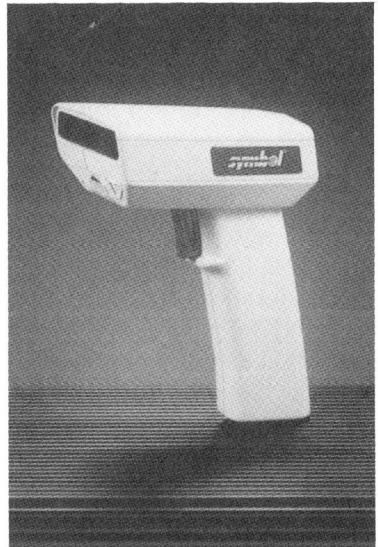
(b)

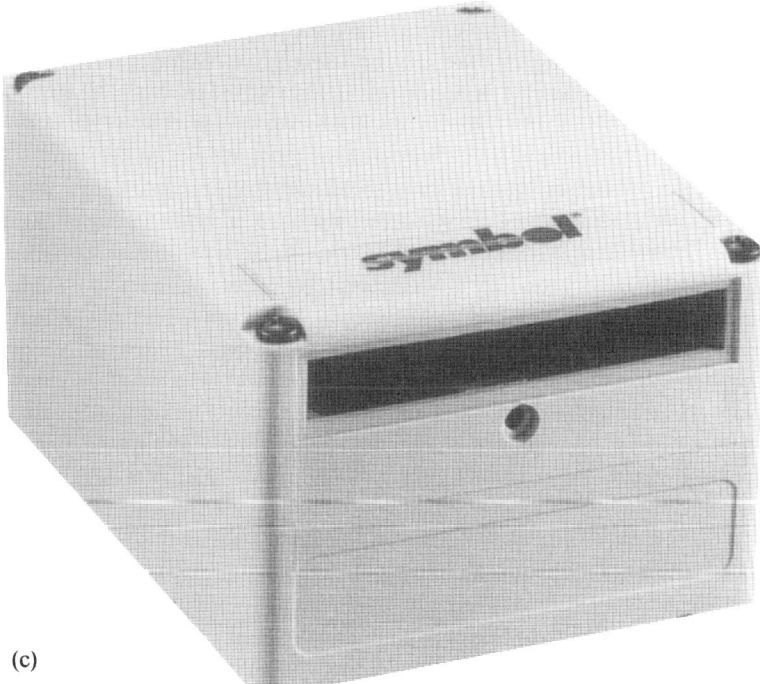
(c)

Figure 7.7 Laser scanners: (a) Laser Scan 5000: fixed, omnidirectional; (b) Laser Scan 2000: hand-held; (c) Laser Scan 6000: fixed mount. Courtesy Symbol Technologies

In each of these readers the laser beam moves across the bar code in an automatic fashion thanks to a moving part in the reader itself – either a rotating drum with mirrored sides or simply an oscillating mirror. This moves the spot of laser light across the bar code, at a speed whereby the spot appears to be a single, unbroken line. The source of the laser is positioned away from the mirror to allow for an opto-electrical detector to be placed in view of the window through which incoming reflected light is received. In order for this to happen a series of fixed mirrors reflect a spot of laser light from the laser itself onto the oscillating mirror or mirror drum.

The advantages of a laser reader, or scanner, over other types are enormous. Firstly, a large number of scans are performed per second. This means the laser reader is likely to achieve an excellent first read rate, even for poorly printed bar codes. Second, a very large depth of field indeed is possible, up to a metre, and today there exist special long-range readers which can achieve working distances of several metres. Third, a variety of light sources is available. The first scanners used a helium–neon laser, or 'He–Ne', which could be quite large and bulky, especially for a hand-held reader. Although solid-state technology was able to produce smaller readers, the first of these used infrared light, which was invisible to the human eye, so that they had to incorporate a tracer beam to allow the user to aim the laser beam at the bar code. Also, with infrared, only carbon-based inks could be read. In the late eighties Symbol Technologies introduced the first visible light diode (VLD) scanner. Such devices are both small and lightweight, and have a lower waveband than their infrared predecessors, which means that they can read most inks.

The major difference between hand-held and fixed-mount laser scanners is in their use. Hand-held scanners are employed in attended applications where the scanner is brought to the bar code by an operator. Fixed-mount scanners are generally used for fully automated processes, with the bar code being brought to the scanner (one notable exception is at checkouts in supermarkets). The implementation of fixed-mount scanners is quite complex in comparison with its hand-held counterpart (Chapter 21), and for now we need only say that in most industrial applications where these scanners are used a number of parameters have to be taken into account to assure good scans. These will include:

- the correct positioning of the label on the item, so that the bar code stays under the reader's beam long enough to be read and decoded before the next bar code comes into range
- the speed at which the bar code is passed in front of the reader
- the depth of field, as items may pass in front of the scanner at different distances
- the size of the bar codes and the number of bar codes to be read on any one item.

The last basis on which we categorize laser reading equipment is the *scan* or *beam pattern*. In order to increase further still the first read rate and thus make fixed-mount readers simpler to implement, many scanners incorporate a number of beams which can sweep a bar code simultaneously at a number of differing angles, in what is known as *omnidirectional scanning*. Such a beam pattern may be a simple 'X', a network of crisscrossed lines or even a starburst pattern. Each pattern type has its advantages, but all have the same aims, namely to increase the number of scans possible in a given time framework, and to allow the bar code to pass through the scanning field at any angle. The latter facility can be particularly useful where items of many different kinds are read, with bar code labels in various positions on them.

7.5 Influences on and the measure of reading success

As mentioned in Chapter 2, the reading success of any auto-ID device is measured by its first read rate (FRR) and substitution error rate (SER). In bar code reading these parameters can be adversely affected by a host of differing factors. Those factors related to printing are examined in Section 8.5; others are as follows.

Ambient light

This is environmental light, for instance office lighting, fluorescent illumination or even sunshine. A high degree of it can adversely affect the FRR for certain reading devices, for example in the case of a glossy label being read under fluorescent lamps, or where a laser scanner tries to read a bar code outdoors on a very sunny day. It is thus necessary to take the lighting environment into account when choosing a reader. For instance, in our latter example, a CCD might be preferable to a laser scanner.

Surface type

When choosing a reading technology it is essential to consider the surface to be read. Many surfaces are unsuitable for contact or near-contact readers. A rounded surface, for instance a jar, may not be suitable for light pens or CCDs. Similarly, corrugated or brittle surfaces should be read with non-contact readers.

Access to the bar code

If a bar code has to be placed on an item where there is little free space to move a contact scanner, then a non-contact scanner should be used. A classic example is a printed-circuit board. Similarly, contact scanners are not very effective when a bar code label is affixed close to the edge of an item. Insufficient access to a bar code is detrimental to the reading process. If a contact scanner is to be used then there must be enough space to allow the free movement of the user's hand. If a non-contact scanner is used then nothing should be allowed to obstruct the beam.

Packaging

Certain packaging can seriously flaw a reader's performance; thus translucent material will itself absorb part of the emitted light. Also, coloured plastics will in some cases adversely affect the required print contrast signal (see Chapter 8).

Decoding algorithms

Decoding algorithms are not all the same. Some are more 'open' or 'aggressive' than others. An *open* decoder is programmed so that its top priority is for a decode always to take place: 'decode at any price'. Thus a high FRR will be attained, but with poorly printed bar codes the SER may be high. A more *closed* decoder will put data integrity as its highest objective and will therefore sacrifice a few non-reads in exchange for true ones. Any vendor will tend to claim that their device has the best of both worlds, i.e. that the decoder is both aggressive and accurate; however, this subject should not be blown out of proportion because such problems arise normally only with bar codes of borderline quality.

8
Quality assurance and analysis

8.1 Introduction

Quality assurance or bar code verification is part and parcel of the production process. It may be enough to print a few bar code labels to start with, verify that they can be read by a bar code reader, and then continue production. Such a brief check can be sufficient for *closed systems*, where the label to be actually used is read by the end-user's bar code reader, but this does not mean that another reader will be able to read that same bar code. The correct approach to bar code verification is to reach a level of quality high enough for all bar code readers, regardless of their technology, to be able to read the bar code with a first read rate of well over 90 per cent. This is quality assurance for an *open system*, and its importance must be emphasized. One great benefit of bar code technology is its portability; the same bar code can be used by different bodies for different purposes. We should bear in mind that with many labels print quality declines with age. With contact scanning the printed surface can deteriorate with every read. Environmental conditions can also take their toll on labels with time, so that it is possible (especially with marginal quality bar codes) for the bar code read today by a particular reader *not* to be read by the *same* reader tommorrow!

At what stage do we check quality? This will depend on the production method used. If the bar code is to be produced by a printshop, it is worth while first to check the quality of the film master positive before printing begins. Next, for all printing methods it is advisable to print a small batch, verify, and, should the results be satisfactory, continue with periodical sampling. For wet-ink printing, just verifying the film master is not enough because ink will spread during printing, so one must ascertain that the ink spread stays within the defined tolerance allowed for a given symbology. Quality analysis should be seen as a compulsory stage for all bar code systems.

8.2 Quality analysis devices

Quality analysis is performed with the help of a *bar code verifier*. There are a number of these on the market today, with some more advanced than others, depending on the reading technology used. A bar code verifier is in fact a bar code reader with a special decoder that not only will decode the bar code but also will provide details pertaining to the bar code's quality. The American National Standards Institute (ANSI), as well as AIM, the association of Automatic Identification Manufacturers, have defined standards for most symbologies that relate to a number of important printing parameters. With the help of a verifier one can determine whether the printed bar code meets the required standard or not. Indeed, some of the more advanced verifiers are able to present the user with the ANSI grade as well as to pinpoint exactly where the bar code fell from grace. The bar code verifier should be seen as a tool whose purpose is not only to tell us where we went wrong, but also to help us correct our mistake too! This, though, can only be achieved with a correct understanding of the relevant parameters (see Section 8.3). The more advanced verifiers incorporate laser scanners that scan the bar code a number of times per second, enabling the verifier to provide a *percentage decode* (PD) value, that is how many reads were successfully decoded out of 100. This result is perhaps one of the best indications as to the quality of a bar code. The less advanced verifiers use a wand or light pen as their reading device; though limited in some areas, they still provide a good indication as to the bar code's quality, and are extremely popular owing to their relatively low cost compared to devices using laser technology.

8.3 Quality analysis parameters

Now let us look at some of the major parameters used to verify a bar code. These parameters can be broadly classified into three basic categories:

- bar width measurements
- reflectance and contrast
- printing defects.

As we know, bar code decoding is based on the absolute and relative widths of the bars and spaces. The width of all bars and spaces are a function of the X dimension. If, for example, a Code 39 bar code is printed with a resolution of 10 mils (0.010 in) and a wide/narrow bar ratio of 2.5:1, we would expect three bars/spaces in each character to be 25 mils (0.025 in) wide. In reality, though, the actual X dimension will differ slightly from the nominal width, as will the wide bars. As we have seen in Chapter 6, this can be for a number of reasons. The term used to characterize this phenomenon is *bar width growth*, (BWG), and the BWG allowable for any particular symbology is known as its *dimensional* or *printing tolerance*. Both ANSI as well as AIM define these tolerances, as well as other important parameters that we look at in this section. The tolerance range (both positive and negative), increases in inverse proportion to the bar code's resolution, and, where applicable, in direct proportion to the wide-to-narrow ratio. How to analyse BWG and other parameters and the steps taken to rectify bad results are examined in Section 8.4. Tolerance also relates to the deviation from a nominal *edge to similar edge* measurement for continuous symbologies.

Reflectance is the amount of light returned from the bars and spaces to the bar code reader. *Contrast* is the difference between the light reflected by the bars and that reflected by the spaces. There exist threshold reflectance values for both bars and spaces, termed *minium space reflectance* and *maximum bar reflectance*. These terms are self–explanatory, if we remember that we wish bars to absorb light and spaces to reflect it. Contrast is measured by one or both of the following parameters: *minium reflectance difference,* (MRD) and *print contrast signal* (PCS). There is a subtle difference between the two, but both these parameters provide important information as to the quality of the printed bar code. Ideally, the difference between the minimum space reflectance and the maximum bar reflectance should be around 50 per cent, while the PCS should ideally be well over 75 per cent, although a good scanner should be able to cope with inferior results.

Printing defects consist of either 'holes' or voids in the bars, and specks of ink in the spaces. A defect should not reach a diameter greater than 0.25 times 0.8X, 0.8X being the assumed spot size of the bar code reader. If a defect, say a void, is quite wide, for example 0.5X, the decoder may interpret it as the start of a space, which in turn may lead to a non-read.

8.4 Analytical methods

Now, how do we make head or tail of the results we receive from a verifier, and more importantly what do these tell us about our production process and how to improve it? It may be reassuring to know that bar code verification can always be left to the experts. Sending samples to an outside contractor for analysis not only saves the headache of learning bar code verification, but also saves the cost of the bar code verifier itself. If the bar code was produced using a film master, the contractor will have to be told what bar width reduction was used, also which printing method is being used, and will, of course, have to be provided with a real-life printed label on the actual media. (This is essential!)

If the contractor's services are to be dispensed with, however, then it is vital that the following factors are borne in mind during the verification process:

96 AUTOMATIC IDENTIFICATION AND DATA COLLECTION SYSTEMS

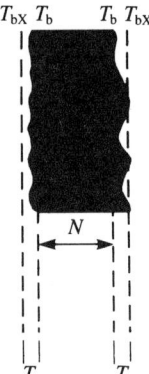

Figure 8.1 Bar width growth, showing an element of Code 39. N = nominal width (20 mil), T = print tolerance ($\pm$ 4 mil), T_b = bar width growth within tolerance limits, T_{bx} = bar width growth out of tolerance limits. Note: wide/narrow ratio 2:0.

– Ambient light may affect the result for PCS and/or MRD; some verifiers require a calibration process to be performed first in order to create reliable terms of reference.
– The results received do not necessarily give a true picture of the complete bar code, rather the area of the bar code that was read. Therefore, should a tall bar code be verified, it is a good idea to read different stripes of it and compare the results.
– One label is not normally representative. A few labels should be verified in order to achieve accurate results.

We can begin with dimensional tolerance as represented by *bar width growth* (BWG) (Figure 8.1). Some verifiers provide results for both the *average BWG* and the *worst BWG* of the bar code. If the latter is out of specification this does not necessarily mean that the bar code is, but if the former is out of specification then we can quite assuredly say that the whole bar code is too. Deviation from the dimensional tolerance can be caused by a variety of factors, depending on the printing method used. With a wet-ink method it could be because the pressure between the plate and substrate was too high, or the ink was of the wrong type, or even because an inappropriate substrate was used. The last factor can also apply in thermal printing (both direct and transfer) where another cause of deviation during printing is the temperature of the printhead, which may therefore require an adjustment. For dot matrix printers either an unsuitable ribbon was used, or again an inappropriate substrate. Some of these printers allow the printhead pressure to be adjusted should BWG become out of specification. What is clear from this is that a solution to the difficulty depends upon

QUALITY ASSURANCE AND ANALYSIS 97

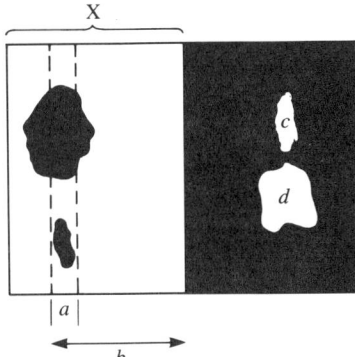

Figure 8.2 Bar code defects. $a = 0.25 \times 0.8X$, $b = 0.8X$, c = 'hole' within tolerance, d = 'hole' out of tolerance

knowledge of the printing method. One final tip is that if a wet-ink method was used, we should make sure that the film master was verified and in specification before deciding on the solution to the problem.

When contrast is poor it is not enough to know that the PCS or MRD is insufficient; we need also to know which of the components of these parameters caused the poor result, or we are left with guesswork. For instance if the maximum bar reflectance was high, then we can look in the direction of the ink, a faded ribbon or incorrect colour. If a low MRD resulted from a low minimum space reflectance, then we should look again at our substrate material. Defects can be caused by a whole host of factors, which once again depend upon the printing method. Common causes are damaged printheads, inferior film masters, incorrect print temperatures and incompatability between the ink and label substrate, (Figure 8.2).

8.5 Common production mistakes

In order to reduce the probability of producing low-quality bar codes it can be quite useful to become acquainted with some of the more common mistakes that can occur during the production process (Figure 8.3).

Undersized quiet zones

This is perhaps the most common of them all. The quiet zone is the area free of print, needed before and after the bar code. The width of the quiet zone is a function of the X dimension, and will vary from one symbology type to another. For instance, the required minimum quiet zone of Code 39 is defined as 10X. Unfortunately one can see many examples of undersized

(a) *1234567890123456111111111*

79710900
(b)

|IIIIII IIIII IIIII IIIII IIIII IIIII IIII IIII|
123456
(c)

123456
(d)

Figure 8.3 Common bar code production mistakes: (a) very long; (b) too dense; (c) too short; (d) quiet zones too small

leading and trailing quiet zones on many bar code labels. While more-aggressive readers might be able to deal with this, others will not and the result will be an exasperated user who does not understand why the bar code is tough to read or not readable at all.

Short bar codes

The shorter the bar code, the harder it is to read. As a general rule a bar code should not be under 1.5 cm in height. If a wand or other contact scanner is to be used, it will be difficult to keep the reader from leaving the top or bottom boundary of the bar code. Similar problems will arise when using a hand-held laser scanner, as it may prove quite difficult to aim the beam on such a short bar code, especially from a distance.

Long bar codes

With contact scanners, the longer the distance the user's hand has to travel the harder it is for the user to keep it steady. The bar code producer should consider breaking a very long bar code into two shorter ones, should such a problem be foreseen.

High resolution bar codes

A bar code with a very narrow X dimension might be totally unreadable or readable only with a scanner of very high resolution. Special care should be taken with such bar codes, especially when they are designed for an open system.

Transparent or translucent backgrounds

We have already looked at problems of contrast resulting from printing errors, However, poor contrast can also come about when the substrate is transparent or translucent. The best way to explain this point is by way of an example. A manufacturer of a chocolate spread produced translucent plastic jars for his product. The bar code, whose bars were black, was readable when the jar was empty. However, when the jar was filled with chocolate spread, the spread showed through the jar, giving a black bar code on a dark background, making it unreadable.

8.6 Existing standards

In the world of bar codes, there exist regulating and advisory trading organizations and technical committees who offer assistance and guidelines to bar code users. The two main technical bodies, ANSI and AIM, have already been mentioned. The latter of these provides excellent literature, in the form of booklets, on all aspects of auto-ID technologies. Other organizations have as their aim the creation of industrial standards for bar code users, with the following aims:

- To allow multiple use of a single symbology by a number of different users in the same industry.
- To reduce the amount of research needed by any single user to implement a bar code system.
- To encourage the development of standardized data collection systems within any one industry.
- To meet the majority of needs of all the users within any one user group or industry.

Perhaps the best-known of these bodies are the *article numbering associations* that are to be found in many countries. These bodies regulate the use of UPC/EAN symbologies, providing a series of unique numbers to any manufacturer who needs to bar-code a product. The EAN bar code data structure contains the manufacturer and product number and it is the article number association's role to make sure that no two manufacturers receive the same number. In the USA, where the UPC symbology is used instead of EAN, this is undertaken by the Uniform Code Council, (UCC).

Apart from this regulatory function, these bodies provide advisory services on a whole host of bar code and bar-code-related subjects. Some of the other bodies that have created industrial bar code standards are:

- ODETTE – the Organisation for Data Exchange by Tele Transmission in Europe. This body has developed a standard transport bar code label, incorporating the Code 39 symbology, for the motor industry.
- IATA – the International Air Transport Authority has adopted Interleaved 2 of 5 for ticketing and identifying baggage and baggage containers as well as cargo handling.
- HIBCC – the Health Industry Business Communication Council, in the USA, has created health care standards for bar coding including Code 39 as well as Code 128.
- LOGMARS – Logistic Applications of Automated Marking and Reading Symbols. This American DOD project has been the vanguard for other military auto-ID projects around the world. Here Code 39 was chosen for a wide variety of bar code logistic applications.

These bodies have added another dimension to bar code verification in a less orthodox sense, for in some industries not only does the bar code label need to meet the required quality in terms of printing standards, but the data conveyed by the bar code also has to conform to a required structure.

PART THREE
DATA COLLECTION DEVICES

9
Programmable controllers

9.1 Introduction

As mentioned in Chapter 1, programmable controllers (PLCs) have traditionally been used in supervisory control environments, where their task has been the control of automated processes. Each unit is programmed directly via an attached keyboard and monitor, or the program can be downloaded to it from a hand-held terminal or host computer. In other words, there have always been serial communications to the PLC itself. Yet the PLC can also be a significant asset in collecting raw data as events happen and immediately or shortly afterwards reporting these events to a host computer. In this chapter we look more closely at the PLC's role in data collection, its architecture, software, communication configurations and man–machine interfaces (MMIs). We do not look in detail at the various functions of the PLC, because this is beyond the scope of this study. For a good review of the PLC's various functional abilities see the Bibliography.

The connection of PLCs to a host computer should be seen within the context of the overall structure of computerized integrated manufacturing (CIM). CIM is usually portrayed as a pyramid, with information systems that support long-term or strategic planning at the apex and computerized control of plant machinery at the base. At one level up from the bottom can be found data collection systems that provide key data to information systems at the higher levels. Some of these intermediate levels are logistic, quality control, factory floor management, account costing, or engineering systems. The data collected in real time is later transmitted to the higher levels, providing them with timely and accurate information. Examples of the types of data collected for different purposes are presented in Chapter 14, but for the time being we can see the general flow of information in manufacturing as follows:

CNC machinery, robots, PLCs, computerized materials handling, etc.

9.2 The PLC as a data collector

As already noted, the PLC traditionally controls automated processes according to a predefined set of instructions programmed in the PLC itself. For instance, if on a production line raw materials have to be loaded into a machine in certain proportions and kept at a given temperature, the PLC does this by controlling the loading process and temperature levels. It is also able to monitor variations in processes and in many cases steer them back on track or else halt the process itself and alert factory floor personnel. These are all purely technical procedures, yet it is in them that extensive and extremely useful information is to be found, for instance:

– data concerning quantities produced and machine cycles
– data concerning scrap and rejects
– quality control data, pressures, temperatures, acidity, etc
– maintenance data, such as frequency of machine breakdowns
– consumption data, raw materials, energy and more.

In many cases all this information is freely available.

The supervisory control of automated processes is not new to industry, but before the introduction of the PLC it could only be accomplished by hardwiring complicated relay structures (hence one of the variations on the PLC's name is PRC, or programmable relay controller). The relative innovation in the PLC is that supervisory control is performed by software and involves very little hardwiring.

A PLC is no more than a specialized microcomputer, specialized in that unlike the personal computer, which is programmed to fulfil a vast range of diverse functions, the PLC utilizes its microprocessor for the input, analysing and output of discrete or analog signals originating from an external device or piece of machinery. These signals enable the PLC to understand its environment and to react accordingly in a predetermined, accurate and speedy manner. It is the PLC's speed that adds another unique dimension to this device. As the PLC controls automated processes it will have to respond to the occurrence of certain events within milliseconds, in other words in real time. This gives the PLC a very specialized role in data collection. Most data collection devices that we examine here require human intervention to report events soon after they have occurred. A PLC gathers, while unattended, data about physical events as they are happening. Other features that distinguish a PLC from a regular microcomputer are:

- Resistance to industrial noise or disturbances, such as electromagnetic fields, sudden surges or drops in electric current.
- Resistance to dirty working environments, especially to dirt particles in the air.
- The existence of a *watchdog*. This device monitors possible disruptions in the function of its CPU due to program failure. Should a failure occur then the watchdog resets the program cycle.
- Built in backup power facilities in case of power loss.

All these features and others are of great significance, as they greatly reduce the chance of the PLC becoming inoperable and thus halting a manufacturing process.

The architecture of a PLC will differ from model to model, yet all PLCs have the following components:

- A power supply unit.
- A central processing unit.
- I/O terminals (channels), from a few points upwards.
- RAM for data, I/O status and certain control programs. (RAM sizes vary from a few kilobytes to a megabyte.)
- ROM for the control program.

A PLC is normally of a modular design, that is apart from the standard power unit, CPU, I/O terminals and basic memory, one can add on other modules. Such modules can be additional I/O terminals, extensions of memory, serial or LAN communication interfaces (see Section 9.3), and other special functions, such as closed-loop-PID (*proportional integral differential*) control units (see p. 107). All these additional modules plug into the backplane of the PLC, (Figure 9.1). The *backplane* is the communications bus for the PLC that allows the addition of a limited number of these special modules. Some of these modules will have their own dedicated

106 AUTOMATIC IDENTIFICATION AND DATA COLLECTION SYSTEMS

Power	PC CPU FVO Battery	■ ■ ■ ■ ■ ■	■ ■ ■ ■ ■ ■	■ ■ ■ ■ ■ ■ ■ ■ ■	■ ■	Power	■ ■ ■ ■ ■ ■ ■ ■ ■
POWER SUPPLY	CPU	INPUT	OUTPUT	INPUT / OUTPUT	COMMUNICATIONS	ANALOG INPUT	REMOTE SCANNER

Figure 9.1 The programmable controllers' modular structure.

microprocessor to relieve the burden from the main CPU. In this situation logic processing is distributed with the main CPU delegating work to other modules. This ability greatly reduces the *scan time* of the PLC, that is the time taken to input, analyse and output signals.

The PLCs input and output devices are of special interest. These input and output terminals or modules receive and give out signals from wires connected to them. Such a signal can be *discrete*, that is on/off (or of 0/1 status), or variable within a predefined range (for instance − 10 V to + 10 V), when it is known as an *analog* signal because it is analogous to the status of an occurring event. For example, varying temperature levels can be input into a PLC, but the PLC is not subjected to the temperature itself; rather, it receives a representation of the actual temperature provided to it by a *transducer* to be considered in the next paragraph. An example of a discrete input can be the presence of an object on a conveyer system. Here the PLC receives the characteristic two-state indication of a discrete signal, in this case object present or not present.

A PLC receives both analog and discrete signals from a host of different devices. Transducers convert one form of energy to another, normally

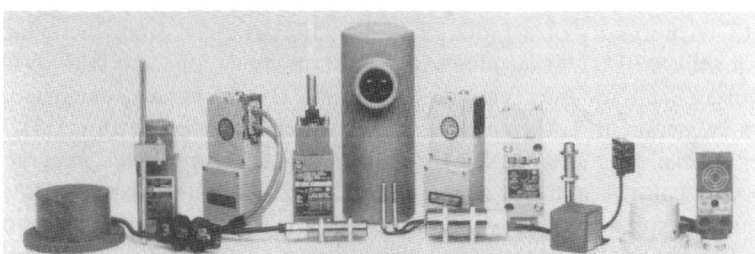

Figure 9.2 Sensors. Courtesy Allen Bradley

providing analog signals, while *sensors* sense the presence or non-presence of items and usually provide discrete signals (Figure 9.2). A brief look at both these types of input devices follows.

A sensor can detect an item in one of three basic ways:

- Physical detection – a mechnical switch.
- Proximity detection – the proximity of an item to the sensor is detected by an electric or magnetic field.
- Optical detection – either a beam of light is broken by a passing article or the article reflects light which in turn is detected.

The most common functions of tranducers can be broadly classified as follows:

- pressure measurement
- temperature measurement
- positioning measurement – displacement
- flow measurement.

Other input devices that can interface to the PLC are various auto-ID readers, the most common of which are the bar code readers.

The PLC's circuitry can be connected to various types of machinery and other devices via its input terminals. Many PLCs are able to input signals from more than one machine simultaneously. Signals received by a PLC are tested and either stored or new ones immediately output. An example of an input signal could be the presence of an object, while the resulting output signal could be the activation of a device that will perform a task on that same object.

The PLC outputs signals in both discrete and analog fashions, depending on the specific requirement. The activation of an external process by a PLC is known as *actuation*, and is normally facilitated by a discrete signal. Yet many PLC units have advanced PID (proportional, integral and differential control) capability. Essentially these features give the PLC the ability to provide different analog outputs as a function of a received input. *Proportional control* means simply that the analog output is in direct proportion to the input signal, *integral control* allows for accurate corrective action to be taken as a result of a given deviation from a predefined course (the integral being the sum of all previous deviations reported up to the time of the corrective action), and *differential control* determines the output signal according to the rate of change of the input signal.

Apart from basic input/output functions, the PLC is able to:

- Keep time, making input/outputs dependent on definable time intervals as well as measuring elapsible time intervals such as cycle times.
- Count events.

108 AUTOMATIC IDENTIFICATION AND DATA COLLECTION SYSTEMS

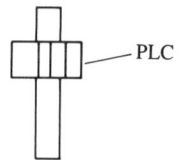

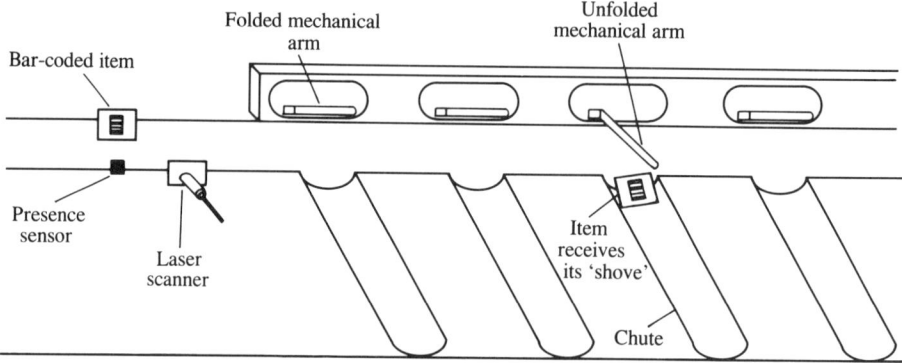

Figure 9.3 Chute and conveyance system

- Perform simple arithmetic procedures.
- Sequence output states using a *drum* controller to facilitate the sequential activation of one or more outputs according to a predefined pattern.
- Search lookup tables, which are areas of RAM that can store data in a tabular fashion. These tables can originate in a host computer and are downloaded from the host to the memory of the PLC. An example of the particular use of such a table is to store production details of a number of different items.

Finally, to conclude this section let us consider the following example of a PLC performing a simple task (Figure 9.3).

A number of different items are transported along a conveyor belt past a number of chutes. The PLC has to push the right item down the right chute. Item-to-chute matching is facilitated by bar-coding each item as well as by installing a number of presence sensors, one for each chute, connected to an input terminal of a PLC. Before the item reaches the chute section of the conveyor system the bar code on the item is read and the item ID is matched to a particular chute in the PLC's memory by the use of a lookup table. When the correct chute's presence sensor inputs the item's presence at the mouth of the chute the PLC outputs a signal to a mechanical arm which gives our item the shove it needs to tumble down the chute.

9.3 Connecting the PLC to a host system

The type of output dealt with in this section is the one that enables the PLC to transmit from its memory registers valuable information about processes that are under its control. This is facilitated by a number of components:

- a physical communication link or cable between one or more PLCs and a host computer
- a communications protocol between the host computer and the PLC (to be considered in Section 9.4).
- application software that specifies and controls data acquisition according to predetermined criteria (to be considered in Section 9.4).

When examining the first component one must keep in mind elements of speed and versatility. Transfer of data is often required to be frequent, and may occur as often as once per second. The requirement for versatility stems from the fact that many industrial systems are dynamic and subject to change, so the chosen solution should be adaptable to future changes.

The physical link

For the physical link between the PLC and the host computer, or between the PLCs themselves, cables of various types can be used. Apart from speed, a cable's ability to isolate the transferred data from possible interference from industrial environments is of the utmost importance. Its versatility, another desirable feature, is expressed by its ability to permit the transmission of a number of channels at once, at different frequencies, for example, the simultaneous transmission of both video pictures and data (made possible by a *broad-band coaxial cable*). High data transfer rates can be achieved by the use of *fibre optic cable*. Both of these types of cable are, however, more expensive than two other widely used ones. A *base band coaxial cable* will only allow a single communications channel yet it has all the isolating properties of its multichannel broad-band counterpart and is less expensive, while a *twisted pair cable* also only permits the transfer of data through a single channel cable. The latter type of cable is susceptible to environmental disturbances from machinery and therefore requires some form of additional isolation.

Communication ports and topology

Various types of communication ports are used to link PLCs to a host computer. The simplest is a direct link via an RS232C serial interface, and most host computers require this form of serial interface. The limitation of the RS232C is that transmission speed is greatly reduced with distance, and distances over one hundred metres are usually not recommended. A *current loop* is more efficient over greater distances, i.e. it is speedier. If this type of communication port is used, then a converter to RS 232C from the current loop will most likely be required at the host computer end. If we wish to connect a number of PLCs to a host computer then an RS 485 port can be used. Such a port allows the connection of more than one PLC over long distances in a *multidrop* configuration. Yet as soon as we have more than one PLC trying to talk to the host computer at any one time the management of data communications becomes a more complex task.

An alternative to the multidrop topology is to connect a number of PLCs to a *multiplexer*, a single unit that gathers data from separate communication lines from each PLC and merges these lines to a single port in the host computer. This configuration does not require complex management of data communications and more than one PLC can send data simultaneously. Similarly the host computer can contain a *multi I/O* communications board that contains a number of communications ports. Each PLC is connected to a separate I/O port on the board, which acts as a multiplexer for the incoming data.

PLCs can also be networked together using either proprietary PLC or industrial networks. The first of these is supplied by the PLC manufacturer, and can include special features such as giving priority to particular PLCs. This form of network may not be suitable for installations using different makes of PLC. Examples of propriety networks are Allen Bradley's Datahighway or Siemen's Sinet. Industrial networks such as the Manufacturing Automation Protocol (MAP) of General Electric Corporation were designed to allow the linkage of a large number of different devices – CNCs, robots, and PLCs – to a single network. Such great versatility, though, comes only at a very high price, and MAP is one of the more expensive networks.

9.4 SCADA – supervisory control and data acquisition

The final step in the integration of PLCs into a data collection system is to define the software link between the PLC's internal registers and the host system, as well as to define which data is to be collected, from where and in which circumstances. This is made possible by the use of a *supervisory control and data acquisition system* (SCADA). As its name suggests, this system has two purposes, one to provide and display all pertinent information concerning one or more automated processes and the other to log data from those processes into data files for further analysis. The first element is termed a *man–machine interface* (MMI), which provides a textual and graphical view of events in real time. The second element is known as a *data logger*. In this section we examine the various key elements of a SCADA

PROGRAMMABLE CONTROLLERS 111

Figure 9.4 Wizcon 2 MMI. Courtesy PC Soft International

system using the example of one of the leading packages on the market today, namely Wizcon (Figure 9.4).

The first task in setting up a SCADA system is the logical creation of an interface from the host system to particular outputs of the PLC. This is done by defining a virtual PLC interface or VPI. The VPI can be of either *read only* or *read/write* status for any particular data item. Greater throughput efficiency can be achieved by transferring data items in communication blocks, thereby reducing network control overhead per item of data. Once the registers or *gates* for any particular PLC are linked to the host computer via a VPI the sample rate of that VPI is determined. The sample rate is the frequency measured in times per millisecond, at which the SCADA system will address and extract data from each gate.

The Wizcon SCADA system, if distributed, provides a technique of reducing data traffic via *push blocks*. These blocks of data are only received by the local station if a remote station detects a change in the value of those gates since the last transmission. A block is a grouping of gates from any PLC. The address of any particular block, and the actual dialogue between the SCADA system and the PLC, will actually vary from PLC to PLC, and it is the task of a *communications driver* to perform the necessary translation of the SCADA control commands to the PLCs and vice versa. Note that there may be a number of communication drivers for one make of PLC, as they differ from model to model. The SCADA system is not only concerned with the technical link up of gates but also with their functional grouping.

Gates are grouped for data-logging reasons; thus a series of gates can be logged together into a chosen data file. They are normally grouped together where there is a functional common denominator between them, such as the production rate of a number of machines. Another example of a gate functional grouping is the *compound gate*, which allows the SCADA system to link the output of a number of gates in order to calculate a result. For instance, a particular compound gate's specification may define some arithmetic relationship between its two component gates. Thus one of the latter ('gate 1') might contain the number of items that pass through a quality control check, while the other gate ('gate 2') might contain the number of items channelled off the production line because they did not pass the test. Such a compound gate could then be specified as follows:

$$\text{Compound gate} = \frac{\text{Gate } 2 \times 100}{\text{Gate } 1}$$

(which is the percentage of rejects between sample times). We should note that the compound gate formula can include constants.

Once data has been received from the various defined gates it can be presented in a number of ways on the monitor of a host computer. SCADA systems like Wizcon excel in their ability to produce a graphic representation of events on the factory floor as they happen. For instance, the SCADA system can show a number of containers filling up with various liquids, each container labelled and each type of liquid colour-coded.

Liquid levels rise on the screen each time the values of the various gates rise.

This brings us to another important point: a SCADA system allows for data to be displayed or logged each time a gate is read, either according to a fixed sample rate or only when there is a change in a gate value. Data can also be represented textually, a particular gate value being assigned a message; this is necessary for alarm messages. For instance should a process halt, and a gate value not change over a given period of time (which is definable), then an alarm can pop up on the screen. This alerting of the user is performed by a mechanisim called an *annuciator*. The annunciator has a whole host of special functions and variations, for instance alerts can be grouped by severity and messages colour-coded. Some alerts will require the user to acknowledge their occurrence, while others are logged and automatically cleared. Data can also be represented in graph form, with the graph continuously evolving as new data arrives from the PLC.

Finally, to conclude this chapter on data collection in real time, we should note the special importance of the operating system under which the SCADA system functions. Clear preference should be given to those systems that allow *multitasking* – as in fact many do. Though multitasking can be emulated under the DOS operating system, true multitasking environments such as OS/2 or *windows* enable the user to perform additional tasks on the same computer or workstation without interrupting the data collection process. In the past a distributed data collection configuration was the only way this was allowed, with one computer acting as a communications server, and others for other processing and data analysis functions.

10
Portable data terminals

10.1 Portable data terminals – a comparative framework

Today's market is literally saturated with portable data terminals, manufactured by different companies. Not all of these have the same capabilities, nor indeed are they intended for the same kinds of applications. Anyone interested in implementing a data collection system that incorporates portable data terminals has first of all to determine the required specifications in order to carry out the task in hand, yet also to keep in sight possible future needs. The following is a comparative framework aimed at guiding the system designer through the maze of what the various vendors have to offer.

Displays

Perhaps one of the major differences between a personal computer and a portable data terminal is in screen size. The display of the portable data terminal can vary from a single line of a few characters up to over 20 lines of over 20 or more characters. There are a number of reasons for this. First, the portable data terminal replaces the traditional form, so unlike a personal computer, whose applications are concerned with more than just inputting data (for instance producing graphic representations of processed data), the terminal need only display the relevant information neccessary to facilitate the accurate collection of data. Second, the end-user normally collects data at the same time as performing a particular task (for example recording inventory as it is being received), which means that the user's eye has to find the relevant input field on the screen in the quickest possible time. However, one should not choose a very small screen unless there is a certainty that the terminal will only run 'small-screen applications', both in the present as well as in the future. Traditionally there exists both 'large screen' and 'small-screen' applications. For instance, most inventory applications can fit nicely into a 2- or 4-line screen, while vansale systems (see Chapter 15) generally need a large screen in order to display all the data they manage. It is, therefore, essential when one is purchasing a terminal to consider whether the intended application will be the only one run on that terminal. One might also assume from the above that 'big is best', but this is not always so; larger screen terminals are usually both bulkier and more expensive than their smaller, lightweight counterparts. Finally, a good terminal should provide both screen contrast control and backlighting for poor lighting conditions.

Keyboards

If one keeps in mind the type of end-user that is expected to operate the terminal then choosing the right keyboard should not prove too difficult a task. Unlike a PC, whose keyboard rarely differs from unit to unit, keyboards for portable data terminals come in a wide range of layouts. As such terminals are small, the keyboard, and more importantly, its keys, are small too. An end-user, already disheartened by the prospect of losing pen and paper, who has wide fingers and is presented with a terminal with lots of tiny keys, may well react with rage and/or despair! Some keyboards are designed to have the same layout as a PC, only with much smaller keys. While this at first may seem advantageous, most keys may not be required for most data collection applications. It might be assumed that the transfer from a regular PC to a portable data terminal will be smoother if the keyboards are the same or at least similar, but as just mentioned many end-users will only have used paper and pen for data collection and not a PC, and so they will not be making this transition. Other layouts commonly available are *numeric only* and *full alphanumeric*, (the alphanumeric keys are normally arranged in alphabetical order). As most data collection applications normally involve the collection of far more numeric data than alphanumeric, the best layouts emphasize the numeric keys, which are normally larger than the rest. Again one should remember that the end-user should spend as little time as possible in searching for a specific key – the data collection device must not become a bottleneck!

Memory

Memory configuration is perhaps one of the most important design considerations in planning a data collection system comprised of portable data terminals. In order to do so, though, one must first understand the different types of memories available. A terminal's memory can be divided into three broad categories: for the terminal programs, system, and for data. The first category is a *non-volatile* RAM in which the user application is stored. This memory type will not be written into during normal use and can only be erased by a special procedure. It is also not dependent upon an external power source, hence its being termed non-volatile. Non-volatile memory can be found in a number of different forms, the most common being *removable EPROM*, (erasable programmable read-only memory), and *EEPROM* or *flash* EPROM. The main difference between the two is that the first is programmed externally by a special device (this same device can erase the program on the chip by exposing it to ultraviolet light). The program is transferred to the device from a host computer, then 'burnt' into the memory chip, which in turn is installed into the terminal. The installation is normally a simple affair and can be performed by the end-user. The EEPROM is programmed inside the terminal itself by connecting the terminal to a host computer and downloading the program into the special memory; no external devices are required for this process.

In some of the older models of portable data terminals still found on the market today the application program is actually downloaded into regular volatile RAM (because in these terminals this is the only form of memory that is available). In order to prevent the corruption of the program during use, this area of memory is *write-protected* after the program has been downloaded to the terminal. However, as with all RAM, should the power source be cut off the program will be lost. The second category of memory, RAM, is the type used for storing data collected by the end-user, and data can be both read from and written to it under the control of the application. While non-volatile memories can range from as little as 16 kB to 512 kB, RAM size can reach a number of megabytes. In Chapter 19, on system design, we discuss the considerations in choosing the optimal memory size. Finally, the portable data terminal's system functions, such as its operating system, are normally stored in read only memory (ROM). This is a non-reprogrammable memory chip.

Processors and operating systems

The 'strength' of a terminal is measured by its processor, as this directly affects the terminal's speed of operation and data processing capability. Older generations of portable data terminals incorporated 8-bit processors, the latest generation having 16-bit ones, (though to put this advantage in perspective, most data collection systems are not required to handle or process large amounts of data at any one time). Data collection systems are characterized as being *transaction-based*; that is, usually (but not always) only the data in a single transaction is processed at any one time. However, a strong processor is required should the data collection application program require extensive searches in large data files of thousands of records, for example in finding an item number from a large item file. The 16-bit terminals are supplied today with DOS operating systems, so it might seem that any program that runs on a PC will also run on a portable data terminal, but this is not the case: most portable data terminals are not PC-hardware-compatible, differing both in their basic input output system

(BIOS) as well as in their screen type and keyboard. This means that although programs can be written for the terminal in a common development language such as Pascal or C, the programmer will have to be aware of these hardware differences. For this reason application programs are developed with both a standard development tool as well as unique libraries of programs to deal with the particular terminal's unique hardware components. These libaries are acquired from the portable data terminal vendors, and will differ for each manufacturer.

Power source

In Chapter 1 we saw that one of the main distinctions between a PLC, time attendance and shop floor terminal on the one hand, and a portable data terminal on the other, is that the latter has an *independent* power source to allow for its portability. The portable data terminal is battery-driven, usually by rechargeable nickel–cadmium cells ('Ni–Cads'). Other terminals can be run by disposable alkaline cells. The most versatile, though, can be powered by both, which is a very important feature in a portable data terminal, since end-users may forget to recharge the terminal when they should; if there is no spare charged battery pack on hand when this happens then the terminal will be immobilized and the data collection process interrupted unless we can replace the rechargeable battery pack with disposable batteries. When the portable data terminal loses its primary source of power, a secondary power source, normally a lithium battery or a capacitor, takes over to prevent data being lost from the RAM. Lithium batteries will back up data for a considerably longer period of time than does a capacitor: 300 to 400 backup hours is not uncommon with lithium cells. A very important feature that most terminals provide is an advance warning to the end-user that its cells need to be replaced or recharged. When considering a particular terminal's power source, note the following factors:

– the time it takes to fully charge the cells and whether the terminal allows trickle charging, that is the 'topping up' of the Ni-Cads periodically without the need to charge them fully
– the net work time between charges.

Communications interface

RS232 serial communications is the standard interface for most portable data terminals. Some terminals have more than one communication port, which can be a significant factor if the application demands that a terminal communicates simultaneously with a number of external devices, such as a printer as well as an electronic scale.

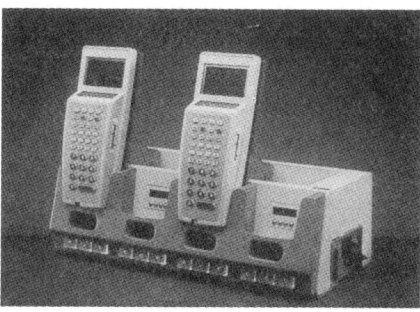

Figure 10.1 Portable data terminal communication cradle: Symbol Technologies' CCM. Courtesy Symbol Technologies

If the proposed system will involve a large number of terminals that will need to communicate with the host computer near, or at the same time as each other, then one should make sure that a *communications cradle* is available for the chosen model (Figure 10.1). The cradle enables the connection of a number of terminals to a single port in the host computer, thus reducing the risk of a data communications bottleneck as end-users wait in line for the previous unit to finish transmission. With this configuration, as soon as one terminal has finished sending its data the next can begin automatically. Some communications packages allow for the *simultaneous* transmission of data to all terminals in the cradle.

The type of communication port offered by the portable data terminal is also of significance. Most offer a standard 25-pin port to which a communications cable is connected, while others offer an *optical coupler*. This latter option receives data by the controlled activation of light-emitting diodes (LEDs). The terminal is placed into a special receiver that receives the light signal and transfers the data to a standard RS 232 communications port, with the advantage that the terminal and communication cable avoid most of the wear that can occur when they are frequently connected and disconnected. Not only this; a terminal with an optical coupler can be fully sealed, which is an advantage if it is required to operate in harsh environments.

Finally, some terminals offer the use of a *memory disk* rather like a miniature diskette. Here data can be transferred to the host without the need for actual data communications.

Durability

Some terminals are particularly durable in adverse environmental conditions. These units normally live up to military standards as regards their durability in dust and rain, and their ability to withstand falls and vibration. This is a major consideration when considering the procurement of a portable data terminal, as unlike non-portable data collectors, data collectors on the move have a tendency to fall and be knocked.

10.2 Auto-ID interfaces

Portable data terminals provide built-in support for many auto-ID readers, the most common of which is the bar code reader. Most terminals contain a built-in decoder (unlike a PC or other computer), as well as providing the current needed to power the reader itself. It is for this reason that many portable data terminals have special ports for auto-ID readers, (as opposed to using an RS232 interface). Wands and laser readers are the most common bar code reading technologies that interface to the terminal, and many are supplied with readers that are an integral part of the unit itself. This 'one-hand solution' is clearly a superior way to implement a combined data collection and auto-ID system (in Chapter 22 we examine a 'no hands' solution). Other auto-ID readers that are supported are magnetic stripe readers and interrogators for RF tags.

10.3 Software design considerations

Portable data terminals are used in the field, by a warehouse operative, a meter reader, a truck driver, a delivery person or a factory floor worker. Such a user may never have worked with a computer before, and may at first be wary of the terminal, or wish to ignore the benefits that this tool confers both here on the job and within the system as a whole; the user may concentrate instead on how the terminal 'complicates' a once straightfoward task. The software designer must take this into account, if the terminal is to be accepted. A portable data terminal is a data collection device with attributes similar to those of a PC, but it is *not* operated in the same environment. A user working in front of a computer monitor is often cut off from the immediate environment, preoccupied with inputting data, running programs or analysing output. The user of a portable data terminal is, by contrast, usually *interactive* with the environment, and is performing other tasks besides operating the terminal. So, the application software which runs the terminal *must* be simple to operate, 'user friendliness' is not just an advantage – it is vital, a basic requirement. This means that the program will:

– *Not* require significant changes to existing working methods.
– Allow the operation of the terminal in the simplest possible fashion, with the minimal usage of special-function keys.
– Be simple enough to allow any user to master its operation in a minimum

amount of time. In certain systems there can be a high turnover of end-users.
- Not allow data already collected to be erased from the memory as a result of incorrect usage. We must accept as a 'golden rule' that if the user is told not to operate the terminal in a certain way, it will be operated in that same way!
- Have an immediate response time for any particular operation. The situation in which the user has to wait for the terminal to complete a particular action has to be avoided at all costs.
- Display clear, unambiguous user instructions and messages.
- Allow the execution of a particular task with the minimal number of keystrokes.
- Not require the user to make too many additional decisions to the ones they already make today.

All in all, the terminal must not be in any way a hindrance to the end-user, but rather serve as an efficient tool. Let us look now at some common software design pitfalls:

- In order to prevent the processing of information based on replicate data, the terminal should not be allowed to send the host computer the same data twice. This can be prevented either by automatically erasing data after a successful communications session or else by marking the data sent in the terminal's memory so that it is not sent in subsequent communications sessions.
- The situation should be avoided where during the data collection process the terminal's memory is filled to capacity. This event will require the user to stop work and send data to the host system, a particularly annoying occurrence if the host system is far removed from the site in which the terminal is operated. The solution is to warn the user well before the memory reaches full capacity, for instance each time the terminal is powered up.
- With manual data collection procedure it is common for users to write comments alongside the data they are recording. This facility does not exist with a portable data terminal; as we already know, it comes with a small keyboard, but we cannot ask the user to learn to type. If standardized comments can be displayed and chosen from a memory file, all well and good; otherwise, the designer must think of an alternative solution.
- The designer should allow, where permitted, the reaccess of previously collected data for updating in the simplest way.

11
Computerized time and attendance, access control and shop floor terminals

11.1 Introduction

In the previous two chapters we have seen how data is collected in real time from automated processes and have examined portable data collection solutions. The last category of data collection devices we have to look at is the fixed-mount data collector. These devices are all similar if not almost indistinguishable in their hardware configuration, yet nevertheless are variously classified according to their functional purposes. Thus a computerized 'time and attendance terminal' might be collecting data about hours put in by employees at one site, while an identical device, this time termed a 'shop floor terminal' is collecting data about work in progress at another. So here we first examine the general hardware and software configuration of such devices before we discuss their different functions in a number of separate sections.

11.2 Hardware configuration

As with all data collection devices, the basic components of a fixed-mount data collector are a central processing unit, a memory, a serial communications interface to a host computer, a power supply and various other I/O drivers. The fixed-mount device normally possesses two levels of backup power, first a lithium battery used to back up the RAM, in which the collected data is stored, and second is a rechargeable nickel–cadmium power cell, which allows the continued operation of the data collector when the main power supply has been cut off. The memories of a fixed-mount data collector fall principally into two categories, volatile memory or RAM, in which the collected data and application programs are stored, and EPROM, in which the basic functions of the data collector are preprogrammed. RAM capacity ranges from device to device, but it is normally found in the range 32 to 100 kB. Serial communications are normally facilitated by a standard RS 232, RS 422 or RS 485 driver interface.

The most common I/O devices supported by the fixed-mount data collector are:

- magnetic card reader
- bar code reader
- relays
- microswitches.

These last two devices allow this data collector both to input and to output discrete event signals, much as does a PLC. Two classic examples are relays that open doors as well as those that cause a bell to ring (a standard function for time and attendance terminals, to tell workers about the commencement of a work break). Relays, therefore, are activated following an event (as in the first example), or as a function of time (as in the second example). Data can be input into a fixed-mount data collector in a number of ways. When an event is reported to the system it is normally done by the combination of automatic identification as well as manual key entry. Very few of these data collection systems rely on just the latter.

Unlike the PLC, the fixed-mount data collector, whether a time and attendance terminal or a shop floor terminal, has very few supervisory control functions. So we might ask ourselves at this stage what special purpose a fixed-mount terminal serves; why not replace it with a regular computer monitor and keyboard or with a personal computer? There are a number of answers. First, the fixed-mount data collector is inconspicuous, taking up very little room. These little terminals can be mounted on a wall, in a control panel, almost anywhere. Their screen and keyboard are normally small (in comparison with a computer monitor or personal computer) and are an integral part of the unit itself. Screens are not normally required for monitoring, but rather merely to prompt users about the data that they are to report, as well as to display simple messages. Terminals are normally very resistant to adverse environmental influences such as electrical interference, climatic factors, dust, oils, etc. Indeed, most contain defence mechanisms against sudden surges in electrical power and against lightning. The keyboard is normally of sealed-membrane type, which stops dust particles getting in and causing the keys to stick. The fixed-mount data collector does not require many of the components of a personal computer, such as disk drives, hard disks, or even a DOS operating system (although some terminals do possess this feature). A fixed-mount unit that periodically uploads its data to a host computer will not in any significant way burden the host system. As we see below, real-time input checks on inputted data can be performed by the data collector without interacting with the host system.

11.3 Communications interface and application software

Computerized time and attendance and shop floor data collection terminals are programmed at two different levels. Basic functions and procedures are preprogrammed in ROM; they will include the definition of certain standard keys on the keyboard, such as ⟨IN⟩ and ⟨OUT⟩, or even the terminal's ID, as well as decoding algorithms for bar codes, data communications management and more. Procedures that differ from one installation to the next are normally programmed on a personal computer using a program generator; these are then downloaded to one or more terminals in the field. In this section we take a brief look at some of the major characteristics of fixed-mount terminal application generators, though different generators will offer their own special features.

The program generator permits us to define the communication link between the host computer and the terminals in the field. The term 'host computer' does not necessarily refer to the final destination of the collected data. In organizations in which a mainframe computer contains the central database, a personal computer is normally used as a bridge between the field terminals and the mainframe. There are a number of reasons for this, a main one being that many terminal vendors normally develop their program generators to run on a personal computer platform. Defining the communications interface, (see Figure 11.1), includes:

- *Line definition*, baud rate, parity, etc.
- *Terminal activation*. Which terminals will be recognized by the system and considered active? The user enters the unique terminal identity for each active terminal.
- *Data transmission policy*. Data transmission can be defined for a single terminal, a group of terminals or all active terminals. Data transmission can also commence automatically at different definable time intervals for different terminals.
- *Data erasure in the terminal*. Data once received by the host is erased in the terminal. The erasure of data in the terminal is not normally an automatic process, rather, though, it is carried out after the user has given the appropriate command at the host end. This feature and other similar ones allow the control of a large number of terminals in the field from a central host computer. Note that after receiving a data erasure command the terminal knows how to distinguish between data that has been sent

124 AUTOMATIC IDENTIFICATION AND DATA COLLECTION SYSTEMS

Active stations			
Station number	Active	Station number	Active
1	Y	15	N
2	Y	16	N
3	Y	17	N
4	Y	18	N
5	Y	19	N
6	Y	20	N
7	Y	21	N
8	N	22	N
9	N	23	N
10	N	24	N
11	N	25	N
12	N	26	N
13	N	27	N
14	N	28	N

Figure 11.1 Communication interface screen

and data that has yet to be sent; in this way unsent data will never be erased.

– *Terminal communications tracking.* It is of vital importance to know which terminals have sent data and when. Terminal communications tracking is therefore an essential part of any terminal communications management routine.

After the communications link between the terminals in the field and the host computer has been defined, the user interface and application program will be configured. The user may wish to download different terminals with different programs. As mentioned earlier, identical models of a particular terminal can be used for quite different purposes. Programming is normally a very simple procedure, far simpler than the programming of a PLC or portable data terminal, so much so that with a little practice most end-users can perform this task. Programming methods will obviously differ from vendor to vendor; what follows is a brief description of one of the more common programming approaches.

Most fixed-mount terminals have keyboards with up to ten or so specially defined function keys. Some terminals possess numeric or alphanumeric keys also. Pressing a particular function key presents the operator with a series of prompts as to the data to enter. For each function key there exists a different set of prompts. For instance, one key might be designated for jobbing while another is for reporting defects. In the case of time and attendance a single prompt is presented, asking the user to enter their ID. In such cases the employee is normally not required even to press

TIME AND ATTENDANCE, ACCESS CONTROL, SHOP FLOOR TERMINALS 125

Key No.	Master table description
3	Work in progress

Parameters	1	2	3	4
Preliminary message				
Input (bar code, Tag, KB)				
Display input?				
Field length				
Obligatory field				
Auto enter?				
Input check #1				
Input check #2				
Input check #3				
Routine number				
Concluding message				

Figure 11.2 Master table

a key, although as we see shortly there are some exceptions to this. Each prompt is linked to an input field, a selection of input checks, messages, and input device definitions. The prompt's associated input field makes up part of the data record that is stored in the terminal's memory.

Programming itself is carried out simply by creating program tables that are part of the terminal's application generator. A generator contains a number of table types, each with a different purpose. Among these tables are to be found:

- *Master table* (Figure 11.2). This table contains a series of prompts and their related parameters (see below). Each prompt is in fact a single step in the application program. Each master table is allocated to a particular function key.
- *Message table*. This table contains all the messages in the system that are presented to the end-user. Each message is assigned a unique code and these message codes are entered into the appropriate entry in the master table.
- *Lookup tables*. An instance would be a list of employees.
- *Input check table*. Each entry in this table contains a particular check to be performed on input data, for instance a minimum–maximum range check. Input check codes are entered into the appropriate location of the master table.

Let us take a brief look at how we might wish to create a master table and thence program a particular function key on one or more terminals. As we saw earlier a master table contains a series of prompts, each one being an independent program step. Therefore most data collection with time and attendance or shop floor terminals are essentially sequential processes with data being entered in a predetermined fashion. Each program step in the master table contains such parameters as:

- The initial message to be displayed at the start of the current step.
- The entry device or devices for this step, e.g. one or a combination of the following: keyboard, bar code reader, magnetic stripe reader.
- The length of input field.
- The type of input field, such as obligatory or non-obligatory.
- Input checks to be performed.
- The record type. With data being recorded for different purposes, each type of data record in the terminal's memory is uniquely marked. The record type is essentially the identity of the function key pressed before data is entered.
- Special routines to be performed once data has been entered, for instance a search in a lookup table.
- The end message to be displayed at the end of the current program step.

By entering values into the master and other tables, simple yet very effective programs can be created. In most data collection procedures the most effective programs are the simplest that do not leave too much room for end-user decision-making in the field. Programs can be updated frequently and redownloaded to terminals in the field. To facilitate the maintenance of the different programs some generators offer a *learning mode* in which the host computer software reads and displays the current contents of a program in each terminal.

11.4 Time and attendance

Orginally it was the need to solve time–attendance and data processing problems that led to the development of computerized time and attendance terminals. Only later on were these used for data collection from the factory floor. Most of us are familiar with the standard time and attendance 'clock-in' card. When an employee inserts his card into a mechanical or electronic time and attendance clock it is date-and-time-stamped. Problems begin to arise at the end of the month when all employees' cards are collected and their recorded hours are summated, for this task is not only laborious but one rife with hazards. A mistake in the total hours worked means that either an employee is under-paid or the company's payroll will exceed its nominal level. Further complications arise when a particular employee has to record each time he leaves a work site during the day, either on or off duty. This can soon make the standard time and attendance card a complete jumble of stampings, and summation even harder. Not only this, but when a number of wage tariffs are used to work out an employee's salary (depending on the number of hours worked and when) then manual calculations are a headache!

The computerized time and attendance terminal solves these problems. An employee's movements are recorded by swiping through a slot reader in the terminal itself a plastic card on which the employee's identity is recorded by either a magnetic stripe or a bar code. The 'in' or 'out' mode of the terminal is set either by the pressing of a function key or by program according to the time of day (for instance the clock can switch from 'in' to 'out' mode automatically at midday). A worker leaving a site on duty presses an 'on duty' key before swiping the card. The computerized time and attendance terminal can also possess a number of basic supervisory control functions in conjunction with an access control system; these are examined in Section 11.6 on access control.

Once data has been collected and stored in the terminal's memory it is fowarded to the host computer. This data has a number of uses:

- *Attendance reports*. There are a number of different types of these, the most common being an employee's monthly attendance report and monthly absentee report.
- *Salaries*. Each worker is employed under agreed terms, which are often based upon a wage tariff per hour (according to the number of hours worked and the time of day at which they were worked). Assuming that the only dynamic component of an employee's salary is the hours worked, then the salary can be computed automatically from the data received from the computerized time and attendance terminal by the host computer, and payslips issued upon demand.
- *Time event tracking*. Time events are those events that fall out of the defined framework of an employee's terms of employment. Examples of time events that can be computed by the system are unapproved overtime or too much sick leave or holiday. These events are harder to track with a manual system.
- *Output files*. As stated earlier, the host computer in a system will not always be the final destination of the collected data. Either summarized or raw data can be exported into ASCII files and imported into a mainframe computer.

Two related time and attendance data uses are examined in the next sections. These are work premiums and access control.

11.5 Shop floor terminals

In Chapter 9 we explored real-time data collection from the factory floor. Yet not all important industrial data can be collected in an unattended fashion. Manual data collection has to be both simple, non-time-consuming and unambiguous. Many reporting tasks incorporate the use of auto-ID technology to reduce the possibility of mistakes. The classic use of a shop floor terminal is for the collection of data used to calculate work premiums (a financial reward for work performed at a rate over and above the standard rate determined for a particular task). This can be measured in one of two ways: either by time taken to perform a task or by quantity produced within a given time period. In order to calculate premiums, production tasks are broken down into *jobs*, with the start and end of each one being reported to the shop floor terminal by workers. Both worker and job identification (the latter is normally linked to a particular work order) are reported with the aid of magnetic stripes or bar codes. Data so collected can be used for other purposes too. Time data can be integrated into the cost accounting of a manufacturing process, thus allowing the price of a product to accurately reflect the work hours invested in its production. In many situations the work-hour contribution to the overall cost of production is based upon outdated standard costing calculated in the past. Jobbing permits the 'fine tuning' of these standards used to calculate the cost of labour. If work orders or jobs are reported on a regular basis then customer order status or production schedule advancement can be verified. That is, we can know where each work order is on the factory floor and thus what stage of production each work order is at. The reported data is used to calculate estimated completion times for work orders, thereby enabling shop floor managers to plan production schedules accurately.

The various function keys on the terminal enable workers to report certain events as they happen. These events, while they are expected, can not be predicted ahead of time: they might be equipment failures, defective products, etc. Once again the worker is guided through the reporting process while providing answers to the questions asked by the terminal (see Chapter 14).

11.6 Access control

Not only are the attendance times of individuals a matter of importance; so too are their actual movements. Access control systems, as their name suggests, are primarily concerned with the supervision of the movements of individuals within an organization. A time and attendance terminal can deny access to an unauthorized individual, by opening doors only for those whose personal identity numbers (PINs) appear in a lookup table in the terminal's memory.

Access control can also be implemented by a special, dedicated controller. This, like the time and attendance device, can be either a standalone unit or one connected by batch communications or in real time to a host computer. The latter case involves an integrated access control solution and is discussed in more detail in Chapter 13; here we look at the other two solutions. Though as with many supervisory control systems data collection was not originally considered a primary aim of access control, nevertheless important data can be collected about who passed through which door and when. Such data is aimed at *people tracking*. *Event tracking*, another data collection objective in access control, records any noteworthy event, such as the access of a particular individual or a door being open for over a given period of time. Data is logged into memory and periodically uploaded to a host by serial batch communications.

By the very nature of this type of configuration both event tracking and people tracking are considered important goals, but not crucial enough to demand the collection of data in real time, as in the integrated solution. The various lookup tables containing authorized PINs and event definitions are downloaded from the host computer. In true standalone situations, where there is no physical link between the terminal or the controller and the host computer, (a rare occurrence for time and attendance terminals), lookup tables can be downloaded and collected data uploaded with a portable terminal.

12
Other data collection devices

In Chapter 1 the basic components of a data collector were itemized; they were:

- the means of inputting data
- an independent processing capability
- memory capacity for storing data
- data communications to the host system.

With these components as criteria for defining a data collector it is clear that most computerized tools can be regarded as data collectors. However, one must not forget that data collection is the initial recording of events as they happen, or shortly afterwards, at the place where they occur. Therefore while most computerized tools have the potential to be regarded as data collectors, it is only those that are *commonly* utilized for these purposes that are categorized as such.

The previous three chapters have presented the three best-known data collectors. There are also other devices that are variations on these, among them specialized fixed and portable SPC/SQC data collectors. The latter belong in a category of their own because they are distinguished from the others by possessing the following capabilities (Figure 12.1):

- direct interfacing with digital and analog gauges
- built-in SPC/SQC analysis
- connection to full-screen monitors.

The fixed station SPC/SQC data collector is typically used by machine operators. They input and analyse characteristics of one or more produced parts directly from gauges, automatically displaying relevant control charts as well as alerting the operator to certain trends or out-of-limit events. Portable SPC/SQC data collectors are designed for the roving quality control supervisor, who collects both variable and attribute data from a number of sources.

OTHER DATA COLLECTION DEVICES 131

Figure 12.1 Fixed-station SPC data collector: Allen Bradley Data Myte model 953. Courtesy Allen Bradley

Examples of gauges that both types of data collectors can interface into are:

– calipers
– micrometers
– gap and flushness gauges
– paint coat thickness testers
– torque testers.

While some data collectors interface only into certain gauge types and possess limited statistical analytical ability, others are able to accept interchangeable gauge modules as well as different program packs.

Among the extensive range of statistical charts and reports that these data collectors can create are to be found:

– X-bar and range
– X-bar and sigma
– histograms
– individual and moving range
– Pareto charts.

Other specialized data collectors to be found on the market today include:

- meter interface centralized units: data loggers for digital meters (water, electricity and gas)
- car data loggers, which collect data concerning travelling events, for example journey logs (times and distances) and speed events (maximum speed exceeded)
- local telephone call loggers, which record call information data for customer supervisory control.

PART 4
APPLICATIONS

13
Military and security related applications

13.1 LOGMARS

LOGMARS stands for logistics applications of automated marking and reading symbols. This is a large-scale US Department of Defense project that was established in the mid-seventies. Its mandate was to set the American defense establishment's standards for automatic identification and data collection for military logistics systems. A great deal of effort was invested in establishing a military standard for bar code labels that are used to mark many different items within the system. Code 39 was chosen as the principal symbology for the identification of items. The choice of Code 39 by the American Department of Defense gave great impetus to the further adoption of this code by other bodies, for two reasons. First, the military's choice was a major vote of confidence in this symbology. Second, the Department of Defense required 40 000 of its vendors to deliver their goods marked with Code 39 bar codes. All label components were specified, with special attention placed on adhesives. Extensive tests and specifications were drawn up for portable data terminals, with the most stringent demands being made on the terminal's durability and its ability to withstand the very harshest environmental conditions.

13.2 Guard patrols

Site inspection for security purposes requires the frequent attendance by a security officer at particular areas within that site. Such areas may include a perimeter fence, gateways, high-security installations, machinery or containers, damage to which can lead to devastating results. Regular inspections of sites such as these are common in prisons, military bases and power installations as well as in civilian industries generally. When guard patrol is required, so too is the accurate collection of data concerning any particular guard's shift. If data is collected in real time, then supervisory control features can be incorporated into the system. For instance the central system can alert a supervisor should a guard not acknowledge his arrival at a given place by a given time. Normally guards are required to patrol an area following a particular route, and positioned along this route are reporting stations at each of which the guard acknowledges his presence. The stations can be connected on-line to a central system, either by hard-wiring of all stations, which might well be infeasible on a very large site, or by radio frequency.

For installations not requiring on–line alerting, two common batch systems are commonly available. The main aim of these is to track a security officer's movements during a particular shift and to ensure that the data collected accurately reflects those movements. If we were to require the security officer to manually report his movements on a form, it would mean our total reliance on that officer's integrity to report these movements in a faithful manner. In order to overcome this problem in the past, guard patrol clocks were introduced. At each reporting station a small cabinet containing a special key is installed. Each key in each cabinet has its own unique identification. Upon reaching the station the guard opens the cabinet with a generic key, withdraws the unique key and inserts it into a special keyhole in the clock itself, which is of robust construction and is normally attached to a strap and carried over the guard's shoulder. When the key is turned in the clock its identity and the date and time are automatically printed onto a small paper strip inside the clock; this strip is later retrieved from the clock at the end of the guard's shift and contains a faithful report of her or his movements.

In the above procedure the identity of the guard was not recorded by the clock, and the collected data still had to be manually entered into a computer. There remained the need to collect data automatically and to fulfil the following requirements:

– automatic identification of the guard and reporting stations
– automatic time and date stamping during identification
– data that is unalterable once it has been reported
– batch data communications to a host system.

There are a number of computerized solutions for this type of system. Automatic identification of the guard is by means of a magnetic stripe card, a bar code or an RF tag. The method of identifying a station depends upon the data collection device used; if the data collection device is a computerized time attendance clock then the reporting station's identity will be the clock's own unique code stored in memory; otherwise one of the three methods mentioned for identifying the guard can be used to identify the station.

The data collection device can be either a fixed-mount or a portable one, each has its own advantages and disadvantages. A fixed-mount solution is more expensive to implement, because at each reporting station a data collection device has to be installed which must be either hard-wired to a central host computer or else able to transmit the collected data to a portable data terminal at given time intervals. In the latter case a supervisor connects the portable data terminal to the time and attendance clock, which transfers the collected data from its memory to the portable data terminal. The latter is later connected to a host system and the data uploaded. The portable device does not have to be a fully fledged portable data terminal (as described in Chapter 10); a small terminal with memory and simple data communications capabilities will suffice.

Finally, a portable data terminal can be used to provide a cost-effective solution for guard patrol, as only one data collection device is required for each guard simultaneously on duty (as opposed to one data collection terminal per reporting station); this solution has the disadvantage, however, of putting the data collector in the hands of a security officer, as with the guard patrol clock. Nevertheless, each reporting station requires only a simple durable bar code or RF tag, and when the portable data terminal reads the station's identity a new record of data is automatically recorded in its memory. This record contains the guard's personal identification number (entered once at the beginning of his shift), the station code, date and the time of read.

13.3 Crowd control

Crowd control is a portable version of access control (Section 13.4). This unique solution is required when access to a particular site or event is barred to groups of individuals. In such situations the installation of a conventional access system is often infeasible, for the following reasons:

– Events can move from site to site.
– Entry points to events are subject to change.
– The environment does not permit the installation of a conventional access control system.

Examples of crowd control can be found at sporting events (indeed such a system was used at the 1992 Olympic Games in Barcelona), or entry through border points (such as the entry of Arab residents from the Gaza Strip into Israel). In both situations a bar-coded personal identity tag is read and matched against a database inside a portable data terminal's memory. When the bar code is read the portable data terminal searches for the individual's ID. The portable database might include all those barred (a blacklist), or only those permitted access. As we may imagine, the memory capacity of the terminal has to be quite large. An on-line solution via radio frequency might expand the possibilities of such an application, although response times would have to be faster than those provided by most existing RF applications.

13.4 Integrated access control

In Chapter 9 we saw how supervisory control and data acquisition systems (SCADA) enable us to collect data in real time from the factory floor, via PLCs. Another application of a SCADA system is the integration of access control equipment to a host computer. In order to better understand the significance of this integration, we need to become acquainted with standalone access control, as described in Chapter 11. An integrated system not only provides powerful access control features that are easy to manipulate, but also provides us with the most timely information concerning the whereabouts of individuals, as well as the occurrence of certain events.

A major difference in this type of SCADA system, as opposed to one found on the factory floor, is in its hardware configuration. While PLCs can theoretically be used for access control, simpler, non-programmable controllers are the standard. The term 'non-programmable' may at first be a little misleading. Of course the non-programmable controller contains a program (otherwise it would not be functional), but this program cannot be modified by the user as it is embedded in a read-only memory (ROM). As such, it is categorized as *firmware*, which derives its name from an itermediate state between hardware and software. The inputs to the controller are more limited than the PLC, the principal ones being:

– the output of a magnetic stripe reader
– microswitches
– serial communications.

The magnetic stripe reader is the conventional way of conveying the PIN of an individual to the system. Alternative ones might be by the use of a keypad or a transponder. The former can normally be used as a backup facility for those who forget their magnetic card, but it might also augment the magnetic stripe reader, with the reader reading an employee's number from a magnetic stripe and the PIN being keyed into the system via the keypad. The latter is a 'hands-free' solution to access control, whereby the transponder conveys the PIN to an interrogator attached to the controller. Microswitches enable the system to detect tampering with equipment or other undesirable activity, such as the forcing of a door. In such situations the system will be provided with an alert. The serial interface to the controller enables the latter to receive various lookup tables from the host system, such as a list of all the PINs allowed access. These tables are dynamic, and therefore an integrated access control system has the obvious benefit over standalone units that a large number of controllers can be updated immediately. The principal output of the controller is the serial communications interface, which conveys data to the host system and relays that activate solenoids that open doors. Other optional inputs to the controller are thermocouples, smoke detectors, etc. Optional outputs can include small displays for conveying messages or connections to devices such as sprinklers (in the case of smoke detection).

For the physical connection of the access controllers to a host computer, some of the cable types and configurations discussed in Chapter 9 are relevant here also. Controllers can be linked in a multidrop fashion via an RS 422 interface, or can be 'daisy-chained' together via a current loop. In most situations the host computer will require an RS 422/RS 232 or current loop/RS 232 converter in order to both send and receive data. The fact that the access control system is integrated and does not stand alone does not mean that it cannot revert to a standalone situation, as it may have to when there has been a disruption in the communication link or the host system is temporarily inoperable. In such situations data is stored in the controller and later uploaded to the host system. Controllers can also indirectly pass messages between themselves, for instance where there is a need to limit an individual to a one-time-only access; thus when that individual passes through a door, the access event is sent to the host, while at the same time all other controllers in the same area can 'pick up' the sent data and delete that individual's PIN from their memory, thus preventing further access.

The various control functions of an integrated access control system are very wide, and a detailed discussion of them is beyond the scope of this text. Briefly, however, they include such features as:

– Anti-passback: the same PIN cannot enter unless it has already exited from an associated door.
– Access of a PIN only with a supervisory PIN.
– Access groups: PINs can be categorized, with access being restricted to certain categories.
– Time zoning: access is allowed only within certain time periods.

The functional aims of data collected from access controllers can be classified into two broad categories, as follows.

People tracking

This is made possible by the collection of data concerning the movement of people and the activation of doors. The aims of this data are:

– Tracking particular individuals, particularly visitors.
– Tracking time spent by individuals in particular areas.
– Automatic roll-call. In case of emergencies one can know where each person is situated.

– Information as to how many people are in a particular area at any one time.
– General access history – of all PINs for all areas.

Event tracking

An event can be any noteworthy occurrence, and is normally recorded as an alarm. Such alarms can require immediate acknowledgement or immediate action, or simply be logged. Alerts can be either loud or silent (an alert is silent when the person triggering the event has no idea that their actions have alerted the system). Examples of events are:

– 'Illegal actions', such as door or device tampering.
– The entry of a particular person into a particular area.
– Overcrowding: too many people in one area.
– Entrance frequency: the alert is made when a particular person has entered a particular area over a preset number of times.
– Duration in a particular zone.

Finally, as with other SCADA systems, people or event logging can be conditional upon a number of parameters. Such parameters might include:

– certain event types
– certain PINs
– an access group, i.e. a group of PINs with a common characteristic, for instance new workers
– a geographical zone
– a time zone, at a particular time of the day
– any combination of the above.

14
Data collection from the factory floor

14.1 Data collection from the factory floor – an overview

Before we look at certain applications of data collection from the factory floor, we need to examine the role of computerized data collection in manufacturing control and information systems. Information models in such systems include:

- an initial business plan and sales forecast
- product design and engineering
- manufacturing process design
- long-term production plan (master schedule)
- material requirement planning (MRP)
- production capacity planning
- an order release schedule

All of these elements are carefully planned information models, yet they are influenced greatly by day-to-day events. For instance, an order release schedule should take into account the actual status of the current orders on the factory floor. Another important characteristic of these information elements is that they are dynamic. What is planned should not be assumed to be axiomatic; changes will occur and information models will be readjusted, particularly in the case of MRP. Some influences on these information models are *external*, that is though they can be detected from within the factory system, they are not under direct control of factory management. Other factors that affect a model's performance and accuracy derive from within the factory. Examples of internal and external influences on various manufacturing information models include the following:

Product planning

Product quality: how do the following factors influence a product's quality?

- raw materials received from different suppliers
- particular manufacturing cells or machines
- manufacturing conditions, length of operation, temperature, acidity, mixing procedures, etc.

Manufacturing process design and production scheduling

Burden:

- actual burden on the manufacturing cells
- number of available production cells or machines (this data is also needed for order release).

Actual machine/worker hours invested in particular work orders (this data is also needed for costing):

- Which machines or processes are most efficient for particular products?
- Do production times vary with variations in the production process of a standard product?

Statistical process control (SPC)

- In which situations do processes or machinery step out of defined tolerance levels?
- Malfunctioning: how frequent is it, and under which circumstances does it occur (product, materials, tools, operator, environmental conditions, etc.)?

MRP

- Actual stock levels in warehouses.
- Materials in progress; where and in which amounts?
- Scrap levels (this data is also required for the other information models already mentioned). High scrap levels will require the maintenance of higher stock levels. This is an example of how an external influence can be detected from the factory floor, as the relative quality of a supplier's raw materials might adversely affect scrap levels. This in turn can affect procurement decisions, including possible discounts or reimbursements receivable for below-standard materials.
- Actual rate of material consumption.
- Order status (also needed for capacity planning and customer order followups).

Capacity planning

Order status: current status of work orders in progress.

– Actual order cycle times and influences on these times (product, materials, tools, operator, environmental conditions, etc.)

Actual setup times for machinery as a function of each product and operator as well as the previous product produced on the same machine

Order release

Availablity of production cells within a given time framework. Work orders are typically not released unless a predicted relatively smooth production flow can be guaranteed.

We should note that the role of a data collection system from the factory floor is to provide the necessary feedback to manufacturing information systems in order to validate, fine tune or even restructure manufacturing information models that are influenced by the above-mentioned and other factors. This feedback can bring about the reduction of inventory levels, knowledge of the causes both of inferior quality products and of production bottlenecks, superior scheduling and accurate customer order status information, and these in turn will lead to reduced costs, better customer service and, not least, stable or improved product quality. The applications to be discussed in this context are:

– production time management and work in progress
– data collection from automated manufacturing processes
– quality control
– warehouse management
– 'just-in-time'.

14.2 Production time management and work in progress

Production time is the actual hours of labour invested in production tasks. *Work in progress* means following the progress of particular work orders on the shop floor. Data concerning both is collected with the aid of shop floor data collection terminals (see Chapter 11), and this can be done using a single reporting method. The shop floor terminals collect data over a period of time, and at the system manager's request transfer it to the host system. Typically this data is imported into production management software, which among other things is able to compare actual production events against planned schedules.

144 AUTOMATIC IDENTIFICATION AND DATA COLLECTION SYSTEMS

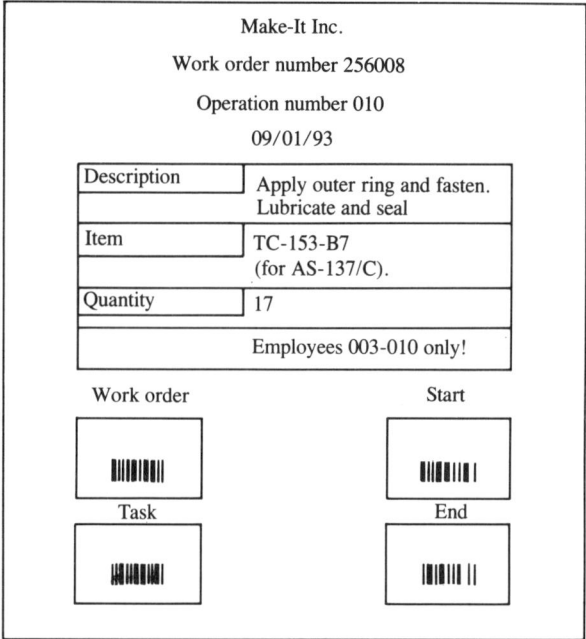

Figure 14.1 Bar-coded work order form

The shop floor terminal can and normally does collect data concerning the time attendance of shop floor personnel, to which end each worker is given an identity card with either a magnetic stripe or a bar code on it. Work orders are typically printed with one or more bar codes, containing the following data (Figure 14.1):

– Work order number.
– Task or production stage code.
– Control bar codes, such as 'start of job', 'end of job', 'job break'. These bar codes can also be found on a standard control sheet by the terminal itself, or in some cases actually printed on the terminal's front panel.

As with most data collection systems, the method of reporting data to the system must be swift, simple and unambiguous. For each production task the following data may be collected (Figure 14.2):

– worker identity
– work order number
– task number
– start of task
– end of task
– quantity.

DATA COLLECTION FROM THE FACTORY FLOOR   145

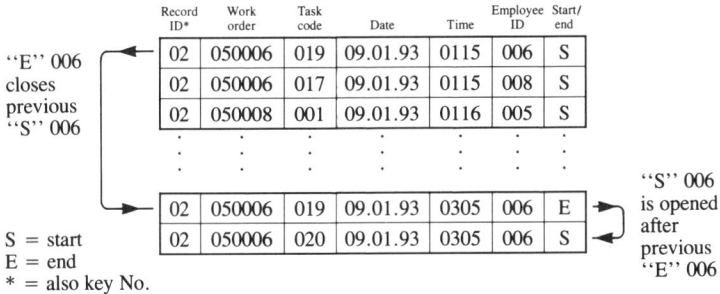

Figure 14.2   Task data records

As with time and attendance, the worker reads his identification into the system when a task is commenced. Similarly, at the end of the task the worker's identification is read, enabling the data collector to locate in its memory the right task to close (i.e. an open task with that worker's identity). The quantity field is normally optional and is filed only if the system requires a report of the amount of units produced. This might be the case if a production task is not completed by the end of the day, when the production worker may be required to report his progress.

The method of reporting can be simplified further. Task details can be reported just once to the system, at the end of each task. When the worker clocks in at the start of the day a task is automatically opened. When a task is closed the task details are reported and a new task is automatically opened. Clocking out at the end of the day closes the current task without opening a new one. This method of reporting has one inherent danger, namely that *idle time*, which is the time the worker spends in the factory in non-productive activity, may be included in the net task time. To overcome this problem idle time is recognized by the system as a task; thus a worker who has taken a break must, before commencing a new task, first of all close a *personal time task*. This task can appear as a standard bar code printed on each work order, or as a key or control bar code on or near to the terminal itself.

At each reporting stage the terminal can perform a number of validity checks, based typically on the following provisions:

– A new task for a particular worker cannot be opened unless the current task for that same worker has been closed.
– A reported work order number must be recognized by the host system.
– The total reported quantity is no greater than the quantity required for a particular work order.
– The worker reporting the task is authorized to perform it.

The last three validity checks are made possible by the storage of control tables in each terminal's memory.

The data collected for production time management purposes also enables the tracking of work orders. This is particularly significant if a work order contains a complete customer order. If so, the central system will know exactly at all times which production stages of a customer order have been completed as well as the number of units finished. This is an important tool in the estimation of the time required to complete a particular customer order.

14.3 Data collection from automated manufacturing processes

In this section we look at two examples of data collection from automated manufacturing processes, in industries where contrasting conditions prevail and yet where factors such as quality assurance and manufacturing efficiency are of cardinal importance.

The biscuit factory

Here certain problems were encountered during the packaging stage of production, but before the introduction of a SCADA system these defied actual and accurate specification. Every one of this particular factory's five production lines, with an output of 600 kilograms of biscuits per hour, can produce up to three different shelf products simultaneously. Each product is distinguished by its own unique packaging, and on every line there exist three automated machines to package the biscuits.

Management faced the following problems:

- overweight and underweight packages
- high and inexplicable levels of scrap packaging materials
- lack of quality assurance data
- lack of machine maintenance data.

Management was sure that the first two problems were artificially keeping production costs high. These divergences from planned costs and the actual circumstances in which they would occur amounted to an unknown factor.

The solution was to automatically collect data in real time about the weight of packaged biscuits and about packaging material consumption, as well as data on machine failure and quality assurance. Thus a data collection solution was implemented (Figure 14.3) in which for every 50 items a package is automatically weighed on a scale, its weight registered by a PLC.

DATA COLLECTION FROM THE FACTORY FLOOR   147

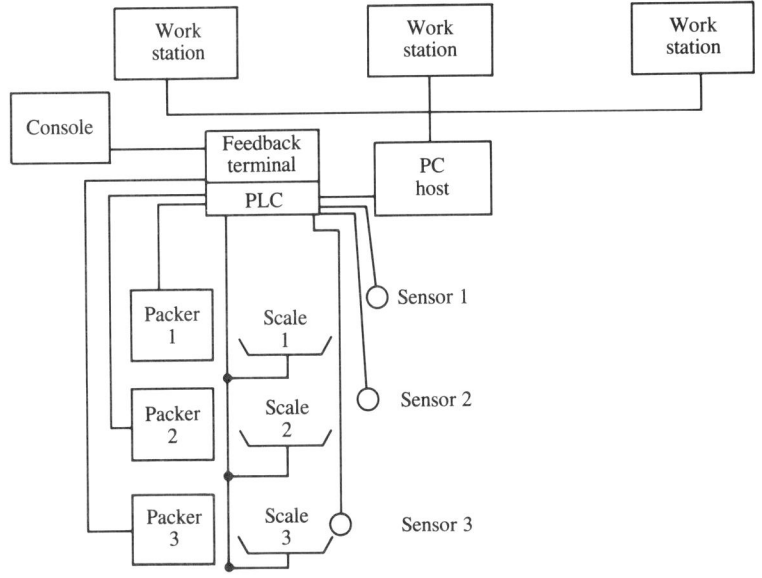

Figure 14.3 Solution configuration

Ten readings are registered before the SCADA system samples the PLC (the sample rate is approximately 6 per hour). The same PLC is connected to each packaging device on a particular production line, the PLC capturing data concerning the number of metres of packaging material consumed by the packager. Presence sensors also connected to the PLC detect the passage of biscuits along the line. From this data the following information can be determined:

– discrepancies from the predetermined weight of a particular product
– actual packaging material consumed per number of packages
– machine stoppage with biscuits present or not present on the production line.

Each PLC is downloaded with a production 'recipe' for every product. These recipes include details such as the number of items to be packaged for any one lot and planned package weights.

The following results have been achieved:

– The production system is now able to detect in real time occurrences of over- and underweight packages, and connect these to other production parameters such as oven temperature, humidity level and so on; production workers are alerted in real time and the discrepancy remedied.

- Package material consumption is actually measured. Previously the number of metres on a reel of packaging material was calculated from the weight of that reel. However, because packaging materials varied in thickness a given reel weight could provide varying lengths. Now, however, management knows the actual length of material on each reel as well as the actual number of packages produced from it.
- Machine stoppages are now reported in real time to the production system (via the connection of the packager to the PLC). If biscuits are not present on the line and the production lot is uncompleted (this information being part of the production recipe), then the fault can be traced to production procedures other than packaging. The frequency of stoppages and the circumstances in which they occur are now made known to the system. (This information is reported by production workers via a feedback terminal connected to the PLC.)
- Quality assurance: the feedback terminals also enable quality inspectors to report to the production system the quality control data so vital in this area.

These data items, with others, provide vital real-time information to a dynamic production system, facilitating not only the accurate costing of material consumption, but also substantial cost savings from the timely detection of overweight items.

The car plant

The automatic identification of vehicles at General Motor's Buick City production plant has, like a SCADA system, a two-fold purpose of supervisory control and data collection. A passive RF tag applied to the chassis of each car is tracked throughout the whole system. The tag contains a unique vehicle identification number (VIN), vehicle description number, tag number and the various build options needed to assemble the car. The tag is reusable, with data being reprogrammed into the tag from the host computer at a special tag load station.

Vehicles are identified at different production stages for different purposes:

SUPERVISORY CONTROL

- A non-sequential manufacturing process is accurately upkept, because jobs can flow out of the original build sequence and then return into the correct sequence later.
- Build instructions are automatically conveyed to PLCs that control automated machinery and robots. Vehicle specifications are sent to processes such as spot welding facilities, for colour mix in the paint shop, etc.

- The encoded vehicle identification number is read automatically to ensure accurate VIN stamping by the VIN stamping machines.
- Manufacturing processes can be run independently of the central computer, data being provided to the processes by the tag.
- Build verification occurs when the RF tag provides car specifications to a vehicle component verification scanner that checks the accuracy of component installation for that vehicle.

DATA COLLECTION

- Individual vehicles are tracked for the management and followup of customer orders.
- Part consumption during production is automatically reported, establishing accurate part requirements on an hourly basis.
- The progress of each vehicle is collected in order to facilitate part ordering just before that part is needed (see Section 14.6).
- Inventory reporting to the materials management inventory system is kept on a daily basis.

The RF tag is particularly suited to the automotive industry, owing to its ability to be updated in real time, to be read in areas where there can be no human access, and to withstand extreme temperatures and other harsh conditions.

14.4 Quality control

The collection of timely data for quality control can and does reduce significantly the time spent on the rework of orders, as well as decreasing the possibility of a customer receiving substandard products. Here we wish to collect data in order to find out the exact causes of deviations from defined manufacturing processes which can then be eliminated before high levels of rejects are produced. In high-volume production environments that may require very high sample rates, the manual collection of both variable and attribute data on preprinted check sheets is sometimes infeasible. Even for lower-volume production the price of erroneous manually collected data can be too high for certain manufacturers. In such situations it will be necessary to collect data with little or no human intervention, and we find that most data collection devices as well as auto-ID technologies and their variations (such as automatic vision inspection – not to be confused with machine vision for identification) have been prominent in increasing the possibilities and scope of quality control.

Data collection devices have become an integral part of statistical quality control/statistical process control (SQC/SPC), data being collected both in real time, on-line, and in batch fashion. Typically the chosen data collection device is linked to a host computer system that contains one of the many SQC/SPC software packages that imports, analyses and reports the results of the collected data (though as we saw in Chapter 12 some data collectors possess preprogrammed SPC analysis capability). The relevant considerations in choosing the type of data collection device to be integrated into a quality control system include the following:

- *Required sample rate.* A manufacturing process or machine might produce data at very fast rates indeed, such as data about scrap levels. Note that the sample rate may not necessarily be required to be at this level. A real-time unattended solution is normally required for high-level sample rates.
- *Level of automation.* In fully automated environments there is a greater possibilty of extracting the required data by data communications. In labour-intensive manufacturing the costs of installing real-time data collectors may be prohibitive; in this situation quality control may also be labour-intensive, but it may be assisted by computerized tools.
- *Required corrective response time.* In high-volume production environments there is a need for a very fast corrective response time (the time between a deviation from quality or process control limits being detected and it being corrected). In these situations a real-time system with a fully fledged alert mechanism is required.
- *Method of inspection.* Some quality control data can only be collected with human assistance, because only an actual person can inspect and determine the values of various quality control parameters. As mentioned earlier, automatic vision inspection systems have already made headway in this field.
- *Amount of quality control parameters.* Sometimes the sheer volume of data to be collected for a particular sample demands the use of fully automated data collection devices.

Let us begin with the collection of quality control data in real time. Real-time SPC/SQC software packages belong to the family of SCADA systems because they possess supervisory control characteristics (see Figure 14.4). With a real-time SPC/SQC system the internal registers of various PLCs are read and logged, and this data is used to dynamically build control charts. Using these, the system compares this data against predefined control limits. Both the type of control chart used and the level of the control limits are defined by the user as part of an overall data collection framework for a given manufacturing process or processes. (Data may be collected into a number of such frameworks simultaneously.) The various control charts that are commonly available are listed in Chapter 12.

There are a number of variations on how and in what circumstances SPC/SQC data should be collected. They include:

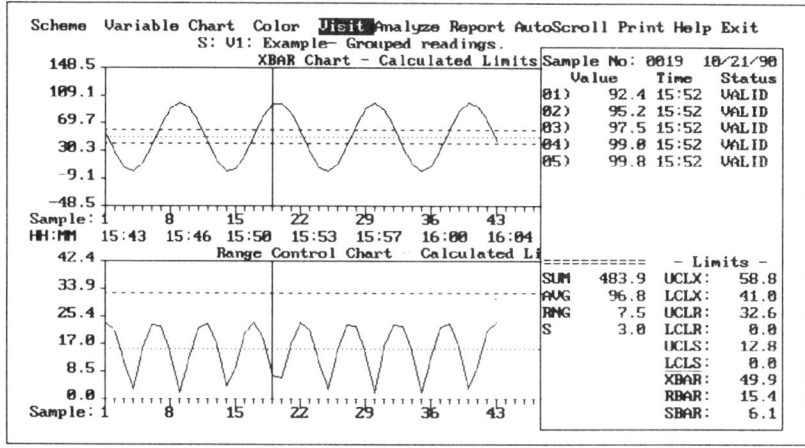

Figure 14.4 SPC MMI: P-CIM SPCIM Guide (AFCON Control and Automation Inc.). Courtesy Afcon

- *Periodic sampling at constant time intervals.* The user defines the time zones within which samples are taken. The amount of samples within each time zone is also user-definable.
- *Event-triggered data collection.* When a certain event or events occur sampling commences. Here too the frequency of sampling is defined.
- A combination of both.

Of these, the first is best for continuous manufacturing processes, the second for batch production. The SPC/SQC real-time software contains an annunciator mechanism (discussed in Chapter 9); when processes get 'out of control' or exceed predefined control limits they can be halted by the SPC software, which issues the appropriate command to a PLC.

A great advance in attended quality control has been the introduction of a portable voice recognition data collection system, which allows the quality control supervisor to keep his eyes on the inspected part without being distracted by the need to type data into a terminal. In critical inspection environments the voice data collection system can operate in real time by transmitting the spoken results via radio frequency to the host system. This solution is quite similar to the one based solely upon portable quality analysers. Instead of check description prompts being displayed on a screen, they are spoken by a portable *voice unit* programmed with the appropriate application software. The voice unit simply asks the questions and the inspector provides the answers. The inspection routine is divided into three sections:

- identification details of the inspector and the part to be tested

Figure 14.5 Quality control with voice recognition system: Monicor voice recognition system. Courtesy *ID Systems* magazine (Helmers Publishing Inc.), Monicor Electronic Corporation and Hackmeister Advertising and Public Relations Co.

– results of the tests or faults found
– corrective measures taken (if any).

In many situations a hands-and-eyes-free system of quality control will lead to a significantly greater inspection throughput, in other words a significant reduction in the work hours needed to carry out this task. One user of such a system has even stated that it has actually improved quality: before the system was implemented some inspectors who rested their clipboards on the bodywork of cars that were being inspected would inadvertently scratch the paintwork, whereas now the worst 'damage' that can be caused by the voice system is a fingerprint mark (Figure 14.5)!

Fixed-mount SPC/SQC data collectors for SPC/SQC have been discussed in Chapter 12. Such units are typically positioned at various stations manned by production workers such as machine operators. For example in the manufacture of screws, machine operators might be required to maintain manually a series of control charts (such as X and R charts that measure the average and range of sets of data), which in turn inhibits productivity. The introduction of a fixed-mount data collecting device, rugged enough to withstand an oily and dirty environment, as well as being easy to use, can significantly improve the situation, increasing both the speed and accuracy of data collection as well as worker productivity. Every half-hour a sample piece is examined with the fixed-mount data collector receiving readings from a number of devices, namely a micrometer, a bore gauge and a dial indicator. Results, X and R, are displayed at the stroke of a key, allowing the operator to reach a decision concerning whether or not to continue production. The stored data from the fixed-mount collector is later uploaded to a host computer. In this way relative machine capability is determined in the most accurate fashion, with jobs requiring greater precision levels being identified and routed to the most suitable machine.

14.5 Warehouse management

Bar code technology and portable data terminals are used for recording all general stock transactions. Their use reaps many benefits, which include:

- *Accurate reporting of all stock transactions* (item numbers, storage locations, etc.) Bar codes as well as downloaded control files prevent the entry of erroneous data to the host system. These are major tools for the accurate calculation of existing inventory value.
- *Greater system sensitivity.* The transfer of stock transactions on-line from the field via RF portable data terminals or via batch communications significantly decreases system response times to inventory events. For instance, backlogged items can be dispatched faster if goods received are reported accurately and without delay.
- *Reduction of operational inventory levels.* Greater system sensitivity decreases required operational inventory levels.
- *Exact and swift retrieval of stored items.* If accurate storage information is reported to the system, then item picking becomes an easier task, because items are found in their expected locations and in their expected quantities.
- *Optimization of storage space.* The portable data terminal is a powerful management tool for the warehouse staff. For example, it can recommend optimal storage and alternative storage locations for particular items.

Let us look now at some of the tasks in which both bar code technology and portable data terminals are incorporated. In the following example the warehouse is managed with defined storage locations. Each item can be stored in one or more locations, and more than one item can be stored in each location. The host computer is able to manage inventory levels on the basis of these locations; that is, it can report the current location of each item and quantity of it stored at that location. Items may, if required, be moved from location to location.

As each item is received into the warehouse it can be marked with a bar code label containing its catalogue number. Bar code labels are produced on–line as items are received, yet they can also be printed in advance, in the appropriate quantities, according to the information received from an advance shipping notice. If printing bar codes for every item received is deemed infeasible then individual locations in the warehouse can be bar-coded, with the bar code label containing the items stored at each location. (This solution is not suitable for warehouses that store items according to storage space currently available.) Location addresses can also be bar-coded with a unique code.

After items are received they are put away at particular locations. The portable data terminal with an attached or integral bar code reader records the *putaway* transaction by location, item and quantity. This information is crucial, as an unreported or erroneous *putaway* typically means that an item becomes 'lost', and may be reordered simply because an inventory system does not contain accurate information as to where it is to be found; inaccurate putaways are a common cause of overstocking. In warehouses where the optimization of storage space is a required practice, the putaway procedure is different. An advance shipment notice can be downloaded into the portable data terminal. The optimal storage location is downloaded for each item as well as for alternative locations (should the optimal location be full). To avoid backtracking the terminal presents each item to be put away, and its putaway location, to the warehouse operator in an orderly route. Once the operator has arrived at a particular location, the location and item bar code are read for verification purposes. If an RF terminal is used, then putaway instructions can be displayed on-line without the need for the repeated downloading of advance shipping notices. Working on-line also permits putaway priorities to be dynamically changed, thus improving system sensitivity (Figure 14.6).

Picking items for delivery similarly requires the verification of items and their locations, against a previously downloaded picking list for batch terminals or on-line for RF systems. If storage optimization is practised, then the portable data terminal will also receive inventory transfer instructions on a regular basis. These instructions help to prevent *storage fragmentation*, a situation whereby a shipment of a particular item is fragmented over a large number of storage locations, thus lengthening picking time. If the host system is capable of recommending the relocation of previously stored items in order to make storage space for newly received items (in single or contiguous locations) then relocation instructions can be sent to the field terminals in advance of the delivery of these items, the system being alerted by an advance shipment notice.

Perhaps the best-known use of portable data terminals and bar codes in inventory systems is inventory taking. (This is often also the first stage to be implemented in a step-by-step phasing-in of an inventory data collection system.) There are a number of variations on this task, from a straightfoward 'wall-to-wall' or 'what is seen is what is reported' approach, to cleverer routines which perform a number of useful real-time verifications. In the latter case, a file containing item locations, item numbers and

DATA COLLECTION FROM THE FACTORY FLOOR 155

Figure 14.6 Radio frequency terminal used in putaway. Courtesy Symbol Technologies

current stock levels is downloaded into the portable data terminal's memory. These stock levels are not revealed to the warehouseperson. The terminal displays each location and item to be counted within an optimal route. The warehouseperson verifies that he or she is at the correct location by reading the location bar code and then the item number. Items are then counted and the quantity is entered, after which the terminal compares this quantity with the current inventory level for that location which is stored in its memory. If the totals match, all well and good, otherwise the user is requested to count again and re-enter the quantity. The terminal will accept a discrepancy between the quantity reported and the current inventory level in its memory should that same discrepancy be entered twice in succession. The real-time verification of inventory levels by the portable data terminal significantly reduces the need for re-counting items or locations after inventory results have been reported to the host system, because inventory discrepancies are detected and dealt with without delay.

14.6 'Just-in-time'

'Just-in-time', or JIT systems have already been referred to in Chapter 1. In manufacturing environments raw materials can be received moments before they are consumed, and finished items can be produced for orders just before those orders are to be dispatched. While this might seem a risky policy, potential savings from its implementation can be enormous, particularly the saving in floor space that would have to be used to store the items that otherwise would not have been received 'just-in-time'. In order to ensure the smooth implementation of JIT (with little danger of 'just-in-time' becoming 'just-a-moment'!), auto-ID technologies and on-line computerized data collection are a prerequisite. One of the major benefits of the AVI system in Buick City discussed in Section 14.3 is that certain unique parts in the manufacturing process which are required for the manufacture of particular vehicles arrive just when they are needed. The RF tags installed on each chasis signal to the host system exactly which job is currently being performed on that vehicle. This provides not only an on-line picture of where each vehicle is on the production line; the information can also be utilized immediately to order parts that will be required at later stages, thus ensuring uninterrupted production.

A JIT environment will benefit from the physical proximity of supplier warehouses to the production plant. However, JIT can be implemented with distanced suppliers if they are willing and able to keep tight delivery schedules. If a plant can schedule production in such a way as to know exactly between which hours jobs are to be performed on particular items, then suppliers can be requested to deliver within a fixed time slot shortly before those jobs are to be carried out. In this situation delivery slot times can be confirmed or initiated from promptly reported work-in-progress data.

15
Trade and service applications

15.1 Retail

It was the retail sector that gave the first major vote of confidence to modern auto-ID technologies, particularly to the bar code. Today not only the bar code but also OCR and magnetic stripe are commonly found in the retail sector. The implementation of these technologies is seen at points of sale (POS), where the cashier reads either a sales tag or the item itself with a special reader in order to identify automatically the product being purchased. The bar code is the dominant technology at points of sale for item identification, but OCR has also made some headway, especially in fashion stores; OCR is also employed as an efficient means of identification for small labels that have no room to contain both computer and human-readable data. Magnetic stripe readers are used at points of sale to enter customer charge and credit card details into the system.

Over and above the obvious benefit of allowing the computer and not the cashier to automatically identify items and look up prices, the combination of point-of-sale terminals and auto-ID facilitates the automated updating of inventory levels. Point-of-sale terminals are normally connected to a back-office computer which receives sales information from the terminals as well as managing the price look-up file (PLU). The back-office computer can thus be used to automatically reorder items whose stock levels have fallen below a predetermined point. Such a system will also have to take into account current inventory levels in the storeroom.

Another popular and efficient method for the replenishment of in-store stock levels is performed with portable data terminals. In this daily routine, one or more workers enter into their terminals the actual stock levels of items on shelves. The identification of each item is normally facilitated by a bar code reader either attached to the terminal or else as an integral part of it. If a product number is manually entered then the terminal can validate the check digit of the product code or validate that code by searching for it in the PLU file stored in the terminal's memory. At

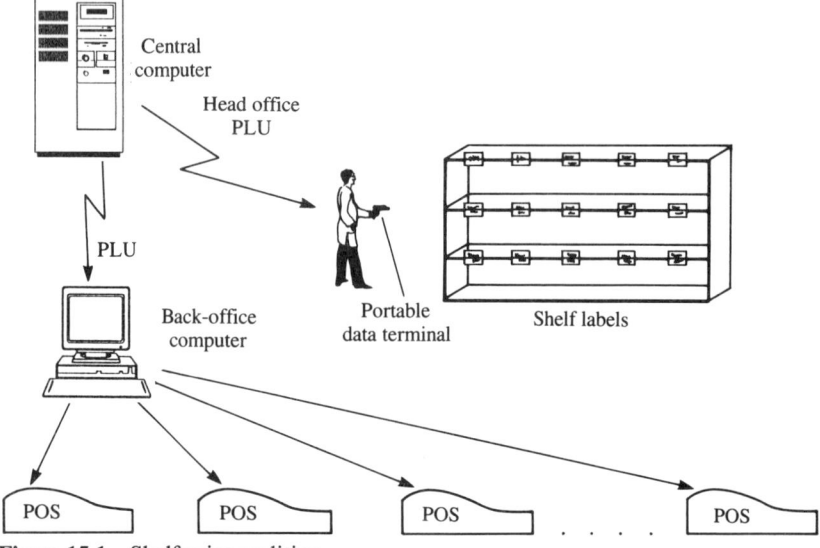

Figure 15.1 Shelf price auditing

the end of this process the counted items are uploaded to the host computer, which compares the actual stock levels against predetermined order levels and if necessary issues orders.

As part of this routine or as a separate process the worker can perform a shelf price audit (SPA). Here the portable data terminal and bar code technology have provided a unique solution for the immediate rectification of pricing discrepancies, which are a common occurrence, (Figure 15.1). Such a system is aimed at significantly reducing the instances where customers are overcharged or undercharged because of discrepancies between shelf and POS prices, for example where the POS or the shelf price is not updated regarding a special offer on a particular product. An SPA is performed by downloading a terminal with the latest PLU, normally from head office. The user reads a bar code on a shelf and the terminal presents the item description and price. If there is a discrepancy between the price displayed by the terminal and the shelf price it is noted by the user and stored in the terminal's memory. As the terminal contains the very latest PLU then a new bar-coded shelf price label may be printed by a portable label printer attached to the terminal itself.

In-store inventory taking is performed in a similar manner. If the terminal is used without a downloaded stock file, then inventory items should be identified automatically. Otherwise a download file can be used for validating not only item numbers but quantities too!

The above applications can also be performed using on–line radio-frequency portable data terminals. This alternative, though more costly, will mean that terminals will always verify the collected data against the latest update of price and stock levels in the system.

15.2 Marketing systems

In recent years there has been a growing awareness of the need for the accurate and efficient capture of sales data as well as for reducing lead times for delivery of customer orders. In an ever more competitive market great weight has been added to the concept of total customer satisfaction. A mistaken order or a delay in its delivery can be greatly detrimental to the attainment of this satisfaction. The portable data terminal has come to the rescue in two increasingly widespread applications, namely *presale* and *vansale* systems.

Presale systems receive the customer's order at his premises. In the past such orders were taken by a salesman equipped with no more than a product catalogue, an order form and a pen. Now, by the regular download to a portable data terminal of a catalogue file, price lists, details of special offers and other relevant information, a customer is provided with the latest details regarding the supplier's products and services. The salesman in the field receives valuable information concerning a customer's current account balance with his company, as well as that customer's credit facilities. Order details are entered into the terminal and are verified against the various download files, greatly reducing the possibility of recording an erroneous order. The greatest contribution made by the system is in the dramatic reduction in the order process cycle made possible by the direct transmission of orders to the host system. In fact, some particular systems allow the transmission of collected orders from the final client *en route* via a public telephone line, by using a modem installed inside the terminal.

Vansale systems manage the delivery of items to a customer's premises. It is here that the final order is approved and supplied and accounts settled, thanks to the portable data terminal's three basic functions:

1 *Van inventory management.* The van is in fact a mobile warehouse and is normally replenished on a daily basis. The terminal records all inventory transactions: loading, unloading and deliveries, and thus can provide the current stock levels in the van when requested.
2 *Portable point of sale.* The terminal deals with all financial transactions and can issue invoices, delivery notes and receipts to the customer. This is made possible by the attachment of a portable printer to the terminal. The final amount payable by the customer can be calculated by the terminal according to a vast range of criteria, including item, client or quantity discounts.

3 *Receipt of future orders and order adjustment.* A customer's order may be downloaded in advance into the terminal's memory. This order can be adjusted before a final delivery note is issued at the customer's premises. The inventory program can verify whether any additionally requested quantities can be supplied according to the van's current stock levels. Moreover, future orders can be collected in advance.

Over and above the reduction in delivery process time, vansale systems offer the following benefits:

- The capture of vital sales information, including consumption patterns, i.e. item sales levels by area or season.
- The immediate issue of summary reports without the intervention of the host computer, for instance a daily sales report.
- Supervisory controls during delivery. Such controls include verification that a customer does not exceed predefined credit limits, or does not receive goods already allocated to other customers *en route.*

15.3 Field service systems

Many companies provide field maintenance services to their customers. This is particularly common with large-scale computer vendors such as IBM, Digital, NCR and Data General. Once again the portable data terminal serves as the predominant data collection device. Service calls can be downloaded on a daily basis to the terminal, or, more frequently, via an internal modem and portable cellular telephone attached to the terminal itself. This allows field technicians to respond almost immediately to very urgent calls and thus increase in a very significant manner customer appreciation of the vendor's services. The terminal performs a number of important tasks:

- The recording of on-site repair and maintainance information.
- The presentation of an item's service record, past service details, etc.
- The automatic recording of the length of a technician's service call.
- The recording of spare parts consumed during the service call.
- The issue of a service delivery note via an attached printer. This document includes details of the work done and parts consumed.
- In some systems, the placement of an immediate order for urgent delivery of lacking parts.

Once the service call has been completed, the terminal uploads to the host system, also via public phone lines, the fact that the particular call has been completed, the call's final status (whether the serviced item is operational or not) and other relevant data.

15.4 Parcel and file tracking systems

Parcel and file tracking systems have a common goal, the location of a particular entity within a system. File tracking is needed, especially in large office environments, such as insurance companies, hospitals, local government, etc., where files so often go astray. The information required from a tracking system can be classified as follows:

- current item location
- time of arrival at current location
- estimated exit time from current location
- next location *en route*
- overall time spent in the system
- identity of current borrower or handler.

The identity of an entity, be it a file, a parcel, or a letter, is normally encoded in a bar code. File tracking is implemented by the installation of bar code readers at each relevant reporting station in a system. These can be at a number of levels:

- building or storeroom.
- department
- department section
- desk.

The bar code readers at these locations can be connected to a host system by various configurations, depending on the solution preferred. An immediate on-line tracking system will interface a bar code reader to a computer terminal or personal computer. If the latter solution is chosen then the personal computers should be part of a local area network, as tracking data will be queried from other locations. If a company has a problem with worker discipline (files do not always get read), or an on-line solution is too costly (owing to the number of readers required) then a *batch* solution may be the answer. Here a member of staff 'makes the rounds' reading the files in every department with a portable data terminal and the data is later uploaded to a host computer. Each department is identified by a unique code chosen from a department file in the terminal, or a permanent bar code label can be placed at the entrance to the department and read prior to reading the files.

The following basic data is collected in a file tracking system in order to produce the required information.

- location
- user
- file identity
- time and date of read.

Some courier companies provide an almost real time tracking service for their customers in a similar fashion, (Figure 15.2). Each customer can receive an accurate forecast as to the expected time of a particular delivery. Also, the tracking system can alert a supervisor should a particular item have spent too much time in the system, thus allowing the courier company to pre-empt a customer enquiry. In order to reduce the number of item reads in the system articles are grouped together in batches (normally by destination), and each batch is provided with a unique code (which may include the destination code as part of it). To begin with, articles are barcoded and these bar codes are then read and linked to a particular batch number. Tracking is facilitated by the reading of the batch number at each stop along the route. Only when the batch is broken are all the article bar codes read again.

In more sophisticated systems a courier is provided with a portable data terminal. When an item is collected from a customer, the customer is given a bar-coded receipt, which is read by the terminal which date- and time-stamps the collection automatically in its memory alongside the receipt number. Back at the sorting depot, this information is uploaded to the host system. Later the receipts for each item are grouped into batches. When an item reaches its final destination its bar code is read again into a terminal by the courier and delivery is automatically date- and time-stamped. The terminal can also record certain events, such as if there was no one to receive the delivery, or an address cannot be found. The delivery times and their final status are uploaded back to the host system after leaving the system.

15.5 Direct mailing

Direct mailing systems involve the production of considerable numbers of copies of printed information, or inserts, which are placed into pre-addressed envelopes. Insertion is a time-consuming and laborious task, with a single mailing perhaps reaching millions of addresses, so it is performed automatically by devices called *inserters*. The address can be printed either on an insert itself and read directly through a window in the envelope, or else on the envelope itself. In the latter case one of the inserts is personalized, which demands that the correct personalized insert must be inserted in its matching envelope. Unfortunately the automatic insertion process can go wrong, and it takes just one mismatch between a personalized insert and a pre-addressed envelope to produce thousands of others with the same problem. If this is not detected quickly the financial loss from mismatched mail can be very high.

In such circumstances human monitoring is quite infeasible, because hardly any one can be expected to concentrate on verifying matching envelopes for long periods of time. The solution to mismatched mail has

TRADE AND SERVICE APPLICATIONS 163

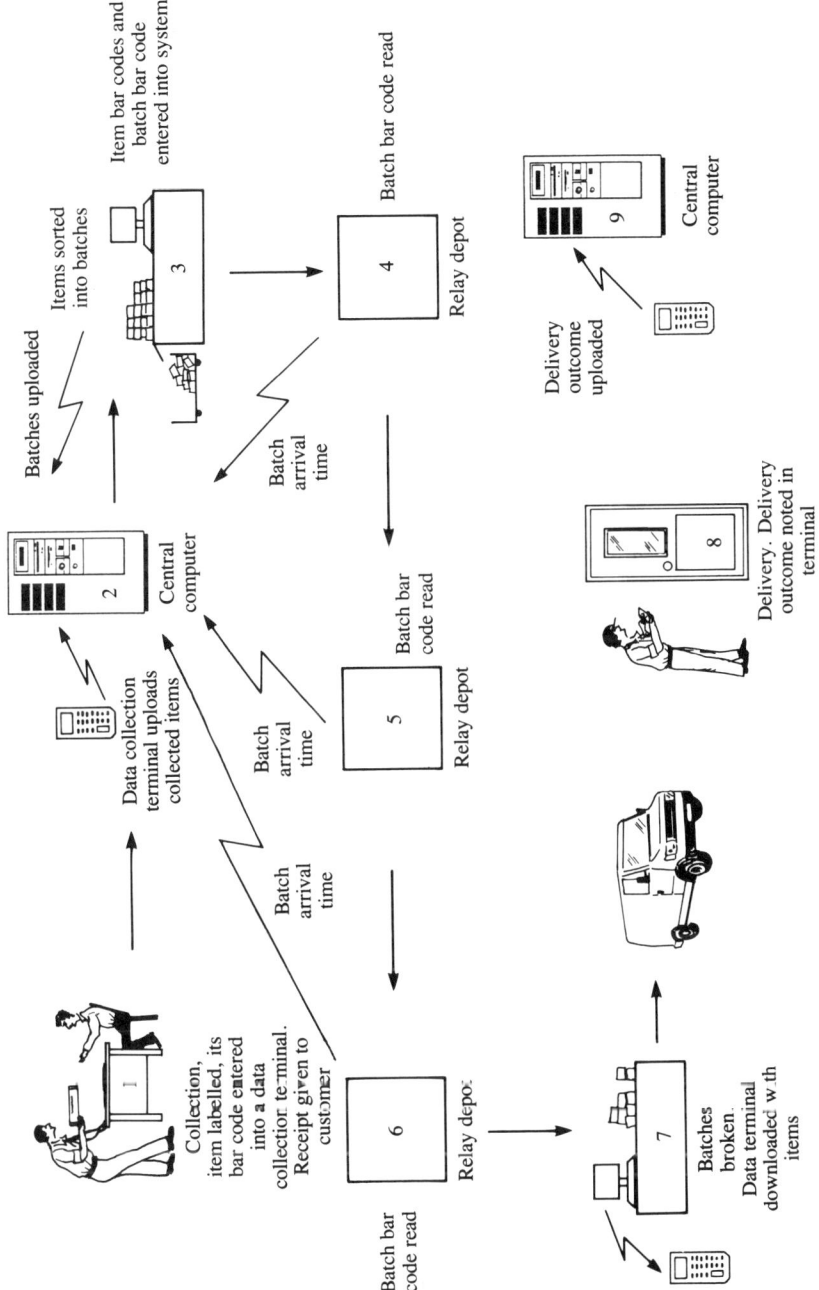

Figure 15.2 Parcel tracking system

been provided by the incorporation of OCR technology into the automatic insertion process. A unique numeric code is printed with the address on each envelope and on the personalized insert. After all inserts for a particular envelope are stacked and ready for insertion a CCD array camera reads the codes on the personalized insert and the waiting envelope. The two codes are compared by host software and if a mismatch occurs the insertion process is halted. In this way mail matching is extremely accurate without any sacrifice of throughput. Cost savings are made by the elimination of mismatch probability.

Optical character recognition is particularly suited to this application, because a limited character set is read from a well defined position on the article itself.

15.6 Automatic identification and data collection in hospitals

Hospital information systems handle vast amounts of material. The cost of erroneous data entering such a system scarcely bears consideration, therefore many data collection tasks are normally performed by trained medical personnel, although this still leaves, of course, the possibilty of human error. Hospitals, therefore, are a natural environment for automatic identification and data collection systems, and these can be found in many areas of hospital management, notably:

– patient identification
– blood banks
– ward drug replenishment
– laboratory sample testing.

Patient identification

Each patient needs to be indentified throughout their period of hospitalization, for example during drug dispensing, laboratory sample tests and for billing. A patient's wrist tag and dossier can be bar-coded, and their dossier may also contain a sheet of printed bar code labels, each one containing patient identification data. Each label is affixed to a document that needs to be attributed to the patient, for instance a laboratory sample test form. The addition of a bar code to each label will hardly alter in any way the previous process of label production: labels are normally printed during admission but now a bar code, containing the patient's identification, is printed alongside the human-readable characters. The price of a good-quality printer to print these labels pales into insignificance beside the potential cost of a patient being incorrectly identified during sample testing or even surgical procedures!

Blood banks

In a similar fashion portions of bagged blood and their derivatives are labelled with bar codes, the bar code containing identification details of each portion, such as blood group, type, and the portion's expiry date. Whenever a delivery of blood is dispatched or received the bar-coded labels are read to verify that the correct portion is being given out or taken in. Bar coding greatly increases the traceability of particular blood portions to their original donators, which is essential when there exists the possibilty that the blood is contaminated.

Ward drug replenishment

The two common problems with ward drug replenishment are:

- A particular ward or department may hold inventory levels for a particular drug over and above its actual consumption.
- One ward may not be supplied with an item out of stock in the main pharmacy when it is actually in stock in another ward.

These problems arise where there is a lack of data on actual ward consumption of particular drugs.

Portable data terminals are used to collect ward and department orders for drug replenishment much as they are used to collect data to facilitate shelf replenishment in supermarkets (Section 15.1). In each ward, every item and its current stock level is collected by the portable data terminal. This data is uploaded to the host system, which automatically produces a replenishment picking list for all the wards according to predetermined stock levels per ward and item. This list is then downloaded into a portable terminal for picking (the terminal verifies that the correct items have been picked – see Chapter 14). The picked quantities are uploaded to the host computer. In this fashion ward consumption patterns for particular drugs can be closely monitored and re-order levels adjusted accordingly. Within a short period of time certain drugs whose consumption in a particular ward is lower than originally determined can be identified. Those same drugs may be more frequently consumed in other wards. In this way a pattern of optimizing drug replenishment can be achieved, (Figure 15.3).

Laboratory sample testing

In hospital laboratories specimen test forms are received with a patient's identification encoded in a bar code affixed to them. A particular sample may be analysed by a number of devices, each providing different results. In the past the many samples received had to be kept in a strict sequential

166 AUTOMATIC IDENTIFICATION AND DATA COLLECTION SYSTEMS

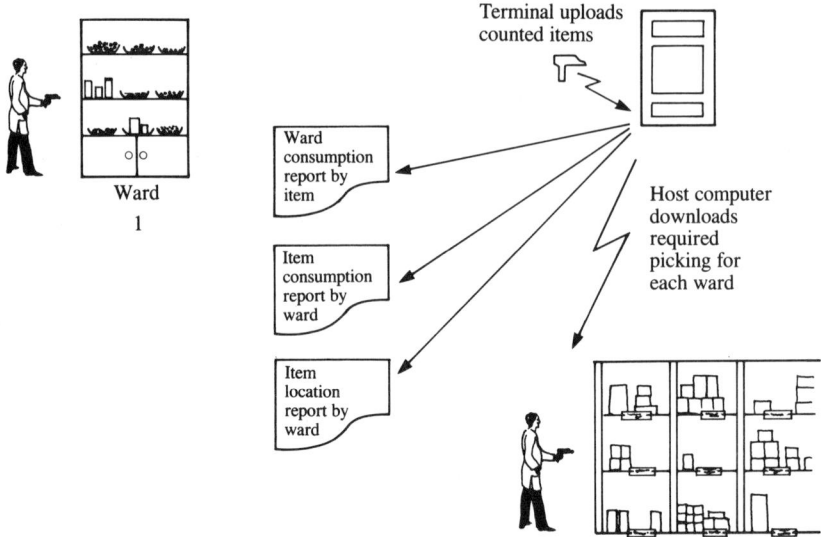

Figure 15.3 Ward drug replenishment system

order during analysis so that each result could be linked with its correct owner. Any deviation from this order in the loading of samples into analysers could lead to one patient receiving another's test result. Today, though, bar-coding of samples and test forms prevents any mixups. The linking of a patient's identity with that patient's test results is now an automated process performed by laboratory software.

16
Specialized applications

16.1 Agriculture

Auto-ID and data collection systems have been implemented in many areas of agriculture, although not as extensively as in manufacturing industry, trade and services. In agriculture the auto-ID challenge has been considerable however: for instance, how is one to identify lifestock, or minute items such as eggs or even bees? Also, in agriculture, environmental conditions may be particularly harsh. In this section we look at some of the more common systems in use, namely:

– insemination and cattle breeding
– milk analysis
– automatic identification of animals
– data collection on battery farms.

Insemination and cattle breeding

Here a record of all cows and bulls is kept near the bulls at the cattle breeding centre, with artificial insemination (AI) taking place on the farm only after careful verification of the ancestry of the animals. For this reason cows and bulls have to be accurately identified. Some systems use bar codes to encode a unique cow identification number, as well as the identification numbers of their parents. This bar code is applied to the cow's registration card kept on the farm. The bull is identified from a file that has been downloaded to a portable data terminal. This file contains details of the bull's parentage. When the cow's bar code is read by a bar code reader attached to the terminal, a test for matching parentage and other details that need to be verified before insemination (such as a similar blood group) is made by the terminal.

The portable data terminal performs other tasks besides a simple parentage cross-reference. Vital data is collected as to which cow was inseminated by which bull as well as the date and time of insemination. This data is later uploaded to a computer, which manages all this information. In this application, small and very rugged terminals are a definite requirement, as they will be splashed and generally get very dirty.

Milk analysis

Auto-ID systems are used for the automatic identification of milk samples in much the same way as hospital laboratories mark theirs. Farms supplying milk have samples regularly collected and dispatched to the milk wholesale authority for testing. Payment to the farm for its milk produce, and the farm's licence to continue producing milk, depends directly on the quality of the milk supplied by it. The milk authorities have therefore to collect and analyse thousands of samples a day from many farms. A slip-up in the identification of the sample and its owner could well lead to the penalization of a quality farmer. The solution has been to bar-code the sample containers. The bar code labels contain details of the farm and the bar code itself a unique farm identification. These labels are applied to the containers when samples are taken and are later read, unattended, as the samples are being processed by the milk analyser. The results of the analysis are then linked to the farm's identity number and later transmitted to the host computer.

Automatic identification of animals

Traditional methods for identifying livestock have included branding, collars, ear tagging or clipping and more. The reasons for identifying animals are many-fold, such as the conservation of endangered species, tracking feeding patterns or other habits, even simply for inventory. The use of RF tags has provided a major breakthrough in this field. In some cases the transponders are tagged to the animal, while in others they are actually implanted into the body of the animal by a surgical process. Indeed, perhaps the most intriguing case of a transponder implantation is in the automatic identification of tropical fish. Each fish is implanted with a minute transponder, which can later be identified with a portable interrogator from *outside* an aquarium. The benefits of the introduction of this technology for the identification of animals are quite impressive; however, perhaps the greatest is the ability to track animals without the need to come into close physical proximity with them, a major advantage in the tracking of wildlife.

Data collection on battery farms

On such farms the productivity of a hen (the number of eggs it lays) is a key factor in determining when it has passed its prime and should be slaughtered. Its weight is another significant factor. The identification and manual recording of a very large number of hens on a daily basis has proved difficult, and the great amounts of data recorded lead to constant mistakes. Portable data terminals, downloaded with the farm's hen file, have proved to be a great boon. The hen is identified by the use of a code; if this data is manually entered then it is cross-checked against the hen file, with erroneous codes being rejected. Use of bar codes read from labels attached to the compartment in which the animal is kept has also been successfully implemented. The collected data, i.e. the number of eggs laid by the hen and its weight, which is time- and date-stamped, is later uploaded to a host system.

16.2 Transportation

Under the general heading of transportation exists a large number of related subjects. Those discussed in this section are parking control and automatic vehicle identification (AVI), while the following section is dedicated to aviation.

The enforcement of local government parking regulations, as well as nationwide laws, is characterized by the recording of a relatively large amount of detailed data by traffic wardens and the subsequent entry of this data into large-scale processing systems. The motorist has to wait a very long time before receiving a reminder of the offence through the post, while one who is lucky enough to find a discrepancy in the reported data, say between the stated colour and registration number of the car, may successfully plead not guilty to the charge.

Two systems based on portable data terminals and smart cards have been introduced in recent years to solve the identification and data collection problems in this field. In the first system a portable data terminal is downloaded with a number of data files, including a list of roads for a particular area, car models, colours, possible offences, and any other files that include data which is recorded when a parking ticket is issued. Most of the data is entered into the terminal by choosing an entry from a file, say a car model from a file of different car models, or by the entry of a code and the verification of that code's description (normally the code itself bears a close resemblance to its corresponding description; for example 'TOY' can represent 'TOYOTA'). After all the relevant data has been collected and verified by the terminal a ticket is printed by a small portable printer attached to the terminal itself. In some systems the printer and the terminal together weigh only a little over a kilogram! The offending motorist receives a clearly printed ticket, data such as date and time of offence being taken automatically from the real-time clock in the terminal.

Even though the software that runs this system in the terminal can be designed in such a way that the data collection process is relatively short, a handwritten ticket will take considerably less time to issue (after the data has been collected the printer still has to print the ticket). Why then have these systems? While ticket throughput is reduced, the accuracy and speed of transferring the collected data from the field to the host system is tremendous and alone justifies the introduction of such a system. The portable data terminal can also perform functions in the advance of law enforcement that were not possible with a manual system. For instance, the terminal might contain a list of the car licence plate numbers of repeated offenders, say those with over twenty unpaid tickets. When the car licence number is entered, the terminal can alarm the warden if the car is blacklisted and instead of issuing a ticket he or she can call the authorities to tow the car away!

An exciting development in parking systems is the integration of both contact and non-contact smart cards that function as portable parking meters, each card containing a bank of preprogrammed hours. After parking his car the motorist inserts a smart card into a 'portable parking meter' fixed to the inside of the windscreen, (Figure 16.1). The meter then begins

Figure 16.1 Piaf portable parking meter. Courtesy of Hello–Innovation Systèmes Urbains

to count down from a fixed period of time, for instance an hour, that has been debited from a stored bank of hours in the smart card (these can be replenished as needed). The remaining time is displayed on the screen of the smart card. A parking warden only has to examine the screen of the portable 'parking meter' in order to determine whether a ticket should or should not be issued.

The use of RF tags in parking control can also be found in the management of parking lots. Those cars that are permitted access to the lot have RF tags attached to them, which are read at the entrance point; a barrier is automatically raised and data concerning which car is in the lot and when it entered is transmitted to the host system. The RF tags are the dominant auto-ID technology used to implement AVI. In the past a VIN was encoded in a bar code and special laser readers were developed to read these bar codes through a vehicle's windscreen. The VIN is a unique number used to identify any vehicle and can be used in a great variety of tracking applications. Yet until the introduction of the RF tag these applications were labour-intensive because in most cases an operator was required to operate the bar code reading equipment. This in turn greatly reduced AVI application possibilities. Apart from parking control and parking lot management, AVI systems can be used for traffic monitoring and control, vehicle tracking, automatic toll collection and more. Most of these applications require extremely fast and accurate data capture with the vehicle on the move, and for this RF tag systems are best, guaranteeing long-range reads, high data transfer rates and superior directionality.

The RF tag can be affixed in a number of possible places on a car, the one chosen depending on the type and position of the interrogator. For traffic control and monitoring applications, interrogators are situated in key areas, at junctions or at various points along strategic roads. In one traffic monitoring experiment in Sydney, Australia, taxi cabs were fitted with RF tags so as to record the time taken to travel from one junction to the next. Similarly, particular cars or fleets of cars can be monitored for a wide range of purposes, as can buses, with commuters receiving up-to-date information as to the expected arrival time of a bus at a particular spot.

Already in a number of countries the application of RF tags on private and commercial vehicles is already being considered for law enforcement purposes. Let us stretch our imaginations for just one moment. You are travelling down a road and the driver in front of you is going a bit too slow. The only other lane is blocked, yet the bus lane, meant for public transport only, is clear. You look both ways and then change into the bus lane. A day later a fine arrives at your home through the post. An interrogator, unseen by you, positioned at some point along the bus lane read your VIN. The ticket was then automatically issued with the details of your offence, including the actual time and place of occurrence. Of course,

Figure 16.2 Automatic vehicle identification at a toll booth. Courtesy Saab Scania Combitech AB Traffic Systems

RF tagging of both private and commercial vehicles is loaded with complex legal implications, and at present would cost a great deal; for these and other reasons it will not be widely introduced at all soon.

Automatic toll collection is already here, however. An RF tag is affixed to the area behind the rear-view mirror and as the driver reaches the toll booth the interrogator there identifies the car and checks that the owner has an account with the toll company, the barrier is raised, and the owner's identification code, date, time and location of entry are sent to a host computer (Figure 16.2). The information is later processed, with the car owner being billed periodically. (Such a system can also be implemented with machine vision, where the reader identifies the licence plate of the car.) The major benefit of automatic toll collection is the dramatic increase of tollway capacity, relieving traffic congestion.

It will no doubt be such applications that will be at the forefront of the ever more widespread use of AVI. Finally, it has also been incorporated for carriage tracking on railways, where tags have been identified on moving trains travelling at speeds in excess of 380 kilometres per hour!

16.3 Aviation

The two main areas in aviation that have incorporated auto-ID and data collection systems are baggage handling and security. In the first, a large bar code label is affixed to each piece of baggage that is to be sent to an aircraft's hold. Fixed-mount laser scanners strategically placed along a conveyer system read the baggage number and flight details, with a controller automatically navigating the baggage to the appropriate container (universal loading device, or ULD). These systems are relatively simple to implement and reduce the risk that the baggage is loaded onto the wrong flight, saving airlines a great deal of money annually in the compensation of passengers.

Aviation security systems use the baggage's bar code to ensure that an aircraft does not leave with luggage in its hold without the owner of that luggage also being on board. The system works as follows. At check-in, bar codes are affixed to each item of luggage. A boarding card that contains a magnetic stripe is also issued. Each bar-coded item of luggage is read at the check-in terminal and in this way is linked to one or more boarding cards (depending on whether the luggage belongs to a passenger travelling alone or to one who is part of a group). When the baggage is loaded into the ULD, the ULD number is recorded and thus linked to items inside it. When each passenger passes through the gate in order to board the aircraft his boarding pass is swiped through a magnetic stripe reader. A few minutes before the flight is closed, software in the host system verifies which passengers have checked in but have not yet passed through the gate. Should such a passenger be found then the system is able to locate this passenger's bar-coded items of luggage as well as the ULD that they have been stored in. This is auto-ID combating terrorism!

16.4 Libraries

The accurate and speedy identification of books has been the moving force behind the introduction of automatic identification in libraries. Each book is simply bar-coded with a long–life label which is read each time it is taken out or returned. The reader's library card can be either bar-coded or else supplied with a magnetic stripe for reader identification. The reading devices are attached to the computer terminals and no adjustments to existing software are normally required. An additional element of security can be added to the system by the use of special bar-coded security labels. These labels, which emit a magnetic field, are demagnetized by a special unit on the librarian's desk before the reader leaves the library, and remagnetized when the book is returned. At the exit to the library a special sensor is positioned which sounds an alarm if it detects the presence of an active label. Today there are hand-held laser scanners on the market that do both jobs: they not only read the bar code and pass the book's ID to the host system but also demagnetize the label so that the book can be removed from the library.

PART FIVE
THE PLANNING, DESIGN AND IMPLEMENTATION OF DATA COLLECTION SYSTEMS

17
Initial stages

17.1 Gathering information

In the first four parts of this book we have discussed the various technologies that are incorporated in automatic identification and data collection systems as well as various applications, more or less common, that have been implemented in the field. This in itself should have provided a comprehensive picture of what has been done, as well as giving a good indication of what is possible. Nevertheless, there is no substitute for seeing the real thing in action, talking to the vendors of the various products, and obtaining the relevant technical specifications. Indeed, this is the first step in the implementation of a data collection system: gathering the relevant information that will act as a sound base for future decisions. As well as obtaining general technical information concerning such systems, it is important to verify the following points:

- the particular auto-ID technologies most prevalent in your industrial sector
- the existence of auto-ID standards for this sector
- the leading vendors of the relevant systems
- popular products or turnkey solutions (should such solutions exist)
- system integrators with the relevant experience in the areas you are interested in
- organizations or companies that have already implemented similar systems, and the extent of their successful implementation
- the time period needed to get such a system up and running
- the required investment needed as well as the possibility of implementing a future system by stages.

All these points will assist the system initiator to conduct a preliminary feasibility study, to 'sell' the idea to management as well as gaining the support and cooperation of future end-users. Furthermore, this information should provide both a base for determining the goals of the future system and a preliminary estimate of the budget and payback period that implementing the system will require. All these issues are examined in this chapter. System vendors themselves are normally only too happy to provide any preliminary technical information about systems that have been implemented. Therefore, a preliminary check with a limited amount of vendors aimed at obtaining some technical information and initial pricing is very useful. Also, a vendor might well at this early stage refer you to one of their clients who has already implemented a system similar to the one you are considering. Such a client could well give you valuable information on their system and might provide you with some more ideas. Moreover, seeing a system in action may settle some of the doubts you may have about its implementation and in turn help you to convince others. It always helps to have seen first personally what you will have to explain later, as opposed to just conveying information provided to you by others.

A complete list of vendors, system integrators, value added resellers and other system houses that specialize in the field can also be obtained from an AIM, the trade organization of auto-ID manufacturers. This same body, based in the USA and Europe, provides excellent educational services as well as written information on auto-ID and data collection systems. It can also help you in verifying existing industrial standards for auto-ID technologies and put you in touch with relevant auto-ID industrial groups.

Finally, trade shows can be a very useful and concentrated source of information about some of the things mentioned here. The major shows are Scan Tech (sponsored by 'Automatic ID News'), held in many countries around the world every year, and ID Expo (sponsored by *ID Systems* magazine). These give an opportunity not only to attend lectures on different aspects of auto-ID and data collection systems, to see the products and to become acquainted with the vendors, but also to meet users of these systems. They are the ideal place to make acquaintances and receive accurate answers to your questions, particularly those concerned with issues of implementation.

17.2 Site surveys of similar installations

We may assume that a visit to an installation on the recommendation of a vendor is to be a visit to a satisfied customer, so that most if not all your questions about the quality of the system and its vendor will receive favourable replies. So what benefits can such a visit confer? The answer is that you should see it as an educational field trip: you can learn a lot by seeing a working installation. The major points to be addressed on such a trip are the following:

THE REQUIRED INFRASTRUCTURE

Until now the proposed system may have been presented in general terms, with certain components perhaps overlooked or the quantity of others underestimated. The installation representative should therefore be requested to itemize every hardware and software component in the system and to explain its function. Their ability to do this will depend very much on who they are: it is quite possible that you will meet a representative of the end-users who is without a clue as to the architecture of the system, so it is important that both end-users and technical staff are present at the system presentation.

THE SIMILARITY OF THE PRESENTED SYSTEM TO THE PROPOSED ONE

While the system is being presented you have your chance to note the similarities between it and the proposed one. Both architectural and functional similarity should exist; that is, not only should the system use the same technology as the one you may be going to implement, but this technology should have been installed in order to attain goals similar to those you hope to achieve.

SECTORIAL SIMILARITY

Is the installation site you are visiting in your industrial sector? While it need not be, it helps if you have a common language and can discuss common problems with the representatives of the installed system, and they are then quite likely to tell you of other uses for these technologies within your industry which you may not have considered.

ENVIRONMENTAL SIMILARITY

Environmental considerations, as we have already seen, are of great importance in the implementation of most auto-ID and data collection systems. The installation presented should be operating in a similar environment. One should take into account elements such as climate, dust and other dirty working environments, the distances at which auto-ID readers read objects, required read speeds, the professional level of end-users and more.

THROUGHPUT

How much data is collected and how many items are automatically identified within a given time period? How many data collection devices are installed at the site you are visiting? What are the installed memory capacities of these devices? How, and how often, is the collected data transferred to the host computer? The efficiency of a particular data communications configuration can only be truly determined, without a test run, by the examination of a system with similar functional requirements.

WORKING PROCEDURES

A company that produces items for stock might have demands on a data collection system that are totally different from those of one that produces for customer orders only. For instance, as regards the frequency and method of data transfer, a company producing items for stock may not require the tracking of lots on the factory floor, and the frequent updating of the host system as to the status of each lot. The introduction of an auto-ID and data collection system may also have required changes or additions to existing working procedures. This should be a subject for discussion with the site representative.

Once you have noted all these points and verified the suitability of the presented system you can put to the site representatives the particular questions that should be asked. The following questions can provide the basis of a more detailed review document that should be prepared before visiting the installation. They have special significance for auto-ID and data collection systems:

- What changes, if any, were made to existing working procedures?
- Does the system in any way slow down existing working procedures?
- Were any organizational or personnel changes required?
- Data transfer: how long does it take to transfer data to the host system? How much data is transferred? By which method?
- Were there any problems of integration between different system components or in interfacing to the host system? If so of what kind were they, and how were they overcome? How long was it before a satisfactory solution was implemented?
- Are there, or have there been in the past, any detrimental environmental effects upon the system's performance, in terms of either identifying objects or the operation of the equipment? If so, how were these difficulties overcome?
- Are there any items of data needed that the system cannot collect? If so, for what reasons?
- If an auto-ID technology was adopted, which type was it? What were the reasons for the adoption of this particular auto-ID technology?
- Were any government licences required before the system could be installed, for instance for RF communications?
- What, if any, were the types of user acceptance difficulties experienced? For instance, have users experienced any difficulties in operating the equipment?
- Has the system been audited? If so did it live up to expectations as regards data accuracy and timeliness?

17.3 Initial feasibilty checks

Gathering appropriate information about others is an important first step, but it is far from all that is needed. Before you present your ideas you must be convinced that the system will work in your own unique working environment. This is the aim of the initial feasibility study, where there are a number of points to consider, most of which fall into the categories discussed in the previous section.

INFRASTRUCTURE

What changes will have to be made to the existing infrastructure? Automatic identification systems generally require a certain degree of order. For instance if items in a warehouse are to be bar-coded, then they will need to be stored in an orderly fashion so that the bar codes are accessible (in order to be read) at all times. Certain engineering solutions might be required for the placement, positioning and connection of auto-ID readers and data collection devices.

WORKING METHODS

The introduction of a data collection system may, and quite often does, mean that existing working procedures will be changed. More data can now be collected and in a shorter period of time. Whereas before the reporting of certain information may have been time-consuming and thus infeasible, the introduction of a data collection system may well now remove the reasons for such non-collection; new opportunities are on the horizon and therefore existing reporting methods need to be re-examined as follows:

– What data has been lacking until now and for what reasons?
– At what frequency is data reported to the system, and can this frequency now be increased?
– Can the number of reporting procedures be reduced by merging some of them together?
– Is certain data redundant at various stages of a process?

An example at this stage should clarify some of these issues. A distributor of agricultural produce receives fruit from different farms every day. This fruit is weighed, checked for type and quality, measured, and washed. At the end of this process the distributor knows if the fruit that a certain farm has sent him is of export quality, good for the local market or just suitable for industrial use. The farm is paid according to the quality of its produce. At every stage of the process data about the farms, their names and the produce supplied by them is copied repeatedly onto different forms, with each form grouping the results for each stage of sorting. By bar-coding containers of fruit when they are received with a unique lot number, a farm's details are only entered once into the system. From then on all these details are automatically retrieved by a data collection system via the farm's ascribed lot number as it is reported at the different stages of processing. This obviously could have been done before the introduction of bar codes into the system, but the high chance of an erroneously reported handwritten lot number made this method of data collection infeasible. Moreover, now that a large amount of data can be captured automatically by reading a single bar code, data can be captured at more stages of the process.

Changes in the host system

The host system might well be required to undergo some changes as the result of the implementation of a data collection system. A classic example of this is the switch from an on-line data inputting process to a batch one. While this might seem a step back in data processing, many collection systems involve the file transfer of data from a data collection device to the host. Whereas before data was input from handwritten forms, either into a data entry terminal or on-line, an existing system may now be required to facilitate the updating of its database by importing external data files.

17.4 Convincing others and gaining cooperation

Now that the necessary initial information about the proposed system has been gathered and analysed, it is time to 'sell' the concept to those who will be involved in giving the go-ahead. In this section we examine some of the obstacles that may arise when the implementation of an auto-ID and data collection system is proposed, as illustrated by some of the more common reactions to be expected from different types of staff members.

THE COMPUTER DEPARTMENT

'Great idea, but too complicated to implement. We are overloaded with work as it is and cannot afford to integrate more hardware or software at this moment in time. The addition of a new staff member for my team could help if this could be done, otherwise forget the idea.' Heard that before? The computer department will need to invest time and resources for the project, but how much depends quite largely on the system vendor and you, the project instigator. If you are willing to implement the system initially so that only existing data collection procedures are automated then the system vendor should be able to supply you with a complete solution by providing an interface to the host system that will require very little or no changes at all to the existing software or hardware configuration. Earlier we saw how some data collection systems will transfer data in files to the host, so a special program will be needed on the host computer to import and validate these files for errors.

In one organization whose computer people said 'No way!' to this proposal, a solution was supplied whereby data files were transferred first to a PC and then in an unattended fashion on-line via terminal emulation to the host system, an IBM mainframe computer. This unique solution was provided by the system vendor, who used a subcontractor and his emulation package. Data was automatically entered into the host system as if it had been manually entered from an on-line terminal. All the existing validation procedures in the host system were left untouched.

THE END-USER – FACTORY FLOOR MANAGER, WAREHOUSE MANAGER AND OTHERS

'Listen, our workload is so great today that we don't have time to study computers. While my kids are quite good at these things, forget about me! Anyway, half of my team have difficulty even in reading the labels on the items and would never be able to operate one of those things in that picture. And who do you think is going to stick those labels on all these shelves?' In many instances gaining cooperation from the end-user is the hardest task, even though this person is the one most likely to benefit from the future system. There follows some basic guidelines to help reduce potential opposition.

Even though, as we see later, the most effective way to gain cooperation is a firm mandate from the top echelons of management, in some cases this is not enough. Workers may cooperate at a certain level yet may also create enough difficulties on the way for the future system not to stand a chance. The solution is to involve a representative of the end-users from the outset and to make sure he is part of the decision-making process. It is also best to emphasize that the invested resources are primarily aimed at his benefit.

Take the end-user representative to a working installation of the proposed system at the earliest possible stage, and most importantly to one that is operative in a similar working environment. The end-user will want to see that the system has already proved itself in an environment that she or he can associate with. If you can find an installation manned by the same number of staff, this may well prove a further persuasive tool.

Avoid at all costs statements that have a potential to be interpreted in a negative light, for instance:

- 'The aim of the proposed system is to stem the tide of errors reported to the computer today.'

- 'Less work hours required ...'
- '... even a monkey could operate ...'
- '... greater control by management of what is going on downstairs'.

Finance department

'Of course, we've heard it all before. By investing a sum of money in computerized systems we gain essential information that until now has been lacking, save on personnel and reduce costs all round. Well, from my experience we will most likely need more personnel, spend a fortune on maintenance and in updating software, lose information due to malfunctioning and generally spend money all round. Anyway, we don't have the budget!' Here you have to be really prepared. To counter these arguments it is up to you to show how much money the organization is losing by *not* implementing the proposed system. This will mean that some preparatory work will have to be done. The various approaches to this work are discussed later in this chapter.

Operational management

Take all the obstacles mentioned up till now and more and then you are ready for your meeting with operational management. The smoothest approach for convincing others is to get a solid mandate from the top. This will probably mean getting the managing director personally involved and making the project his 'baby'. Again, if you can arrange a trip for him to an existing installation this will definitely help, as will a visit to one of the trade shows. Finally, if your competitors are benefiting from this technology, this should be brought to management's attention; after all, who wants to be left behind?

17.5 Establishing a budget

Accurate costing can only be determined after answers have been supplied to the following questions:

- Which technology is to be chosen for implementation?
- Regarding the extent of the project, will the project be implemented in stages, and if so what is the extent of the first stage? For example, how many auto-ID readers or data collectors will be required?
- How much preparatory work is involved? Is system analysis needed?

Only after all these points have been clarified can a budgetary framework be created. This framework should include the cost of the initial planning stages, hardware and software (which might have to be specially customized), installation and current running costs, plus an annual service contract for hardware and software. All these details should be supplied by the system vendor as part of his detailed proposal (to be discussed in Chapter 19).

17.6 Defining system objectives

Defining what we actually want to achieve from the future system in a concise fashion might seem an unnecessary, time-consuming procedure. However, most systems are audited at some stage of their life; that is, a thorough test is made to see whether the system has lived up to everyone's expectations. It is, therefore, important to get down on paper exactly what those expectations are. Remember that in the future you may wish to extend the system further or to introduce similar technologies into other related areas. If it can be shown that the initial stages of implementation fulfilled their aims, then further extension should be justifiable.

How, briefly, should these objectives be phrased? Avoid general phrases such as 'significant reduction in work hours' or 'increased profitability'. Make sure that clear units of measure to determine success or failure are defined *and are measurable*. We have already seen how quality information is a key objective in a data collection system. Quality information is based on two key factors – time and accuracy. Try to obtain data concerning these two factors in your existing system. For instance, many data processing systems provide reports of all erroneous transactions reported to the system, at least where these can be identified. Also, check cycle times for certain procedures, such as the average time from the receipt of an order until its dispatch, as well as the time taken until a certain batch of transactions is actually reported to the host system. This data is a useful basis for the auditing of data collection systems.

17.7 Economic justification

A project will only be deemed feasible if within a defined period of time the initial investment made is returned by either reducing existing costs or increasing productivity or market share. The type of benefits to be gained depends very much on the nature of the organization in which the system is to be established. The basic economics and calculations are quite straightforward and therefore are not detailed here. What is detailed here, though, are the areas that should be considered potential sources of benefits.

Quality

As more detailed data is collected, decision-making will be based upon accurate and timely data as opposed to estimations and outdated standards. For instance, a data collection system can facilitate the capture of data concerning many process parameters that affect the quality of a product during its manufacture. As we have seen in Chapter 9, this data can be collected in real time directly from automated processes. In this way poor-quality products can be directly and accurately linked to individual variable elements of the production process, in other words to assignable causes of variabilty. Real-time data collection facilitates the immediate detection of processes that fall out of defined tolerance limits, hence allowing for remedial action without delay and thus preventing dreadful waste of production resources due to continued production. Find examples of how many items have been produced before a faulty series has been detected.

Throughput

Calculate existing throughput (as defined in Section 18.3). Can this be increased by the speedier and more accurate identification of items? If so, by how much? An estimation can best be approximated either by a simple pilot experiment with the cooperation of a system vendor, or where this is not possible, through trying to obtain details from a similar working environment that is already benefiting from an auto-ID and data collection system. Increased throughput means increased capacity with existing resources, a great attraction for an organization with growth in mind.

Human resources

Can labour-hours be reduced or channelled to more productive areas? For instance, interfacing a data collection device to the host system cancels the need to manually input handwritten data. Also, the introduction of automatic or semiautomatic data collection may reduce the number of workhours invested in manual tasks. A classic example is inventory-taking aided by bar codes and portable data terminals. Workhours are significantly reduced because:

– Item names or numbers are not written down; rather the item is identified in a split second by a bar code reader. The time reduced is equal to:

$$N(T_w - T_{ai})$$

where T_w = the average time taken to write down on a form an item number or name

T_{ai} = the average time to identify an item automatically (including

aiming the bar code reader at the bar code label)
N = number of items to be registered

– Real-time validation on counted quantites can be performed by the portable data terminal. This will significantly reduce the number of recounts demanded of particular items.
– Total elimination of the time taken to enter the inventory manually into the host system.

Most computerized data collection systems for inventory return their initial investment after only one inventory taking!

Space

Reductions in stock levels can be achieved as more timely information is received about actual stock levels and their locations. Procurement and ordering systems will respond more quickly as the result of the timely receipt of current stock levels; also, as order cycle times are reduced, so will be the required stock levels for many items, thus increasing the storage space for newer ones.

Sorting

Auto-ID systems provide a pathway to automatic sorting, again reducing the need for this time-consuming and laborious task.

Accurate costing

The costing of the manufacture of products is a dynamic process based on a multitiude of parameters. Accurate models of costing require fine tuning with time. An automized data collection process eliminates the cost of inaccurate estimates of how many worker and machine hours, energy and scrap have been invested in production.

18
Analysing the existing system

18.1 Introduction

In this chapter we discuss those issues of special relevance to the analysis of a system prior to the design and implemention of automatic identification and computerized data collection. For example, special emphasis will be placed on existing and future throughput in the system. The documentation of information flows with data flow diagrams and other pertinent tools are not discussed. It is not that these diagrams are irrelevant to data collection systems or that calculating throughput is not carried out when analysing more conventional data processing systems; rather, throughput simply has *special significance* to the systems discussed in this book.

The following example should clarify this point. If the throughput (as defined in Section 18.3) for an existing organization is miscalculated for a data processing system, it is still unlikely that the chosen hardware solution will be deemed unsuitable. The most likely result will be slower response times (which may be compensated for by software, hardware or communication modifications). An auto-ID and data collection system will be more sensitive to this issue. Data collection devices generally possess small and non-upgradable memories, while auto-ID readers can read and respond at given maximum speeds. Moreover, in most situations auto-ID and data collection systems are operable while a physical event takes place, so a detailed analysis of those events and their timing is required in order that the auto-ID and data collection system will not become an operational bottleneck. For this reason the term *'design by response time'* has been adopted by some designers of auto-ID and data collection systems.

Special emphasis is also placed on stages where common pitfalls tend to occur in analysis. There are many reasons why these pitfalls are more common in data collection than in data processing. Perhaps most important is a lack of awareness by system planners of large systems which incorporate auto-ID and computerized data collection, as to the importance of the design stage for these elements of their system. While the actual cost and extent of the hardware and software configuration for a data collection system might be much smaller than that of the host, let us not forget that the point of departure of this book is quality information. A system's size should not be confused with its importance.

18.2 Defining system boundaries

System boundaries are the conceptual framework within which the proposed system will function, for instance a shop floor management system. Within these boundaries, information might be based on a number of sources of data, some of which might fall outside of these very boundaries. By way of an example let us consider a data collection system for inventory control. On face value it would seem that all collected data would originate in the warehouse. This indeed may be the case, yet should the proposed system include the labelling of items with bar codes we might be required to prepare a stock of pre-prepared labels for these items before they arrive at the warehouse. If the warehouse stores finished goods for a manufacturing concern, then we will need to know exactly what the production schedule is for a given period ahead of time in order that the labels can be printed in advance. The inventory data collection system will therefore be required to interface into the factory's manufacturing planning system. For this reason the boundaries of the analysed system might be wider than the future system to be implemented.

18.3 Calculating existing throughput

The importance of the accurate calculation of throughput has already been discussed in Section 18.1. It now remains for us to define exactly what throughput is, as well as how to calculate it.

> Throughput is the sum of data kernels that pass through a system during a given period of time.

Note that the conventional approach to the definition of throughput replaces the number of data kernels with the number of physical items that pass through a system in a given period of time. Yet each physical item is accompanied by data, therefore for our purposes we have related to this data.

Take, for example, the number of orders received by a company on a daily basis. Here the kernel of data might be the information written down on the order form. In order to arrive at a correct result for a system's throughput, a serious effort must be made to correctly identify and define data kernels. For example, an incorrect estimation would be if the system planner took into account only the total number of orders received by the firm every day, and ignored the number of items that normally make up an order. The general rule for calculating throughput is to identify a general data grouping, in our example the order, and then reach the lowest level of that data grouping, the kernel. The lowest level or kernel can then be defined as:

> The data items that will be written into a new data record each time one of the values of those items changes.

In our example, should the warehouseman write a new line for each different product in an order, the data kernels are those data items that are written for each product. If a product repeats itself in the same order form then instead of writing a new line for each reoccurrence of that product, the existing line can have its quantity updated. If, however, the order is made up throughout the day, the hour that the data is actually written might be considered significant. In this case, the data kernel would be written down for every reoccurrence of a previously recorded product, instead of just updating quantity; in other words, the data kernel would include the hour that the data is recorded. Throughput would then be equal to:

> sum (orders) × sum (different items) × (sum entries for any item)

Note that the third element in this calculation is a probability (therefore making the calculation susceptible to the test of time). Where possible maximum figures should be used to calculate throughput, because data collection systems will be required to perform well even at peak times.

Finally, how should we go about collecting data on throughput? The most common and also the most unreliable method is simply to ask end-users a series of statistical questions. The received answers might or might not be accurate. Here are some guidelines that can be implemented in order to gain better results:

– Obtain from the host system summary reports, such as sales reports for different periods of the year (since quantities may differ on a seasonal basis).
– If you have to rely on word of mouth, then make sure you receive the answers from more than one source.

18.4 Analysing current working procedures

As with the introduction of any automated or computerized system, special attention must be paid to preventing the new computerized process from contradicting or detracting from the performance of existing working methods. Moreover, this might also be a good time to examine the efficiency of existing work procedures and even to consider aspects of the reorganization or redefinition of some of them. This holds true especially when auto-ID and data collection systems are designed. Up till now data collection has consisted largely of manual tasks involving plenty of form filling, human identification of items and data entry to a computerized host system. Now, with the introduction of auto-ID readers and data collection devices, much of this work is to be streamlined and new possibilities are open to the organization that may not have been there before. At the managerial level important information may possibly be derived from the host system based on data that up till now it was not thought possible to collect. On the shop floor level, manual tasks can be automated or semiautomated, while, as already mentioned, certain procedures may be merged or even eliminated. When analysing current working procedures the following points should be noted:

- When are particular tasks performed? Are they dependent on the prior completion of another procedure? Timing can be a crucial factor, and as was mentioned earlier the auto-ID and data collection system should not slow up existing procedures.
- Which data is collected? When and how is data reported, and to whom? Is certain data reported in certain situations and not in others? Try to gain a complete picture concerning this last point, because it is perhaps one of the most common pitfalls in the analysis of current working procedures preceding the design of a data collection system. System designs based solely upon standard operating procedures can, when implemented, miss the mark and prove ineffectual.
- Look for data collection redundancy and repetition; this can normally be found where similar data kernels are collected simultaneously at different reporting stations.
- Look for *all* data collection bottlenecks (data flow diagrams might help here), not just those pointed out by the end-users. Sometimes there can exist a chain of bottlenecks with the end-users only aware of the one that directly affects them. This could mean that the proposed auto-ID or data collection device will not be of great benefit unless other bottlenecks are dealt with first.
- Lastly, the general rules of systems analysis are as true for data collection systems as for any others. For each procedure and the data collected in it, answers should be provided to every question of 'When?' 'What?' 'How?' 'Who?' and 'Why?'.

18.5 The existing computerized infrastructure

As we will see in Chapter 19 interfacing systems can be a complex task. Before listing the required specifications of the proposed system, information concerning interface possibilities within your system should be gathered and later presented to the system vendor. It is also advisable that those responsible for your information system should give you their preference for interfacing. Interfacing can be analysed at two main levels, hardware and software, and the information that should be gathered for this purpose is as follows:

- *Hardware interfacing*:
  - Host computer type, vendor, model and configuration, including memory configuration.
  - Existing and potential communication ports, their types and availability.
  - Terminal type (VDU), and the existence of a communication port on the terminal itself.
  - Number of host system users.
  - Distance between the host itself and where the data is to be collected.
  - Existing data communication infrastructure, type and configuration, for instance a local area network.

- *Software interfacing*:
  - Operating system, network manager (including the version number).
  - Will the collected data be sent to an existing software package? If so, give the name of the package, the version and the vendor.
  - Type of data files, ASCII, EBCDIC?
  - Does the host system have the possibility of importing and exporting the required data into external files?

This checklist is aimed at facilitating the prediction of major interface problems before they arise; for example a vendor's communication package might not run under a particular operating system, or an auto-ID reader might not connect up to a particular computer terminal. The land-mines are there, so collect this information! In the next chapter we see how to draw up a specification sheet for the system vendors.

19
System design and specification

19.1 Introduction

System design and specification are the stages in which we define exactly what our system will do, how it will do it and what is needed for it to be done. Specific design issues of special relevance to this text that are discussed in this chapter are:

- hardware specification
- software specification and design considerations
- interface design considerations
- data structures
- the request for proposal.

Not all auto-ID and data collection systems will require detailed design work before their implementation. There are a wide variety of turnkey solutions on the market, particularly for time-and-attendance systems, because both hardware and software configurations do not vary greatly from installation to installation.

19.2 Hardware configurations

In the chapters on data collection devices, the possible hardware configurations of those devices have been examined. These possibilities should be related to in deciding upon the final hardware configuration of the future system. Hardware configurations can be divided into three broad classes:

- *Overall system configurations*. These include the type of data collection devices that will be used (possibily more than one type will be used in any one system) and the specific auto-ID technology, (already discussed in Chapters 1 and 2).
- *Individual device configuration*. Under this heading comes reading speeds, memory capacities, input types, backup facilities, screen sizes, keyboard

types, type of housing and durability in adverse conditions, power sources, and more.
- *Interface configurations*. These determine how we are to link up all the devices with the host system, as well as with each other. This last category is examined by itself in Section 19.4. The final hardware configuration of the future system is influenced by application as well as working procedure issues. What then are the major considerations to be taken into account in specifying a hardware configuration? (The hardware elements are marked by 'HW'.)

The application

How much data is to be collected in any given time period?
HW   Memory capacity

Which type of data is to be collected?
HW   Keyboard, numeric vs alphanumeric data.
HW   Discrete, analog inputs

Does collected data need to be processed before being transmitted to the host?
HW   Processor type and level of intelligence (programmability). Ability to perform searches for data in a large file, etc. Processing modules, timers, counters, etc.

Does data need to be displayed; if so how much at any one time?
HW   Sceen size.

Which auto-ID technologies have been chosen for implementing the application?
HW   Capability to interface a number of auto-ID technologies. Communication ports, firmware.

The number of data collection stations in the system.

How many data collection points are needed?
HW   The ability to network data collection devices.
HW   How many I/O ports are available for auto-ID readers on any one data collection device?

Working environment

What will the working environment be like?
HW   Type of casing or housing for the data collection device. Are international or military standards met?

Is the data collection device to be operated in poor lighting conditions?
HW   Availability of screen backlighting.

Procedural issues

Is the solution portable?
HW   Physical dimensions and weight of data collection device.

How often will data be transmitted to the host?
HW   Memory capacity.

Is the unit required to work on an independent power source at any time, and if so for how long?
HW   Net operating time between battery charge or replacement.

What will be the predicted throughput?
Response times.
Access time.

19.3 Software specification and design considerations

The software dealt with in this section is the programs that run within the various data collection devices as well as those that control the communication interface to the host system. These can be broadly classified into two main categories: development tools and application programs. The development tool is a special program or language used to write the application program itself for the data collection device. Such programs totally control the device's processor, memory, keyboard, screen and communications interface, as well as any auto-ID readers connected to the device itself. In many cases we will not be concerned with the data collection device's development tool, because the system vendor will provide us with a turnkey solution in accordance with the system specification drawn up during the planning and design stages. There are, though, a number of situations where the type of development tool offered by the system vendor is of significance, in which cases it is important to become acquainted with the tool offered before a decision is made to acquire the data collection device. Such a situation arises when:

- Application requirements are dynamic and changes to them will be required on a frequent basis.
- Application software development will be done in-house. In this case the tool has to be user-friendly as well as flexible to meet most system requirements.
- The application has some unique requirements. Can the data collection device's development tool support these? Of course the question here is: What is unique? Only someone with much experience in the field can

really come close to giving an answer to this one, and even then various vendors may disagree. So instead of treading on dangerous ground let us play safe by looking at some pointers to the various aspects we should examine when we are considering different development tools.

Again, what follows relates specifically to development tools for data collection devices.

– *Is the development tool a common software language or specifically developed for the data collection device? If the latter case is true, is the tool an application generator or a programming language?* A lot of data collection devices, especially portable data terminals, have had special languages developed for them. This means that time is needed to study and become acquainted with the development tool. Not only this; because so few people know the language, the user is normally quite dependent on the vendor. Normally, specialized languages are more costly than well-known ones such as C or Pascal. If the development tool is an application generator, conferring an environment that simplifies greatly the development process of an application program, then program development will be simpler and speedier, so much so that certain end-users may wish to program the device themselves. However, program generators can limit the possibilities of the program; for instance, how many special-function keys or even data files can be defined as active simultaneously? When complex programming specifications have been drawn up for the data collection device, preference may be given to a common program language.

– *Does the development tool allow the data collection device to have any measure of control over auto-ID readers?* Some auto-ID readers simply plug into the data collection device, while others are an integral part of that device. In the latter case there should be a certain amount of software control over the readers. In other words, the actual functioning of the reader can be application-specific. An example of such a feature is the length of time a laser scanner will scan a bar code before declaring a non-read.

– *How much control does the development tool have over the data collection device's hardware?* Some examples are character size on screen, redefinition of keyboard, and power control including timable automatic shutoff facility. Can the real-time clock be addressed dynamically even when the unit is powered down? For instance, can the data collection device wake itself up according to a preset time? This is especially useful for remote data communications sessions where each device independently sends data to the host system at different time intervals.

If a decision has been made to develop an application in-house or to have the application developed by a vendor with close involvement by the end-user in the design stage, certain design considerations should be taken into account. These considerations are also useful when evaluating a turnkey solution; they are:

- A particular event can be recorded or a function performed with the minimum number of keystrokes. Data collection has to be not only accurate but *fast*, and that means efficient. When evaluating a number of packages that perform the same type of application, choose a particular function or transaction and see how many keystrokes are required to perform it. Differences can be significant.
- Again with reference to speed and efficiency, data collection devices that are human-operable must be clear and easy to understand. The user's eye must be able, at any time, to catch immediately the required information on the screen. Unlike in a computer terminal where large amounts of information are displayed simultaneously, a large amount of displayed information can become a hindrance to the end-user in the field. Remember, in most data collection environments the end-user is both collecting data and performing another manual task. Only the most relevant data should be presented at any one time on the screen.
- There must be simplicity; good human engineering is not enough in itself. Even a user-friendly program can fail if the proposed application is too complex for the end-user. First, do not require the end-user to perform a whole new set of data collection tasks that were previously not there, merely because he has received a computerized tool. If more data collection tasks are required then the software application should be modular so as to allow its implementation by stages. If possible keep to a minimum the number of options available to the user, for example the different number of special-function keys. Remember that a lot of data collection personnel have up till now had little or no experience in operating a computerized tool. Also, the number of decisions that have to be made by the end-user should be left to a minimum. Procedures should be short, precise and unequivocal.
- Messages to the user should be unambiguous, whether audio or visual. Special warning messages and beeps should be given in a consistent fashion, with the warning displayed always on the same part of the screen, and the same type of beep sounded and different from other beeps in the system.
- All data collection systems should advise the user as to the following situations:

 — memory nearly full
 — low power – charge or battery required
 — good read (from an auto-ID reader).

Finally, be wary of an 'off-the-shelf' package's ability to meet your own requirements. Sometimes these requirements will have to be sacrificed in order to benefit a turnkey solution. This is legitimate, as with all such packages. However, if changes to the package are required, get a detailed proposal. Some 'simple' changes might be quite expensive and sometimes both the cost of these changes and the cost of the sacrifices made to certain system requirements can outweigh the actual cost of customized development.

As mentioned earlier, the communication program for the data collection device is part of the application software. In evaluating such software check the following points:

- the operating system and host computer that the program can run under
- data transfer speed, protocol type and data integrity checks
- prevention against sending the same data twice
- tracking facilities: which devices send data where, and when.

19.4 Interface design considerations

The main criteria in choosing an interface type are:

- the required level of updated information in the host system
- the amount of information to be sent in any single transmission
- availability of interface options for a data collection device
- the necessity of linking a number of data collectors
- existing working environment
- budget.

We can now discuss the various interface options presented in Chapter 3, in the light of these criteria.

Batch communications

This is a common and versatile solution. However, it demands some form of tracking and control program where large numbers of data collection devices are involved. This solution is very suitable for the periodic update of the host system by file transfer. If a direct physical connection is available between the data collector and host computer then large data files can be transferred at great speed (40 kbps is not an uncommon speed). Nearly all data collection devices support direct batch communications, and many will allow indirect communications to the host over a telephone line using a modem. In this situation, though, lower transmission speeds are used in order to maintain a high level of data integrity and, for this reason non-direct batch communications is not an efficient solution for large data files. Direct batch communications become expensive when data collection devices are spread over a wide area. Hard-wiring becomes a complex task and additional relay equipment such as boosters may be required.

On-line communications

This is ideal for fixed-mount devices (and is rarely implemented with portable solutions unless radio frequency is used), where the host system demands immediate updating. Not all data collection devices support this method of data communications. On-line communication is commonly a hardwired solution, with that solution's inherent problems. Recently, though, radio-frequency data communications is being incorporated into fixed-mount units, where the cost of hard-wiring is prohibitive. On-line radio-frequency communications requires a great deal of detailed planning and may not be suitable for systems with a very high throughput of data. Both direct and non-direct on-line solutions are deemed unsuitable for the transfer of large amounts of data in a single transmission.

Real-time communications

Here collected data is sent continuously to the host computer without waiting for the logical validation of the data sent. This form of data communications is normally implemented where it is of the utmost importance to capture data about events as they happen, normally from automated processes as part of a supervisory control system (see Chapters 9 and 13). In this situation the linkup is direct, with very small amounts of data being transmitted at any one time from any data collector. The cost of this option is a function of the complexity of the chosen configuration (use of networks, etc.), and it is normally available only for PLC or other types of controllers.

To conclude this section special emphasis should be placed on the 'user friendliness' of any chosen interface solution. Data communications is often carried out by the end-user, knowingly or not. For instance in a radio-frequency solution, when the user has recorded a transaction and pushes the ENTER key on his terminal he is in fact giving the command for that transaction to be sent to the host. As stated in Chapter 3, response times are crucial for this solution; a user who has to wait for lengthy periods of time between transmissions will soon lose patience with the system. A badly designed batch communications interface is one that contains too many user interactions with the system. For instance, should data be sent to a mainframe computer via a PC, the end-user might be required to perform two sets of file transfers, data collector–PC and PC–mainframe. If the latter can be left to the computer department, all well and good; otherwise, both transfers should be combined into a single process to simplify matters. Moreover, if the file transfer of data from a data collector to the host computer consists of a number of stages, then one of these stages may be forgotten by the end-user. This may also create a bottleneck in the transfer of data to its final destination.

19.5 Data structures

By *data structures*, we mean both the organization of the data received and sent by the data collection device and that inside the data collection device's memory. The main parameter in the analysis of data structures and their effects on the rest of the system is *time*, for example the response time of the data collection device, the duration time of transmission sessions with the host computer, or the net work time between data communication sessions (as a function of the correct exploitation of memory resources).

Data that is sent to a data collection device via data communications from the host in the form of a file will have one or both of the following uses.

Translation tables

A translation table contains a list of codes and their description for entities or events with common characteristics, such as item numbers in a catalogue file, or client codes in a client file. Its purpose is to facilitate the entry of data in codes (as opposed to typing descriptions). The code is entered into the data collection device and the code's description is output to a screen or another output device (but not normally sent to the host system, as we will soon see).

The origin of a translation table is normally the host system, although some systems allow for the creation and updating of such tables directly on the data collection device itself. A translation table should only contain the least possible information needed for the operation of the data collection device, owing to the time consideration mentioned above, as well as the fact that some data collection devices possess small memories. Because the translation table normally derives from the host system's files, irrelevant additional data fields should be filtered out from the file before it is received by the data collection device. Such fields are solely of importance to the host's more encompassing software, which uses this additional data for other processing tasks.

Control files

This type of file is one of the central means of assuring data integrity, as it contains all the necessary information to facilitate various validity checks on data entered into the data collection device. The structure of the file may be similar to that of the translation table, but its purpose is different. For instance the control file may well contain item numbers and their description, but will also contain additional information that collected data will be compared with in real time, such as prices, stock levels, and other defined ranges of values. One of the main characteristics of a control file is that it will be searched on numerous occasions for a particular string of data or *key*. A very common example of this is the price lookup file, or PLU, as used by computerized cash registers in supermarkets. An item code is entered and the description and price are looked up by the system (this is more than a translation table, because one of the purposes of the PLU is to assure that an erroneous code is not entered into the system). For this reason a control file should normally be indexed or structured in such a way as to allow swift access to any one of its records and to assure a quick response. (There are a variety of well-known techniques for this, but they are beyond the scope of this study.) As with the translation table, only relevant data fields should be contained in the file.

Other guidelines for the management of translation tables and control files include the following:

- Descriptions should be kept short. Item descriptions stored in a data collector normally have a different functional usage from that in the host system. They exist in the data collector to facilitate code recognition (the code's translation). This, in many cases, can be achieved by the storage of a shortened form of the standard description supplied by the host, thus saving on memory resources. The possible exception to this rule is if the data collector is required to produce a document via a direct connection to a printer. Here, as with the host system, a full description is normally given.
- Repetitive occurrences of the same data should be avoided. This can happen when a particular file contains a record for each different item or event in a system, even when most of the data fields in those records have identical values. If possible, records should be grouped together under a heading that consists of those identical data fields (the *header*). The other kind of record will contain all the data fields with variable values. There are alternative techniques for saving or even compressing data, and these should be looked into, for as we have already seen, most data collection devices possess a limited amount of memory storage space.

Memory files

The next group of files are the memory files into which the collected data is written, and there are two main variations on these. First, there is the *appended* file, which is built dynamically while data is collected, normally a separate record for each event. In other words, the file is empty when the data collection commences and grows as data collection proceeds. It is later sent and erased from memory, only to be built again from scratch with new data.

The other main type of memory file is the *update* file. This is basically a file that is received from the host as an input file and is dynamically updated during data collection. Update files contain records with most of the expected event's data already recorded ahead of time; only a single or a very few data items are missing, to be recorded as an event actually takes place. A classic example of this is the computerized picking list. A data collection device will contain a record for each item to be 'picked' for a given order. Each record contains all the information for each item in the order except for the actual quantity that will be supplied, which is not known until the item has been picked. The file is therefore sent to and returned from the data collection device with exactly the same structure; only the relevant field, in this case 'quantity supplied', has actually been updated.

Some guidelines for the organization of these files now follow:

- Unlike in the case of *update* files, the sorting of *appended* files is not of great significance. Normally the order the data is collected in is the order in which it is stored and sent to the host. The host system can later sort the file into any particular order that is required. *Update* files are normally kept in the order in which they were received.
- Memory files should contain codes as opposed to descriptions, in order to save data communication time and precious memory storage space. There is no need to store the same 20-character item description a thousand times, where a simple 5-digit code will suffice. Translation tables can translate the codes where necessary, both internally in the data collection device and also in the host system.
- The final structure of the memory file is a product of the analysis of which data is to be collected, as well as how the host system will wish to receive this data. Sometimes the way that data is collected and stored in the data collection device will not be suitable for the host system. An example could be the input of an item number via an EAN 13 bar code, in which a unique item number needs to be identified by only 8 out of the total 13 digits of the bar code. For this reason, a truncated item field might well be sent to the host system.
- Where possible, use should be made of *data group identifiers* (DGI). A data collection system will initially collect data about a particular event or entity and then can allocate to this data a unique code that identifies it for future reference. Further along the system, complete events or entities can be collected simply by inputting the DGI into a memory file.
- As mentioned earlier, the way data is collected is not necessarily the way that the host system will wish to receive it. When structuring a memory file, the designer must attempt to identify data that does not vary regardless of the particular event or transaction being recorded. Such data

does not need to be stored in memory; an example is the laboratory number in which data is collected. This sort of data item can be entered into the data collector as a parameter and appended to data sent during transmission to the host.

19.6 Vendors – request for proposals (RFP)

At the end of the design stage, after system specifications have been finalized, we will need to approach the various system vendors in order to receive their proposals. The first point to note is that the quality and accuracy of the vendor's proposal will be in direct proportion to the quality and accuracy of the system specifications they receive. A vendor will find it very difficult to translate a vague discription of the future system into detailed and accurate costs. Generally a vendor's proposal should faithfully comply to the required information itemized in the request for proposal (RFP). Indeed, it is recommended that the RFP requires the vendor to structure his proposal according to its framework; this practice will ease the process of tabularizing and comparing the results of the various offers. The RFP should require the system vendor to detail the following points:

- A brief outline of the vendor's history, market position, products and services.
- A detailed description of the hardware offered, in strict accordance to the itemized hardware specifications supplied with the RFP. If any hardware component itemized is lacking it should be clearly declared. If the vendor deviates from or wishes to improve any aspect of the hardware configuration then this too should be clearly detailed.
- A description of the offered application software – package or customized. This description should include a preliminary specification of the various screens, routines, functions, database, etc. If the software is to be tailored, in which programming language will it be developed? Is it the company's policy that new models of equipment will support applications that run on older models?
- A description of the communication interfaces to the host system. Whose responsibility is it to make sure that the collected data reaches its final destination, i.e. the host software? In many cases the vendor will not provide the facility to import collected data into your host software, and in some cases the collected data will not be transmitted in the structure demanded by the host. Make sure that the system vendor offers an interface to your hardware platform, should it not be a personal computer.
- Other services, such as the preparation of a detailed software design document before programming commences, also training services, equip-

ment installation, and the initial accompanying of the system users immediately after the system has been installed.
- Warranty conditions. What is guaranteed, for how long and under what conditions? Which perishable components are not covered by the warranty or have only a shorter warranty period?
- Technical support, hardware and software. Are units serviced on site or only in the vendor's service facilities, and within what time framework? Are all spare parts regularly kept in stock, or are units sent overseas for repair? Does there exist a helpline for users' questions after installation? For how many years after installation will the vendor supply technical support for the offered system (against the payment of a service contract)?
- Documentation: ask to see examples.
- Previous vendor experience of similar or identical systems. How many of the offered hardware units have been sold in the past by the vendor?
- Customer list and references: emphasis should be placed on the customers with similar systems. Names and telephone numbers of contacts should be provided.
- Hardware costs. These will include both the initial cost of the units themselves and the costs of all system components that will need to be replaced on a regular basis.
- Software costs. The price of the offered software only has relevance if it is accompanied by a detailed specification, or by a declaration by the vendor that his offered system will be supplied in strict accordance to the software specifications detailed in the RFP. The vendor should also itemize costs of a programming work hour, should changes to the system be required in the future.
- The price of all interface devices.
- The cost of a yearly service contract at the end of the warranty period.
- Any additional costs involved in the implementation of the system.
- A declaration of compliance with any standards required in the RFP.
- Delivery time for all parts of the system. A penalty clause is sometimes included for delayed deliveries.

20
Implementation

20.1 Implementation and integration pitfalls and how to avoid them

Data collection systems are almost never independent by nature, and at some stage or another each one will interface with a host system. Such systems are rife with potential integration problems, but most of these need never arise if a good planning technique is used at the design stage. There are some good general guidelines which if adhered to during the design of a system may reduce potential implementation and integration pitfalls significantly. These are as follows:

Design in detail: screens, data structure, logic routines, data communications

Do not ignore issues in the hope of 'crossing a bridge when we come to it'. Some decisions described on paper should be tested in the field by the way of a prototype before software is written or hardware purchased. By way of an example – and there are many examples – if a particular file is to be uploaded to a host computer by the data collection device, a test file can be built with an ASCII text editor and imported to the host, as if it had originated from the data collection device. This test can be done before a single line of specialized software for the data collection device is written. If the system manager of the host system has demanded a certain file structure, check his structure out ahead of time!

Cross-check the data to be collected with that managed by the host system

This is a classic integration pitfall. If the data collection system was designed without fully analysing the host system we might reach the ridiculous situation where the data collection device collects data that the host system cannot handle. In one case, a data collection system vendor was handed a specification document that detailed the various data to be collected by the future system. Only later did the enthusiastic system designer discover that he had solved the data collection problem by creating a new data processing one!

Check the host's hardware configuration well ahead of time

Here is another classic pitfall! Even though the host computer may be of a generic variety, hardware configurations may differ from one installation to another. This is common with data communication interfaces. Such problems can be as simple as the non-availability of a free communication port for the data collection system, or non-matching connectors. Yet more serious problems can arise should the hardware configuration for the generic host computer (such as a PC) differ radically from the expected. For instance if a PC is to be the link between the data collection device and the mainframe computer it should not act as a file server in a network. Sometimes in these situations problems may occur with data communications.

Determine the expected growth of the number of data collection devices in the system

What happens when we increase the number of data collection devices active in the system? The system designer must not assume that the planned number of devices will be the final amount in the system. In many cases a large increase in the numbers of active data collection devices will demand more intelligent data communications routines as well as the definition of procedural guidelines to prevent bottlenecks during the updating of the host.

Integrating technologies

This is a subject of such wide scope that the discussion of integration problems special to bar code systems has been left until Section 21.1; however, general auto-ID technology integration pitfalls include the following.

ENVIRONMENTAL INTEGRATION

The auto-ID reader does not suit the actual working environment. For instance, the actual working distance of an interrogator may prove too short to read an RF tag on the move. Once again, do not leave key elements of the system untried in the field until the implementation stage. If a system's success rests on the guaranteed performance of an auto-ID reader, check that reader's performance during the design stage.

INTERFACING TO A DATA COLLECTION DEVICE OR TO THE HOST TERMINAL

As mentioned in Chapter 2, some auto-ID readers connect up to the host terminal by way of keyboard emulation. Yet not all terminals have exactly the same keyboard emulation type, and moreover some from the same series or family have different keyboard emulations. Merely specifying the type of computer is not always enough; the model number of the terminal or keyboard type will have to be specified too. Once again, preliminary field tests for all types of connections at the planning stage reduce this kind of potential integration problem.

SPEED OF READ

Some auto-ID systems are fully automated, so that the item to be read is brought to the reader and not the reader to the item. At what speed will this be done? We may recall from our previous discussion of the economic justification of data collection systems (Section 17.7) that one of the major considerations is improved throughput. But what if the conveyor brings items to a reader that cannot stand the pace? This sort of information can be read from the specification sheet of most readers, yet the real test of access time is in the field. If a decoding algorithm is customized for a particular application, then its prototype should be tested at the earliest possible stage.

Check the type of text files to be used in the system

Most data collection devices send and receive ASCII files, a standard representation of characters in text form, but not all host systems can automatically offer or accept ASCII files: some use EBCDIC characters, another standard representation of characters in text form common to IBM mainframe computers. Therefore the *type* of text files offered by the host has to be verified ahead of time and, if necessary, a file type converter will have to be incorporated into the system.

It should be clear by now that most implementation problems are caused because the technical feasibility of planned solutions on paper were not actually tested during the design stage. This is a critical factor in auto-ID and data collection systems because, unlike in other, more conventional data processing systems, different technologies that communicate in different fashions are required to interact together. Thus each key interaction should be tested out early on, which does not normally require many hours' work. Simple prototypes can be set up immediately, and in many cases the system vendor can be required to do this.

20.2 Assuring system reliability and backup data collection procedures

Yes, it can happen: the data collection device or auto-ID reader can transmit corrupted data to the host system. Worse still, data collected over a period of time can be lost, erased from a data collection device's memory. These two points contradict the very *raison d'être* for automatic identification and data collection systems. How can such disasters happen, and how can they be prevented?

Corrupted data

Corrupted data is data that has been altered in memory or during transmission by 'noise' or external disturbances. For the purpose of this discussion corrupted data is assumed to be recoverable, that is revertible to its original state. Severely corrupted data, which is unrecoverable, is considered as 'lost-data', (see p. 209). All auto-ID devices have the potential to mis-read encoded data (assuming that the data has been encoded in the correct fashion). Note the difference between a 'non-read' and a 'mis-read'; in either the data is incorrectly decoded, but in the former the auto-ID reader catches on to the mistake, and the mis-decoded data is not transmitted.

All auto-ID systems tackle the problems of corrupted data. There are a number of basic principles that guarantee this, the best one being that 'no data is better than incorrect data'. This means that should for any reason a miscode take place, then the reading device should give a *'no-read'* response. There are two types of no-read response, *active* and *passive*. In the former the reader actually signals the user that a read attempt has been made but the data has so far not been successfully decoded. In the latter case there is no response from the reader. In most situations the former solution is preferable.

Corrupted data originates in substitution errors (discussed in Chapter 1). Auto-ID technologies have taken solutions to detect substitution errors from other areas of computer science, principally data communications, and some more advanced technologies even offer forms of error correction (see Chapter 22). The system designer must pay careful attention to the existence of substitution error checks or the possibility of a partial decode of data. Most auto-ID vendors will be able to supply information on the types of data integrity checks made by their equipment.

Some of the solutions lie in the encoded data itself, and the check digit (Section 4.5) is an example of this. Not all encoded data has a check digit; indeed sometimes the check digit option has to be specified during the planning stage of an auto-ID system. Most readers will handle standard check digit algorithms that are part of the standard encoding specifications, such as in bar coding. Yet sometimes customized check digit algorithms have to be included as part of the host software.

Length checks on data are a common solution, which is normally handled by the host software. Quite simply, this practice defines a given length for each piece of data received by the host. Less than this means that some data was lost on the way. This technique is obviously limited to situations where we know the data length for each item.

Parity checks are used in bar coding. Here, for each character in the character set, an odd or even number of bars is determined, which can vary according to the position of that character in the bar code.

Similar checks can be used to prevent the transmission of erroneous data from a data collection device. This will form part of the communications protocol, which is the way in which two computerized devices pass information from one to another. Special control characters are sent before and after predetermined amounts of the data, so that these control characters are said to 'envelope' the collected data. There are many protocols on the market, and different devices use either standard or proprietary protocols. The system designer should ascertain that the protocol used is sufficient for the projected system's needs. This can be done by determining into which class falls the protocol that the data collection device uses.

There are three broad classes of communications protocol: *one-way*, *half duplex* and *full duplex*. One-way is aptly nicknamed 'send and pray': the communication session is basically a one-way street, in which the data collection device sends data at given intervals but does not wait to receive a response from the host concerning the integrity of the data. Both half duplex and full duplex protocols, on the other hand, allow a dialogue between the data collection device and the host: with half duplex each device waits for the other to stop sending before it sends; with full duplex both devices send simultaneously. If data has been corrupted while being sent it can be immediately re-sent automatically, before the remaining data is transmitted.

Lost data

We noted earlier that RAM is based upon some power source. Once that is lost so is our data! Severely corrupted data, which has been so corrupted that it has become totally unrecoverable, will also be termed 'lost' for the purpose of this discussion. Our working environment can destabilize RAM, for instance because of a strong magnetic field or a sudden drop or increase in the power supply. There are a number of devices that can produce a magnetic field capable of corrupting memory, powerful electrical transformers being one example. Sudden drops in power supply can also be caused by the weather. Bearing this in mind we can try and reduce the potential damage that will be caused in such an event. Here are some guidelines:

- Make frequent transmissions to the host system. Do not 'hoard' data unnecessarily in data collection devices.
- Perform an environmental site survey. Can we identify ahead of time any potential sources of high electromagnetic fields?
- Fit current stabilizers. If the data collection device is of fixed-mount type and connected to the mains, make sure that a current stabilizer is used to prevent sudden drops or surges in current.
- Use insulators from electromagnetic fields. Correct housing materials should be provided by system vendors where necessary.

Finally, every data collection system must include manual backup procedures. In other words most systems should never rely solely on the use of data collection devices, for if these units malfunction then so does the data collection process. This may seem rather obvious, yet some automatic data collection systems have been planned without manual data collection backup procedures, in other words with no way to input data into the host system except via a data collection device. Moreover, those who collect the data should be made aware of the emergency procedures, such as which forms are to be used, what is the minimal amount of data that has to be collected for any transaction, or when the data should be collected.

In order to clarify this point here is an example. Many data collection systems facilitate the collection of large amounts of data in a mimimal amount of time, especially when auto-ID technologies are involved. Should this option be temporarily removed, the end-user cannot always be expected to collect the same amount of data as was collected in the past, in the same time and with the same accuracy. It is therefore highly recommended that a minimal kernel of the most essential data for each transaction be defined. If and when the data collection system is down, only this kernel will be collected.

21
The design of bar code systems

21.1 Symbology, printing and reading interdependence

In Part Two was presented a basic introduction to bar code technology and its various symbologies, printing and reading methods, their concepts and terminologies. In this chapter we discuss a conceptual framework for the design of a bar code system.

The key to the successful implementation of a bar code system lies in an awareness of the interdependence between the symbologies, the reading and printing technologies. It is when this interdependence is ignored or has not been fully taken into account that a system can flounder. All bar code systems have a common operational goal: that the bar code is read quickly and with very little effort. Unfortunately, though, this does not always happen; different bar code technologies are not always successfully integrated into the same system, as we have already seen from the examples in Part Two, more of which are provided in this chapter. Not only this; on a general level we should note that:

- Not all symbologies can be read by all reading devices.
- Not all printers can print all symbologies.
- Not all reading devices can read bar codes printed from all printers.

What then are the correct parameters that make up our bar code formula? Some parameters are simply factual: for instance, infrared laser readers cannot read bar code labels printed from direct thermal printers because the frequencies of the light waves are incompatible. The other parameters are quantitative or qualitative, such as printing speeds, reading distances, etc.

Symbology and reader

As mentioned above, not all readers are able to decode all symbologies. This is because the decoder is not a universal device, and is actually programmed to decode a limited number of symbologies. One must ascertain that the reading device's decoder can actually decode the chosen symbology (Section 21.2 is devoted to how to choose a symbology). A problem can arise with new or old symbologies. Because certain symbologies such as *Plessy bar* or even *Codabar* are being replaced by new and more advanced ones, some new decoders have dropped these older types from their programmed list of symbologies. On the other end of the scale, certain new symbology types have yet to be included in certain decoders, 16K and Code 49 being cases in point.

Symbology and printer

The above also applies to printers and printing software. Certain printing methods cannot handle the production of continuous symbologies, and are able to print only discrete ones. Letterpress, a wet-ink technique, is a case in point. Not all bar code printers contain every encoding algorithm. All bar code printers and bar code label software (used in conjunction with regular printers) will list the selected symbologies that they can produce.

Print and reading resolution

In order to achieve a bar code of a particular width the symbol can be printed at different densities. For instance, should a bar code that encodes 10 characters be too wide for a particular label, it can be printed at a higher density, in other words the X dimension is reduced. System designers must take into account two factors here. First, whether the printer can actually print the required X dimension, and second, that the reader can read it. Both readers and printers define their resolution range, which is normally measured in 'mils' (thousandths of an inch). A mismatch here will lead to non-readable bar codes and a very frustrated end-user.

Distance and print resolution

The wider the X dimension the greater is the distance from which the bar code can be read. If an application specifies a particular print resolution, as well as requiring a guaranteed minimum working distance between the bar code and the bar code reader, then a check must be made to establish that this distance will not be compromised by the chosen print resolution. The best checks are not those made on paper (although a rule of thumb states that the maximum reading range is equal to a thousand times the X dimension), but rather those made in the field with the actual bar code and bar code reader.

Resolution and print tolerances

Every symbology specification states the relationship between the print resolution and the print or bar width tolerance for that symbology. This relationship is an inverse one, with tolerance being reduced the higher the print resolution (the narrower the X dimension). Bar width tolerance can be as little as 1 mil, so it is important to determine that the chosen printer can print within the tolerance limits dictated by the chosen print resolution.

Colour of print and light wavelength

All bar code readers emit light that is absorbed by the dark bars of the symbology. This light can be emitted at different wavelengths, yet not every material or colour can absorb every wavelength. The major ranges of wavelengths (measured in nanometers) are:

– 633 to 750 nm: visible light
– 750 to 900 nm: non-visible or infrared light.

For example, infrared readers demand the use of carbon black ink, and are ineffective with some colours, notably red. The light absorption wavelengths of the label substrate and the ink must be matched with the reader's light-emitting wavelength.

Unattended reading: scan rate, bar height, tilt, scan pattern, and conveyance speed

Finally, some of the most complex systems to plan are those where the bar code is brought to the reader by an automatic conveyance system and is read unattended. Our main aim here is to ensure that the bar code will be decoded within the period of time that it remains within the reader's working range. The relevant parameters here are those just listed in the heading to this subsection. A full analysis of this subject is beyond the scope of this work, but planning should normally be left to the vendor, who will have expertise in this field. Yet our purpose is to maximize the number of scans per inch of bar code without compromising throughput. Towards this end:

– Bar codes should be positioned at 90° to the reader's beam, *ladder fashion*, thus ensuring that the bar code stays longer under the laser beam.
– The taller the bars, the longer the time the symbology will remain under the scanner's beam if positioned in the above fashion.
– Tilted bar codes should be avoided. Labels should be straight.
– Omnidirectional and raster scan patterns, as opposed to a single beam, will significantly enhance reading.

– The faster the conveyor, the more aggressive the system will have to be in scans per second, beam patterns, bar heights, etc.

21.2 How to choose your symbology

We have already seen in Chapter 5, where the most popular symbologies were discussed, that one of the main characteristics that distinguishes various symbologies from each other is their character set. Some character sets are numeric only, while others are made up of digits and a limited number of alphanumeric characters. Others, such as Code 128, not only have a very full range of characters but possess more than one character set! Why then are there so many different symbologies, and why should we concern ourselves with those with limited character sets?

The answer to the first question is historical: as more versatile symbologies were developed, the more limited ones had already been adopted as industrial standards in many sectors, and as we all know, standards are hard to change. In answer to the second question it may be stated that the character set is not the only consideration when choosing a symbology. Another decisive factor is the size of the area available on which we wish to print the bar code. Not every symbology is as efficient as all the others, and if we were to encode the same data using different symbologies, we would receive bar codes of varying lengths. This is significant, as we are often confined to a limited area in which to print the bar code. By way of a summary, the two main considerations in choosing a symbology are:

– Which data do we wish to encode (i.e. which character set is required)?
– How much space do we have in which to print it?

Other factors are:

– The existence of an industrial standard. Certain industries either recommend or demand the adoption of certain symbologies (see Chapter 8).
– Open versus closed system. If the system is open, that is if the bar code will be read by organizations other than our own, then a widely used symbology should be chosen to increase the likelihood that all decoders will be able to decode it.
– Reliability: all bar codes are intrinsically reliable, but some more so than others. For instance, Interleaved 2 of 5 has the potential to be only partially read unless special preventive measures are taken (Chapter 8). Other symbologies have built-in parity checks.
– Is it likely that the required number of characters to be encoded will increase in the future? If so, then we should be wary of choosing a fixed-length symbology, but if one is chosen then the current number of characters should be less than the maximum allowed by that symbology in order to allow for growth.

In every case the chosen symbology should be printed and tested for quality before production is undertaken. If the printed result is wider than the label area at our disposal then we can take the following actions.

- Increase the label size, though this is not always possible.
- Print the bar code at a higher resolution. Remember to distinguish between open and closed systems: if the bar code is to be used in an open system, high-resolution printing should be avoided, as not every reader can handle this.
- Print a 'ladder': print the bar code at 90° if the label is tall enough to accommodate this.

21.3 Bar code label software

In-house bar code printing normally requires software to design and print the bar codes themselves. Most bar code printing software packages are PC-based. A good package would normally have the following features:

- It will allow for the complete design of the label, including simple graphics. Superior programs incorporate the use of an image scanner to allow pictures, logos and other graphic work to be imported and 'pasted' into the design of the label.
- The software will include all major symbologies, or at least those covered in Chapter 5.
- Resolution. Printing resolution is software-controlled. Many packages do not allow the full exploitation of the printer's printing capability. Such packages will offer a number of predefined resolutions as opposed to allowing the user to define the absolute resolution of the X dimension.
- Data. Does the software package allow easy access to external data files (ASCII files)? Does the program work with any file structure, or does a particular one have to be adhered to? Can labels be numerated, in other words can a range of numbers be defined, with the software incrementing the number automatically for each label, within this range? Can numbers be decremented? What level of database management does the bar code software offer? Can particular records in an entire database be selectively accessed for a particular print run?
- Industry label standards. Some packages come supplied with a number of predesigned formats, such as the Odette label.
- Print log. A useful feature on some packages is the *print log*, which documents which label designs were printed, on which day, at what time and in what quantities.
- Emulation. Though listed last, this is a go/no-go item. Different printers print in different ways; each uses a set of print commands known as its

print emulation. Not all bar code packages support all emulations! If you are to print in-house, check which emulations are available from the bar code program and then check that one of these is supported by your printer.

21.4 Choosing a label

In Chapter 4 we discussed the structure of a label. Part of the bar code system design procedure is to choose a suitable label that will meet all application requirements. The main consideration in deciding which label to use is durability. Durability factors are:

- *Life span, both operational and storage* (*shelf life*). One year, two years, three months? The required life span refers to both the label stock, including the adhesive, and the final printed label.
- *PCS*. Not only should a PCS (print contrast signal – see Chapter 8) be high – it has to be stable too. The PCS should be maintained over the whole of the label's life. The label vendor should guarantee that, given the right printing conditions, PCS will not fall below a given level throughout the label's life span. Of course, the PCS is also a function of the printer and the ink used to print the label. However, a good verifier will be able to pinpoint the exact PCS problem, whether it is in the label or in the ink. Some labels have the tendency to yellow with age, which tends to reduce the PCS.
- *Temperatures*. What is the operational and storage temperature range in which the label will have to survive? This information should be supplied to the label vendor, as extreme temperatures can affect both the substrate of the label and the life of the adhesive.
- *Dust and other air particles*. Is the air in the environment in which the labels are to be affixed free of dust, sand, soot or other particles? This is not a prerequisite, but polluted air can affect certain labels.
- *Direct sunlight*. Ultraviolet rays will affect the quality of certain label stocks.
- *Condensation and humidity*. Both of these will affect the label substrate, adhesive and ink. Try affixing a paper label to a carton and then putting it in a freezer for a few hours; the result is that the paper crinkles up and the ink starts to smudge! Solutions do exist for coping with such environments, however.
- *Chemicals*. What happens when grease, oil or other chemicals are applied to the label? There are certain working environments where this might happen. Potential spills of substances or even a worker's dirty hands should be taken into account.
- *Rubbing*. Does the printed label survive rubs? It is quite likely that during the label's life it will be rubbed up against by someone or something!

21.5 Future uses for your bar code

During the planning stage of any bar code system, careful thought must be given to the possible future uses of the bar codes themselves. Systems are dynamic and needs may change over time. Current data may be lengthened, for instance an item number might increase from 8 to 10 digits, or more data items might be needed to be encoded in the bar code. This might be the case especially should the bar code system be expanded to include users outside the existing system. In order to help plan for the future, reserve digits or characters can be included in the bar code. This will mean that the bar code is at first longer than is required, but that new requirements can be addressed in the future without the need to change the structure of the bar code itself. For instance, for a bar code system introduced into a particular department of a large factory, a bar code label was produced that encoded the identity of raw materials used in that department. Two extra zeros were encoded into the bar code. When the bar code system was expanded into other areas of the factory, those same two zeros were used to encode the location in which the raw materials were used.

PART 6
A LOOK AHEAD

22
Future trends and developments

22.1 Future trends for automatic identification

Automatic identification technology has progressed with leaps and bounds during recent years. Existing technologies are still being advanced and refined, while extensive research and development is being invested in new methods of automatic identification. Clear trends can be defined in the furthering of these technologies, namely:

Increased data capacity

Whereas in the past enough data was encoded to provide a key or unique address to access an existing database, or at best the encoded data contained in a single record of data items, recent efforts have been made to create portable databases. One of these contains all the relevant information concerning an entity or group of entities and can be encoded within a single symbol or auto-ID media item. Two-dimensional bar codes, high-capacity smart cards and RF tags are a case in point (the first are discussed in Section 22.3).

Increased data storage efficiency

In order to make greater data capacity feasible, larger amounts of data have to be encoded within the same amount of media. In other words greater data densities are required.

Lengthening optical reading distances

Optical auto-ID readers, principally laser readers, have been developed with greatly extended depths of field. Today non-contact bar code readers reach distances of several metres!

Greater resilience of non-optical reading

Non-optical readers, such as interrogators and voice systems, are being designed to be more resilient to environmental noise. For instance, in the latter case more sophisticated voice systems use a number of microphones as well as intensive signal processing techniques that filter actual speech from overall noise.

Increased reliability

The greatest problem for all automatic identification technologies is reliability, principally to bring about the non-existence of substitution errors. While more conventional auto-ID technologies such as the bar code and magnetic stripes are renowned for their reliability, OCR and other technologies have been slower in reaching the required levels. In order to overcome this problem the combination of more sophisticated decoding algorithms with higher-resolution readers (as in the case of machine vision) has led to superior decoding and overall performance. The use of neural networks in the decoding of OCR fonts is a case in point.

Greater data recovery

Most automatic identification technologies do not provide means for recovery should encoded data become damaged in any way. The latest two-dimensional bar codes provide efficient means of data recovery. That is, all encoded data can be decoded from a symbol that has been partly destroyed (see below).

Reduced cost

Cost has been the major inhibiting factor in the widespread use of automatic identification technologies. While certain readers, such as OCR page readers, are still extremely expensive, their use only being economically justified for mass scale readings, other previously high-cost technologies are becoming more affordable. Quality bar code printers, laser readers, smart cards and RF tags all fall into this category.

Greater diversity of identification possibilities

Besides the use of the existing technologies discussed in Chapter 2, extensive investment has been made during recent years in the search for other methods of automatic identification. Some very interesting developments have been made in the realm of *biometric* identification, the use of biological characteristics to uniquely identify living species. Examples of such advancements are the automatic identification of retinal patterns and fingerprints, (Section 22.5). Similar processes are involved in the recognition of handwriting and in particular signatures (Sections 22.4 and 22.6).

Greater integration of automatic identification technologies

A greater number of integrated solutions can be found on the market today. These products incorporate more than one automatic identification technology, which work together to provide a complete solution for particular identification problems. One example of an integrated solution is the combination of bar code, voice recognition and radio-frequency data communications technologies. For instance General Motors has implemented an integrated auto-ID solution for plant paint quality inspection. Vehicle identification numbers are read using bar code readers; subsequently the voice system guides the inspector through a series of inspection points with the inspector replying to each point. The collected data is transferred from the field to the host system via radio-frequency data communications.

22.2 Future trends for data collection

Advancements in the design of data collection devices can be categorized as follows:

Increased memory

Larger memory configurations are being offered. Ironically, now that radio-frequency data communications is becoming more widely implemented, enabling data to be sent on-line to host computers, larger memory capacities will be of less significance in the future for some data collection systems.

A move away from proprietary systems

Both portable and fixed-mount data collector vendors are now offering programmability with known development tools such as the languages C and Pascal. Moreover, there is a move away from proprietary operating systems as more devices run under DOS.

Ergonomics

Data collectors are becoming smaller and more powerful. This is particularly true of PLCs, which offer a large number of input/output channels and specialized modules in a much smaller device. Just recently there has been considerable development in the design of portable data terminals. Improved ergonomics are to be found with some terminals allowing the unit to be held and the keys to be pressed all with one hand! In Section 22.7 we look at a hands-free portable solution where the data collection device is actually worn by the user.

Auto-ID interfacing possibilties

Data collection devices have traditionally facilitated the interfacing of bar code and magnetic stripe readers. Recently a greater number of auto-ID interface possibilities have become available. These include the capabilities of interfacing to RF tags and to handwriting, signature and voice recognition systems.

In the next sections we discuss selected advances in automatic identification and data collection technology.

22.3 Two-dimensional bar codes

During the eighties significant efforts were made to increase both the data capacity and the information density of bar code symbologies. The result of these efforts was the development of the two-dimensional bar code. The first two developments were *Softstrip* and *Vericode*, the former being designed to encode program listings in computer magazines. These bar codes have a very high capacity and data density performance: Softstrip (Figure 22.1) can encode up to 600 alphanumeric characters per inch, Vericode over 100. Both these codes, as well as other similar ones developed later on, are known as *array* or *matrix* symbologies. Typically, they are based on a dot matrix pattern. Instead of evaluating the widths of bars and spaces, the decoder determines the presence of light and dark cells in the matrix and decodes data according to their position. For instance, Data code (Figure 22.1), which came onto the market in 1989, is decoded in the following manner. After the complete matrix pattern is read, the two

Softstrip   Data code

Figure 22.1 Matrix symbologies: Softstrip and Data code. Courtesy Norman R. Weiland, Monarch Marking Systems

PDF-417   Code 49

Figure 22.2 Stacked symbologies: PDF-417 and Code 49. Courtesy Norman R. Weiland, Monarch Marking Systems

solid lines are measured, and their angles of intersection determined. Next, the number of light and dark cells along the other perimeters are counted. This enables the decoder to determine the angle of read, as well as the individual cell size. Then the positions of all the data cells are determined, with each individual cell's midpoint being tested for colour, light or dark. In this way a bit pattern is created which can later be translated into ASCII code. Array or matrix codes are read with area CCD cameras (as opposed to single-array cameras). Softstrip is read by a specialized contact reader.

Two-dimensional bar codes of the other type are known as *stacked* symbologies because they are composed of stacked rows of short individual bar codes (Figure 22.2). The decoding process determines the transition from one row to the next, as well as their correct order. In this way a series of data items can be linked together into a single portable database. For instance Code 49, which was introduced in 1987, is composed from 2 to 8 rows of bar codes. This symbology uses the parity of each row to determine that row's number as well as the number of the row before it. Another stacked symbology, PDF-417, uses three subsets of bar/space patterns or *clusters* for each alternative row, with each cluster repeating itself every third row. In this way the decoder knows how to identify the transition from one row to another. PDF-417 can encode up to 500 ASCII characters per square inch and reach a total of 1850 alphanumeric characters per symbol! Stacked symbologies can be read with a wider range of reading devices: single-beam lasers, (Code 49, Code 16), raster lasers, and linear and area CCD cameras.

Today there are quite a number of two-dimensional bar code symbologies on the market; in addition to those already mentioned can be found Code One, Upscode, Cryptocode (all matrix codes), as well as Indencode MLC-2D, Code 16, Codablock (stacked symbologies). How then does one decide which two-dimensional bar code to implement? There are a number of factors to be taken into account:

- Not all two dimensional symbologies are in the public domain; those that are not (i.e. proprietary ones) can only be produced under licence from

SECURITY LEVEL 3 - 1·58 sq.in.   SECURITY LEVEL 6 - 2·27 sq.in.

Figure 22.3 PDF–417 sizes according to security levels. Courtesy Norman R. Weiland, Monarch Marking Systems

the vendor. This means there is only a limited amount of hardware (printers and decoders) that can handle proprietary symbols.
- While all two-dimensional bar codes are intrinsically high capacity symbols, some have a higher data capacity than others. Data capacity variation can be quite drastic, from 49 characters to over 5000 characters per symbol.
- Character set size will also differ from one symbology to another. Some symbologies contain user-definable character sets, that permit for example the user to encode foreign language characters such as Japanese or Arabic. Data code, for instance, enables the encoding of executable binary code.
- Matrix codes have some inherent advantages over stacked symbologies. As differing element widths are not significant for these codes, dimensional print accuracy is less crucial. Moreover, matrix codes do not require strong print contrasts.
- Certain two-dimensional symbologies, such as Vericode, Data code and PDF–417, permit the recovery of lost data from a damaged bar code. PDF–417, for instance, provides a number of *security levels* (Figure 22.3), which are user-selectable. Each security level defines the amount of area that can be restored, this amount increasing with each level. Of course this will mean that the actual bar code size for a given amount of encoded data increases as the security level is raised.

The potential uses of two-dimensional bar codes are extensive. Large amounts of data can now be swiftly and accurately read. Whereas in the past, shipping labels contained a number of bar codes, today a single bar code can encode a whole manifest. Greater data capacity allows the two-dimensional bar code to be a complementary tool for the implementation of EDI (see Chapter 3). The bar code can contain a complete EDI message, and provide an efficient backup in the case of the non-transmission of an EDI message to the host system. For instance, by scanning a bar code label on a delivery note, an EDI message can be entered into the host software as if it had derived from a data communications transmission. In the same way as smart cards and RF tags can convey manufacturing instructions to PLCs and automated machinery, so now can the two-dimensional bar code label, and the label costs far less (although it will not be suitable for some manufacturing environments). Finally, two-dimensional bar codes can be one of the swiftest ways of transferring critical information between different computer systems. Examples of such critical data are a patient's medical file and material or chemical safety sheets.

22.4 Signature recognition

In Chapters 11 and 13 we discussed access control systems. Traditional methods of automatic identification used in access control are the magnetic stripe, the bar code and, more recently, RF tags. However, all these solutions have one inherent weak point, the transferability of the means of identification. While some access control systems provide means of preventing the transfer of identification cards (antipassback control is one example of this), there is no guaranteed method of ensuring that one individual will not transfer his identity card to another. Moreover the transfer of stolen cards, such as credit or charge cards, costs the banking sector vast sums every year in insurance premiums.

Only a form of identification inherent in each individual can solve the problem of transferability. This is the subject discussed in this section and the next.

One such form of inherent identification is an individual's signature. This possesses unique characteristics which can be captured, digitalized and stored for future recognition. Voice recognition systems 'learn' our voice pattern, while signature recognition systems learn our signature. The user signs his signature a number of times on a piece of paper that rests on a special pad. This pad is connected to a controller that in turn is connected to a personal computer. After signing his signature a number of times, a final set of values that characterize that signature are stored by the host computer and linked to a unique user code. These characteristics include:

- the time taken to complete the signature
- the speed of signature
- the force applied to the pad while the signature is signed
- a general outline of the signature.

If signature recognition was solely based upon the last parameter then a competent forger would be able to bypass the system. Signing one's signature is to a great extent a reflexive action. The first three parameters listed above represent this reflex. For instance, a forger may be able to produce an exact copy of another's signature, but can this exact likeness be reproduced within the same time period taken to produce the authentic signature? The time taken to sign our signature does not vary greatly. We also tend to apply greater pressure to certain parts of the signature than to others. We may even lift the pen off the paper at certain points of the signature. All this information is captured by a sensor pad and a pen that uses magnetic ink. This ink helps the controller to map the form of the signature as well as to calculate the strength of handwritten symbols at various points.

Signature recognition has great potential, and can be implemented for a number of applications other than traditional access control. These might include access permission to sensitive databases, and as document authorization and validation.

22.5 Automatic recognition of fingerprints

Another form of inherent or intrinsic identification is the fingerprint, which has been traditionally used by police and other government agencies to identify individuals. This automatic identification technology is used for both the classification and subsequent matching of fingerprints. Classification is based upon a number of fingerprint characteristics or unique pattern types, which include arches, loops and whorls (Figure 22.4). A match or positive identification is made when a given number of corresponding features are identified. After the fingerprint image has been captured and digitalized (a tonal threshold is determined in order to establish which image pixels are to be classified as '1' and which '0'), it is analysed. The analysis stage includes:

– feature extraction
– classification
– matching.

Features are first identified and then extracted from the overall image. These features are essentially bit strings. Next, the bit strings are classified by statistical methods into their respective categories. Finally, the classified features are compared in order to determine a positive identification. After a given threshold of matches is passed a positive identification is determined.

Digitalized fingerprints can be encoded within existing large-capacity and high-data-density auto-ID technologies. Smart cards have great potential for the storage of fingerprint and other biometric data. The portability of such information allows for genetic identification and validation without the need to interface to a central database. For example, in one future application an ATM might require the validation of a fingerprint before it dispenses cash. The user's fingerprint would be optically captured, digitalized and then matched to the digitalized fingerprint stored in his own personal smart card.

22.6 Pen computing

Pen computing refers to the automatic identification of handwritten characters and signatures. The principle of pen computing is that the data

FUTURE TRENDS AND DEVELOPMENTS 229

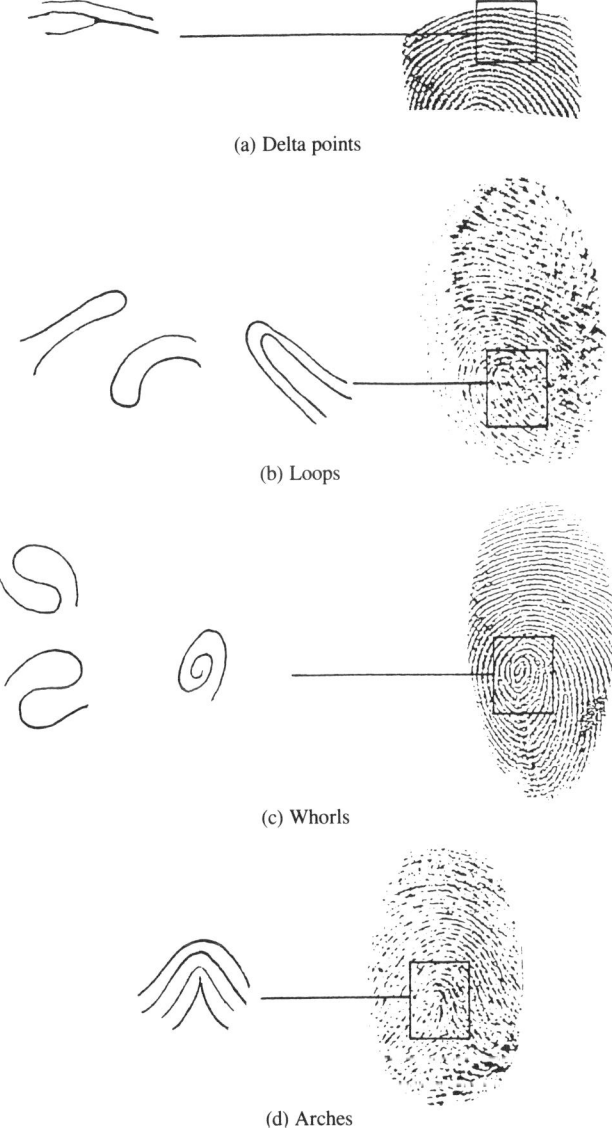

Figure 22.4 Recognition features of fingerprints: (a) delta points, (b) loops, (c) whorls, (d) arches. Courtesy of Electronic Engineering Group, Department of Physics, Keele University

collector and data collection process should closely represent the traditional use of paper and pen. Portable data terminals have already been developed

230 AUTOMATIC IDENTIFICATION AND DATA COLLECTION SYSTEMS

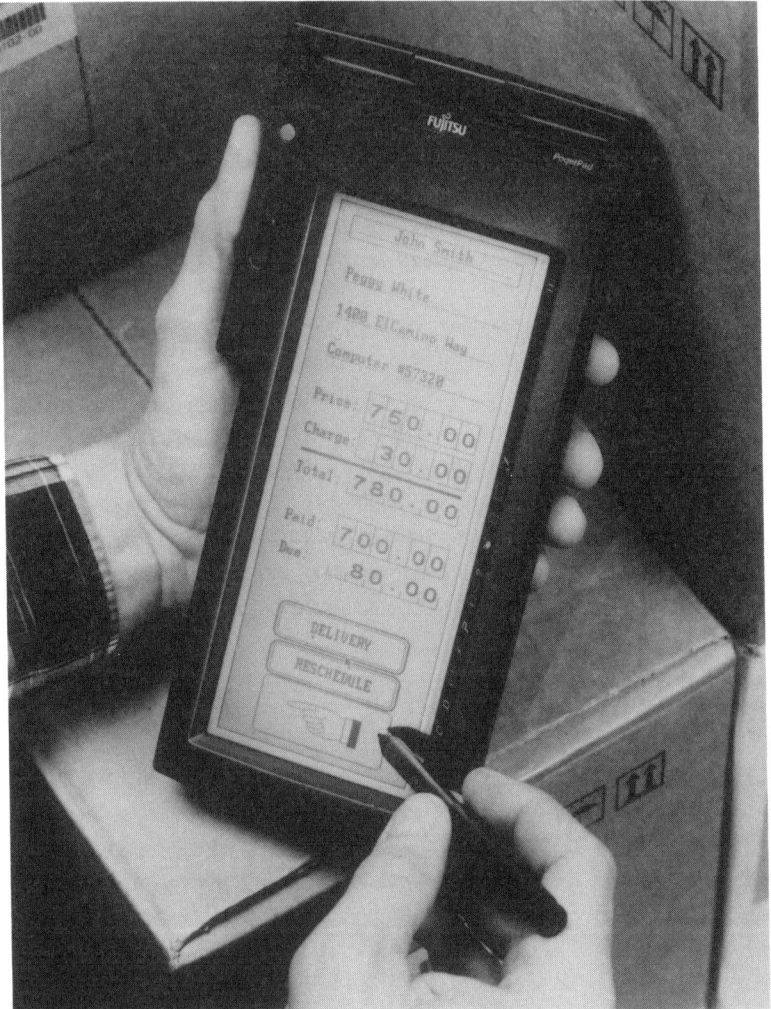

Figure 22.5 Pen computer: Poqetpad. Courtesy Fijitsu Personal Systems

as pen computers. These terminals are characterized by their large screens and are supplied with special pens (Figure 22.5). The terminal's user interface is an electronic form (the interface also makes use of menus, graphics, and more). All the user has to do is fill out a form in the traditional way.

Handwritten character recognition has not as yet reached a level of 100 per cent accuracy. In order to achieve a reasonable level of accuracy, restriction of both the character set and the screen location where data is actually entered is practised. The end-user has also to learn to print characters in a fashion that will be recognized by the system. Yet one can design very effective data collection applications with pen computing data collectors if the application integrates a number of auto-ID technologies, each technology being implemented for its most suitable use. For instance in receiving shipments the data collector can receive in advance the shipment details via data communications. The shipment code can be verified via a bar code, and the lines in the delivery note in the terminal's memory can be confirmed via a simple tick alongside each line. At the end of the process the user can sign on the paper and the electronic delivery note. 'Checklist' applications are a natural use of pen computing. Pen computing will no doubt eventually be at the forefront of attended data collection applications.

22.7 From hardware to hardwear

In Chapter 10 we discussed some hardware variations of the portable data terminal. One of these included the integration of a bar code reader as part of the terminal itself, a 'one-hand solution' to portable data collection and bar code reading. Even a 'one-hand solution' can, in certain circumstances, be cumbersome, especially if we remember that the portable data terminal is typically used while physical transactions such as the movement of inventory are being undertaken. Recently a number of companies have introduced new hardware that is worn by the user in the field. The former's solution consists of a bar code scanner strapped to the back of the hand, and a screen and keyboard that are worn on the forearm, all of them connected to a DOS-run portable data terminal worn on the waist (Figure 22.6). In this fashion the user can handle materials without having to put the portable data terminal down or reholster it. As the terminal's screen is

Figure 22.6 Hands-free data collection: Symbol Technologies' ASP 3395. Courtesy Symbol Technologies

mounted on the forearm, it can be viewed comfortably, without the user having to flip it up after reading a bar code in order to see the collected data. The laser is activated when a finger is pointed at a bar code label; this activates a special trigger that emits the laser beam.

Metrologic's *Scanglove* is a back-hand-mounted laser reader worn as a glove. This device is triggerless: an infrared sensor senses the presence of an object in close proximity before emitting the laser beam.

Both of these configurations provide an ergonomic solution for mobile data collection.

22.8 Conclusion

There is perhaps no limit to the possible implementation of auto-ID technologies and data collection devices, other than one's imagination. And it is imagination that is so greatly needed in order to advance further both in this field and in other areas of information technology. Many of the latest developments in this field have been initiated by end-users, system integrators and other individuals and bodies, rather than by the vendors themselves. It is they who have been able to define for the vendors the data collection problems and even to suggest possible solutions. What is clear from the efforts of the last few years is that auto-ID and data collection technological advancement will continue as long as this partnership does.

Bibliography

Ames, Ron, 'Radio-frequency identification (RF/ID) systems', *Scan-Tech Conference Proceedings*, session 2C, AIM USA, 1989.

Baldwin, Philip, 'Automotive vehicle identification at GM's Buick City', *Scan-Tech Conference Proceedings*, session 8B, AIM USA, 1989.

Bartee, Thomas C., *Digital Computer Fundamentals*, 6th edn. McGraw-Hill, New York, USA, 1986.

Bedworth, David D., Mark R. Henderson and Philip M. Wolfe, *Computer Integrated Design and Manufacturing*. McGraw-Hill, New York, USA, 1991.

Belliveau, Daniel A., '*Voice system passes inspection*', *Automatic I.D. News*, October 1988.

Berge, Paul, *IATA and Automatic Identification Standards for the Airlines*. Bar Code Symbologies, Standards and Technology Updates, AIM UK, 1987.

Black, Uyless D., *Data Communications and Distributed Networks*, 2nd edn. Prentice-Hall, Englewood Cliffs, New Jersey, USA, 1987.

Braun, Jerry, 'Quick response', *Scan-Tech Conference Proceedings*, AIM Europe, 1989.

Bright, Roy, *Smart Cards: Principles, Practice and Applications*, Ellis Horwood, Chichester, 1988.

Collins, David Jarrett and Nancy Natsui Whipple, *Using Bar Code – Why It's Taking Over*, Data Capture Institute, Duxbury, Mass., USA, 1990.

'*Data Code – The Global Symbology . . . Naturally*, ID Matrix'. International Data Matrix Inc.

Datamyte Handbook, *A Practical Guide to Computerized Data Collection for Statistical Process Control*, 3rd edn, Datamyte Corporation, Minnetonka, Minnesota, USA, 1987.

Dick, Donald F., 'An application of OCR in the mailing industry', *Scan-Tech '91 Proceedings*, session 2D – OCR, AIM USA, 1991.

Dorrance, Frank, 'Automatic vehicle identification and radio frequency identification in the transportation industry', *Scan-Tech '91 Proceedings*, session 6D – RFID applications, AIM USA, 1991.

Dyer, Stuart M., 'The basics of radio frequency (RF) data communications', *Scan-Tech '91 Proceedings* – session 2B/3F, AIM USA, 1991.

Evans, Stuart, 'Radio frequency (RF) coded tag systems', *Scan-Tech Conference Proceedings*, book 1, AIM Europe, 1988.

Farrell, Richard, 'Applications for two dimensional symbologies', *Scan-Tech '91 Proceedings*, session 12C, AIM USA, 1991.

Goukler, Barry, 'OCR – an alternative data entry method', *Scan-Tech Conference Proceedings*, book 1, AIM Europe, 1988.

Harmon, Craig K. and Russ Adams, *Reading Between the Lines – An Introduction to Bar Code Technology*, Helmers Publishing Inc., Peterborough, New Hampshire, USA, 1989.

Hemphill, Denton, 'Saturn paint quality inspection by voice', *Scan-Tech Conference Proceedings 1991*, session 7C, AIM USA, 1991.

Itkin, Stuart and Josephine Martell, *A PDF Primer – A Guide to Understanding Second Generation Bar Codes and Portable Data Files*, Symbol Technologies Inc., Bohemia, N.Y., USA, 1992.

Jeffries, Frank, *RFDC Technology and Systems Considerations*, Symbol Technologies Inc., Bohemia, N.Y., USA, 1990.

Keats, J. Bert and Douglas C. Montgomery (eds), *Statistical Process Control in Manufacturing*, Marcel Dekker Inc., New York, USA, 1991.

Keith, Matthew, 'Issues in the design of radio frequency identification' (RF/ID) applications', *Scan-Tech '91 Proceedings*, session 6D, AIM USA, 1991.

Marriot, Mark, *International Bar Code Standards*, Bar Code Symbologies, Standards and Technology Updates, AIM UK, 1987.

Marriot, Mark, 'Quick response – an overview', *Scan-Tech Conference Proceedings*, AIM Europe, 1989.

Morand, Giorgio, 'Magnetic stripes', *Scan-Tech Europe*, book 2, AIM Europe, 1987.

Naujokas, Joseph A., 'Introduction to magnetic stripes. Twenty years of development', *Scan-Tech Conference Proceedings*, AIM USA, 1989.

Naylor, P. 'Automatic inspection systems using machine technology', *Scan-Tech Conference Proceedings*, AIM UK, 1988.

Palmer, Roger C., 'The basics of automatic identification', *Scan-Tech Conference Proceedings*, session 1 – Basic Auto-ID, AIM USA, 1989.

Palmer, Roger C., *The Bar Code Book – Reading, Printing and Specification of Bar Code Symbols*, Helmers Publishing Inc., Peterborough, New Hampshire, USA, 1989.

Palmer, Roger C., 'High density symbologies', *Scan-Tech '91 Proceedings*, session 3D, AIM USA, 1991.

Patel, Vijay and A. Furness, 'Automatic fingerprint recognition – an introduction', *Scan-Tech '91 Proceedings*, session L, AIM UK, 1991.

PC Soft International Ltd, *Wizcon/2 User Manual*, version 1.1, Tel Aviv, Israel, 1992.

Peat, Kim, *Bar Coding – Its Application within the Motor Industry*. Bar Code Symbologies, Standards and Technology Updates, AIM UK, 1987.

Plimmer, Jeremy, 'Optical character recognition', *Scan-Tech Conference Proceedings*, book 1, AIM Europe, 1989.

Quail, Douglas, 'RF/ID in transportation', *ID Systems*, May 1992.
Quinn, Paul, 'Auto ID goes out on a limb', ID Systems, September 1992.
Radio Frequency Identification, AIM USA, Pittsburgh, PA., 1987.
Richter, Werner, 'New trends in auto ID technologies: automatic character recognition and voice recognition', *Advanced Update on Non Bar Code Technologies*, book 2, AIM Europe, 1987.
Robertson, John, 'Vision based automatic identification', *Scan-Tech Conference Proceedings*, session 2D, AIM USA, 1989.
Sheppard, Joseph J., 'Magnetic stripe technology: equipment', *Scan-Tech Conference Proceedings*, AIM USA, 1989.
Sheppard, Joseph J., 'Magnetic stripe technology software-hardware-media', *Scan-Tech '91 Proceedings*, session 5E, AIM USA, 1991.
Singleton, Marcel R., 'How to evaluate industrial OCR applications, software systems, and suppliers', *Scan-Tech '91 Proceedings*, session 2D – OCR, AIM USA, 1991.
Sloan, Bruce P., 'Current hospital state of the art technology: moving toward full utilization of HIBCC standards', *Scan-Tech Conference Proceedings*, session 7E, AIM USA, 1991.
Smedt, Emiel De,'Quick response', *Scan-Tech Conference Proceedings*, AIM Europe, 1989.
Smith, Graham M., 'Milk analysis: the impact of barcode technology on high-volume testing', *Scan-Tech '88 Proceedings*, book 5, AIM UK, 1988.
Teunon, Ian, 'RF tagging: technologies, applications and benefits', *Scan-Tech Conference Proceedings*, session book 5, AIM UK, 1989.
van Riel, Peter J. H., 'Patient identification with barcode creates better care at lower costs', *Scan-Tech Conference Proceedings*, session 7, AIM Europe, 1989.
Warnock, Ian G., *Programmable Controllers – Operation and Application*, Prentice-Hall, 1988.
Weatherall, Alan, *Computer Integrated Manufacturing: from Fundamentals to Implementation*, Butterworths, London, 1988.
Webb, John W., *Programmable Controllers – Principles and Applications*, Merrill, Columbus, USA, 1988.
Weiland, Norman R., '2-D symbologies – application considerations', *Scan-Tech '91 Proceedings*, session 3D, AIM USA, 1991.
Zenko, Wence, 'Spread spectrum radio for indoor wireless networks', *Scan-Tech '91 Proceedings*, session 8A, AIM USA, 1991.

Index

Access control, 127, 128–129, 137, 227, 228
  event tracking, 129, 140
  integrated access control, 129, 138–140
  people tracking, 129, 139
  physical connection, 139
  special features of, 139
Access time, 20, 35, 195
Agriculture, 167–169, 181–182
  automatic identification of animals, 167, 168
  battery farms, 167, 168–169
  insemination and cattle breeding, 167–168
  milk analysis, 167, 168
Ambient light, 38, 91, 96
American National Standards Institute (ANSI), 27, 94, 99
Article Numbering Association, 67, 99
Automatic identification:
  biometric, 222, 228
  components of, 16
  environmental flexibility, 20
  future trends, 221–223
  guidelines for choosing, 17
  integration, 223
  methods of encodation, 19
  of animals, 167, 168
  programmability, 19
  updating, 17–18
  reading, 19
  use of devices, 8
Automatic Identification Manufacturers (AIM), 94, 95, 99, 178
Automatic Vehicle Identification (AVI), 148–149, 156, 169, 171–172
Aviation, 172–173
  baggage handling, 172–173
  security, 173

Backplane, 105
Bar code, 9, 13, 17, 18, 19, 20–21, 36, 50, 55–100, 108, 123, 127, 128, 136, 137, 144, 151, 153, 154, 155, 157, 158, 161, 164, 165, 167, 168, 169, 172, 182, 189, 196, 211, 222, 223, 227, 231
  access to, 91–92
  bar width growth, 75, 77, 94, 95, 96
  bar width measurements, 94–95
  bar width reduction, 77, 95
  character set, 55–56, 64, 69, 72, 73, 83, 84, 85, 214, 226
  check digit, 64, 67, 69, 72, 157
  choosing your symbology, 214–215
  codabar, 73, 212
  codablock, 225
  code 1, 225
  code 16, 212, 225
  code 39, 56, 59, 64, 69–70, 94, 97, 99, 100, 135
  code 49, 212, 225
  code 128, 70, 72, 73, 99, 100, 214
  colours, 61, 213
  comparison to other auto-ID technologies, 20, 21, 24–25
  contrast, 37, 61, 94–95, 97, 99, 226
  country code, 69
  Cryptocode, 225
  data capacity, 21, 224, 226
  data code, 224–225, 226
  data density, 21, 59, 60, 75, 79, 80, 81, 212, 224
  data identifiers, 65, 73
  data security, 18, 21
  discrete symbology, 56, 69, 73, 76, 212
  EAN 13, 17, 56, 58, 67–68, 69, 99, 202
  fixed-length symbologies, 56, 66, 214
  full ASCII symbology, 56
  idencode, 225

238 INDEX

Bar code (*continued*)
  in agriculture, 167–169, 181–182
  in aviation, 172–173
  in hospitals, 164–166
  in libraries, 173
  in parcel and file tracking, 161–162
  in retail, 157–159
  intercharacter gap, 56, 60, 69, 70
  interleaved 2 of 5, 64, 66, 70–72, 100, 214
  in warehouse management, 153–156, 181, 186, 189
  linear bar codes, 21, 68
  materials, 61–63
  matrix symbologies, 224, 225, 226
  maximum bar reflectance, 95, 97
  minimum reflectance difference, 95, 96, 97
  minimum space reflectance, 95, 97
  MLC-2D, 225
  module, 56, 59, 68, 70, 72, 73
  modulo 43, 64
  n,k code, 56
  non-self-checking, 64
  plessy bar, 212
  print contrast signal, 92, 95, 96, 97, 216
  quality analysis, 93–100
  quality assurance, 93–100
  quiet zone, 58–59, 60, 64, 86, 97
  PDF 417, 225, 226
  printing, 21, 59, 64, 74–82, 214
  reading, 21, 83–92
  reflectance, 94–95
  reliability, 62–64, 214, 222
  resolution, 59–60, 75, 84, 86, 94, 95, 98, 212, 213, 215
  scanners, 50, 55, 64, 81, 83–92
  self-checking, 64, 68, 70, 72, 73
  softstrip, 224, 225
  stacked symbologies, 225
  standards, 17, 21, 27, 69, 94, 99–100, 135, 214, 215
  structure, 58–59
  supplementary code, 69
  symbologies, 55–59, 63, 64, 67–73, 76, 85, 93, 94, 99, 213
  UPC, 17, 56, 58, 67–68, 69, 99
  Upscode, 225
  Vericode, 224, 226
  verification, 93–100
  verifyer, 94, 95
  wide/narrow ratio, 60, 70, 94, 95
  X dimension, 55, 58, 60, 68, 73, 75, 79, 84, 85, 94, 97, 98, 212, 213, 215
  zero-suppressed, 67
Basic input output system (BIOS), 116–117
Biometric identification, 222
  fingerprints, 223, 228
  retinal, 223
Bit map, 22

CCD array camera and line camera, 225
  for machine vision, 36
  for OCR, 23, 164
  in direct mailing, 164
Charged coupled device (CCD), 88, 91
Computerized integrated manufacturing (CIM), 40–41, 103
Computerized time and attendance and shop floor terminals, 12–13, 28, 117, 121–129, 136, 137, 143, 144
  application software, 123–126
  communications interface, 123–126
  data erasure, 123
  functional differences, 12, 121
  hardware configuration, 121–123
  input check table, 125
  input/output devices, 122, 126
  keyboard, 122, 123, 124, 126
  learning mode, 126
  lookup table, 125, 128
  master table, 125–126
  memory types, 121–122
  message table, 125
  output files, 127
  program generator, 123, 125
  programming methods, 124–126
  screen, 122
  terminal activation, 123
  terminal communication tracking, 124
  use of data, 12
  user interface, 124
Convincing others, 182–184
Crowd control, 137
  on-line solution, 137
  reasons for, 137
Customer order status, 4, 12, 128, 142, 143, 146, 149

Data capacity, 18, 21, 27, 30, 32, 35, 221, 224, 226, 228

Data collection:
  bottlenecks, 191, 206
  definition, 3, 13, 130
  distinction from auto-ID, 7–8
  event triggered, 9, 151
  from automated processes, 6, 7, 121, 143, 146–149, 186, 199
  from the factory floor, 4, 12, 126, 128, 138, 141–156
  future trends, 223–224
  reasons to automate, 4–7
  redundancy, 191
Data collector:
  components of, 7, 13, 130
  definition of, 7
  features of, 7
  in quality control, 150
  SPC/SQC, 130–131, 150–153
  specialized, 132
Data density, 18, 21, 24, 59–60, 212, 221, 224, 228
Data entry, 3, 4, 8
Datahighway, 110
Data restoration, 19, 21, 25, 222
Data security, 18, 19, 21, 25, 29, 30
Data structures, 51, 69, 193, 200–203, 205
  appended file, 201, 202
  control file, 146, 200–201
  data group identifiers, 202
  memory files, 201–203
  translation tables, 64, 200, 201, 202
  update file, 202
Direct mailing, 162–164
  and OCR, 164
  human monitoring, 162
  inserters, 162

Economic justification, 185–187
EEprom, 116
Electronic data interchange (EDI), 4, 48–52, 226
  advantages of, 51–52
  ANSI X12, 51
  clearing house, 51
  communication connection, 51
  communication protocol, 51
  components of, 50–51
  EDIFACT, 51
  example of, 48–50
  message translator, 51
  standard formats, 51
  value added network (VAN), 51
  X425, 51
Entity type, 15, 18
Eprom, 116, 122
Establishing a budget, 185–186

Field service systems, 160
Firmware, 138, 194
First read rate (FRR), 16, 17, 21, 24, 90, 91, 92, 93
Fixed beam scanner, 86

Gathering information, 177–178
Guard patrols, 135–137
  batch systems, 136–137
  system requirements, 136

Handwriting recognition, 223, 224, 228–231
Health Industry Business Communication Council (HIBCC), 100
Hospitals, 164–166
  blood banks, 73, 164–165
  laboratory sample testing, 164, 165, 166
  patient identification, 164
  ward drug replenishment, 164, 165

Identification, 15, 56
  biometric, 222–223
  goals of, 15
  importance of, 16
ID Expo, 178
Implementation and integration pitfalls, 205–207
Industrial standards, 17, 21, 27, 29, 51, 69, 88, 94, 99–100, 135, 177, 194, 214, 215
Initial feasibility checks, 181–182
Interfacing, 40–52, 180, 183, 191, 195, 203, 204, 205, 206, 207
  auto-ID readers, 41–43, 55, 85, 107, 119, 126, 161, 194, 207, 224
  batch, 43, 136, 182, 198, 199
  cable types, 109, 139
  communication driver, 112
  communication protocol, 45, 51, 46–48, 51, 109, 198, 209
  configuration possibilities, 43–44, 109–110, 194

Interfacing (*continued*)
  control characters, 45
  current loop, 110
  CSMA, 46
  data integrity, 44
  data transmission policy, 123, 198, 210
  frequency, 46
  handshaking, 45
  hardware, 192
  interface design, 193, 194, 198–199
  keyboard emulation, 41–43, 207
  line definition, 123
  multidrop, 44, 110, 139
  multiplexer, 44, 110
  networks, 110
  on-line, 43, 199
  optical coupler, 118
  physical link, 109, 139
  polling, 46
  radio frequency data
    communications, 7, 41, 43, 45–48,
    136, 137, 151, 153, 154, 159, 180,
    199, 223
  real time, 43, 199
  RS 232, 42, 43, 46, 109, 110, 117, 118,
    122, 139
  RS 422/485, 43, 46, 47, 110, 139
  serial communications, 9, 41, 42, 43,
    103, 105, 109, 117, 122, 129, 138,
    139
  simultaneous transmission, 105, 110,
    118, 123, 198
  software, 192
  specification, 192, 193
  speed, 45, 47, 109, 198, 207
  spread spectrum transmission (SST),
    46
  software wedge, 42
  terminal communications tracking,
    124, 198
  terminal emulation, 183, 207
  topology, 109–110
  virtual PLC interface (VPI), 112
International Air Transport Authority
  (IATA), 100

Just-in-time (JIT), 4, 48, 51, 143, 156

Labels, 7, 50, 59, 61–63, 74, 75, 80, 81,
  85, 90, 91, 92, 93, 95, 96, 135, 153,
  154, 158, 161, 164, 165, 168, 169,
  172, 173, 183, 189, 211, 212, 215,
  216, 217, 232
  adhesives, 62–63, 80, 135
  chemicals, 62, 216
  choosing a label, 216
  components of, 61–62
  condensation and humidity, 216
  direct sunlight, 216
  dust, 216
  facestock (*see* Substrate)
  laminate, 62
  lifespan, 62, 216
  rubbing, 216
  specialized, 75
  substrate, 61–63, 76, 77, 78, 79, 80,
    81, 82, 95, 96, 97, 99, 153, 154, 157,
    164, 168, 169, 172
  surface coating (*see* Laminate)
  temperatures, 63, 216
Laser technology, 9, 88–90, 94, 119, 171,
  173, 196
  beam pattern, 88, 91, 213, 214, 225
  categories, 88
  fixed-mount, 88, 90, 172
  fixed-mount implementation, 90
  hand-held, 88, 90, 98, 173, 232
  helium–neon, 90
  infrared, 81, 85, 90, 211, 213
  laser light source, 88, 90
  omnidirectional scanning, 91, 213
  readers (scanners), 50, 55, 64, 81, 83–
    92, 88, 90
  visible light diode, 90
Libraries, 73, 173
Licence plates, 18
Light pen (*see* Wands)
Logistic Applications of Automated
  Marking and Reading
  (LOGMARS), 100, 135

Machine vision (*see* Vision systems)
Magnetic ink character recognition
  (MICR), 17, 25
  data security, 19
Magnetic stripe, 12, 13, 17, 20, 25–29,
  30, 32, 34, 42, 86, 119, 126, 127,
  128, 136, 138, 144, 157, 173, 174,
  222, 227
  5-bit BCD, 27
  ALPHA 7-bit, 27
  ANSI/ISO BCD, 27

biphase encodation, 26
bit cell, 26
coercivity, 27, 28
data capacity, 27
data density, 26, 27
data security, 29
drawbacks, 27–28
electromagnetic reciprocity, 26
encodation, 25–26
flux reversals, 25–27
jitters, 28
materials, 29
reader types, 28–29
reading, 26, 28
reliability, 28
solenoid, 25, 139
track locations, 20, 27
Man–machine interface (MMI), 103, 110
Manufacturing Automation Protocol (MAP), 110
Marketing systems, 159–160
presale, 159
vansale, 114, 159–160
Memory card, 17, 32
comparison to other auto-ID technologies, 32
data appending, 17
Memory disk, 118
Microswitches, 122, 138

Optical character recognition (OCR), 16, 22–25, 36
comparison with bar codes, 19, 24–25
data security, 19
decoding methods, 24, 37, 222
fonts, 22, 222
in direct mailing systems, 164
in retail, 157
ink and media, 23–24
reader types, 23
Optical coupler, 18
Organisation for Data Exchange by Telecommunications in Europe (ODETTE), 99, 215

Parcel and file tracking systems, 15, 16, 115–116, 161–162
batch solution, 161
information required, 161
on-line solution, 161

real time, 161–162
Pen computing, 228–231
Percentage decode, 94
Personal identification, 15, 16
Personal identification number (PIN), 12, 18, 30, 128, 129, 137, 138, 139, 140
Photodiodes, 83, 84, 88
Portable data files, 18, 30
Portable data terminals, 10–12, 14, 50, 103, 114–120, 124, 129, 135, 137, 187, 224, 229
auto-ID interfaces, 12, 119
communication interface, 117–118
communications cradle, 118
comparative framework, 114–119
components of, 10
development languages, 117, 196
displays, 10, 12, 114–115, 229, 230, 231, 232
distinction from PLC, 10
durability, 118–119, 135
hands-free solution, 224, 231–232
keyboards, 10, 12, 115, 224, 231
in agriculture, 167, 168, 169
in crowd control, 137
in field service systems, 160
in guard patrol, 137
in hospitals, 165
in marketing systems, 159–160
in parcel and file tracking, 161–162
in pen computing, 229
in retail, 158–159
in transportation, 169–171
in warehouse management, 153–156, 186
memory, 10, 115–116, 118, 120
operating systems, 116–117
PC-compatability, 116–117
processors, 10, 116–117
radio frequency terminals, 10
software design considerations, 119–120, 196
Printing bar codes, 59, 64, 74–82, 214
anilox drum, 78
blanket drum, 78
common production mistakes, 97–99
continuous deflected, 82
cost, 75
dimensional (printing), tolerance, 94, 96, 213

Printing bar codes (*continued*)
  direct thermal printing, 80–81, 96, 211
  doctor blade, 78
  film master, 76, 88, 93, 95, 96
  flexography, 77–78
  fountain drum, 78
  framework for analysing printing techniques, 75–76
  impact dot matrix, 21, 80, 96
  impression drum, 78
  inorganic, 81
  inkjet, 82
  interdependence, 211
  in warehouses, 152–154
  ion deposition, 78–79
  ladders, 213, 215
  laser, 78–79
  letterpress, 77–78, 212
  lifespan, 76, 81
  line printer, 80
  magnetography, 78–79
  numbering wheel, 78
  offset lithography, 77–78
  off-site, 21, 74, 75, 78, 80
  on-site, 21, 74, 75, 78, 79
  organic, 80
  photographic composition, 79–80
  print log, 215
  printer emulation, 215–216
  printing defects, 94–95
  rotogravure, 77–78
  serial printers, 80, 81
  software, 215
  speed, 76, 78, 79
  thermal transfer, 62, 81, 96
  toner, 75, 78, 79
  toner printing methods, 78–79
  wet-ink methods, 21, 76, 77–78, 93, 96
  where to print, 74–75
  xerography, 78–79
Production time management, 143
  definition, 143
  idle time, 145
  personal time task, 145
  validity checks, 145–146
Programmable controllers, 6, 8–9, 14, 103–113, 122, 124, 138, 146–148, 150, 151, 199, 223, 226
  actuation, 107
  analog input, 10, 105, 106
  as a data collector, 9, 103, 104–109
  as part of a SCADA system, 9
  components of, 105
  discrete input, 9, 105, 106
  distinguishing features, 10, 105, 117
  drum controller, 108
  interfacing, 9, 105, 106–107, 109
  modular design, 105–106
  networking, 110
  PID unit, 105, 107
  traditional role of, 8, 103
  virtual PLC interface, 112

Quality analysis, of bar codes, 75, 93–100
  analytical methods, 95–97
  basic parameters, 94–95
  calibration, 96
  verifiers, 94, 95, 96
Quality control, 7, 103, 104, 112, 143, 149–153
Quality information, xiii, 185, 189
Quick response, 4, 48, 51

Radio frequency data communications, 7, 10, 41, 43, 45–48, 136, 137, 151, 154, 159, 180, 199, 223
  accuracy, 47
  approval, 48
  base station, 45–46, 47
  components of, 45–48
  CSMA, 46
  in retail, 158–159
  insulation, 47
  microcells, 47
  network controller, 45
  performance parameters, 47
  polling, 46
  radio frequency communications protocol, 46
  radio frequency unit, 45, 47
  range, 47
  repeaters, 47
  response time, 47
  speed, 47
  spread spectrum transmission, 46
  system configuration, 47
  throughput, 47
  turn around time, 47
Random access memory (RAM), 10, 105, 108, 115–116, 117, 209

non-volatile, 115
volatile, 116, 121, 122
write protected, 116
Reading bar codes, 68, 83–92, 161, 162, 232
   bar height, 213, 214
   bi-directional reading, 68, 70
   contact scanning, 21, 86, 91, 92, 93, 98
   conveyance speed, 213, 214
   depth of field, 85, 86, 88, 90, 221
   devices, 83–92
   in libraries, 173
   influences on, 91–92
   interdependence, 211
   near contact reader, 88, 91
   resolution, 84, 86, 212
   scanners (and readers), 50, 55, 64, 81, 83–92
   scan pattern, 213, 214
   scan rate, 213, 214
   tilt, 213
   unattended reading, 213, 214
Relays, 122
Request for proposal, 193, 203–204
Retail applications, 157–159
   point of sale, 157, 158, 159
   price look-up, 157, 158, 201
   replenishment, 157
   shelf price auditing, 158–159
RF tags, 18, 29, 32–36, 40, 119, 136, 137, 206, 221, 222, 224, 226, 227
   access time, 35
   active tags, 34, 35
   approval, 35
   choice of system, 35
   comparison to other auto-ID technologies, 34
   components of, 33
   data capacity, 35
   encoding, 33–34, 36
   frequencies, 34–35
   implementation, 34–35
   in automatic identification of animals, 168
   in carplants, 148–149, 156
   in just-in-time, 156
   in parking control, 171
   in toll automation, 172
   in traffic monitoring, 171
   inductive tags, 36

interrogator, 33, 34, 35, 138, 168–171, 208, 222
passive tag, 34
radio frequency unit, 33
range, 35, 171, 206
read only, 33
read/write, 34
spacial directivity, 36, 171
Read only memory (ROM), 105, 116, 123, 138

Sample rate, 113, 147, 149, 150
   event triggered, 9, 151
   periodic sampling, 151
Scanning bar codes (*see* Reading bar codes)
Scan Tech, 178
Scan time:
   of bar code reader, 196, 214
   of PLC, 106
Sensors, 12, 106–107, 108, 147, 173, 232
Sequential validation, 6
Signature recognition, 223, 224, 227–228
Sinet, 110
Site surveys, 178–180, 210
Slot reader, 86, 127
Smart card, 19, 20, 29–32, 40, 222, 228
   advantages of, 30–32
   basic smart card, 29
   comparison to other auto-ID technologies, 30, 32
   components of, 29–30
   data capacity, 30, 221
   data security, 19, 30
   IC card, 29
   in parking control, 169, 170–171
   keyboard and screen, 30
   memory division, 30
   reading devices, 30
   update ability, 30
SPC/SQC, 130, 142, 149, 150, 151, 152
Substitution error rate, 16, 17, 21, 23, 24, 63, 91, 92, 208, 222
Supervisory control and data acquisition (SCADA), 9, 110–113, 138, 140, 146–148, 150, 199
   annunciator, 113, 151
   communications driver, 112
   compound gate, 112
   data logger, 110

Supervisory control (*continued*)
  elements of, 111–113
  gates, 112
  multitasking, 113
  pushblocks, 112
  recipes, 147
  virtual PLC interface (VPI), 112
  Wizcon, 111–113
Symbologies, 55–59, 63, 64, 67–73, 76, 85, 93, 94, 99, 135, 213
  array symbologies, 224, 225
  basic structure, 58–59
  character set, 55–56, 64, 69, 72, 73, 83, 84, 85, 214, 226
  characteristics, 55–59
  check digit, 64, 67, 69, 72, 157
  choosing your symbology, 214–215
  clusters, 225
  continuous symbologies, 56, 70, 72, 76, 95, 212
  control characters, 58, 59–60, 72
  codabar, 73, 212
  codablock, 225
  code 1, 225
  code 16, 212, 225
  code 39, 56, 59, 64, 69–70, 94, 97, 99, 100, 135
  code 49, 212, 225
  code 128, 70, 72, 73, 99, 100, 214
  continuous symbology, 56, 70, 72, 76, 95, 212
  country code, 69
  Cryptocode, 225
  data code, 224–225, 226
  definition, 56
  EAN 13, 17, 56, 58, 67–68, 69, 99, 202
  edge to similar edge, 84, 95
  fixed length symbologies, 56, 66, 214
  full ASCII symbologies, 56
  Idencode, 225
  interdependence, 211–212
  interleaved 2 of 5, 64, 66, 70–72, 100, 214
  matrix symbologies, 224, 225, 226
  MLC-2D, 225
  module, 56, 59, 68, 70, 72, 73
  n,k code, 56
  non-self-checking, 64
  parities, 68, 69, 72, 209, 214
  PDF 417, 225, 226
  plessy bar, 212
  principal symbologies, 67–73
  public domain, 225
  quiet zone, 58–59, 60, 64, 86, 97
  self-checking, 64, 68, 70, 72, 73
  softstrip, 224, 225
  stacked symbologies, 225
  supplementary code, 69
  t distance, 84
  two-dimensional bar codes, 21, 221, 222, 224–227
  UPC, 17, 56, 58, 67–68, 69, 99
  Upscode, 225
  variable length symbology, 56, 71
  Vericode, 224, 226
  X dimension, 55, 58, 60, 68, 73, 75, 79, 84, 85, 94, 97, 98, 212, 213, 215
  zero-suppressed, 67
Symbol technologies, 90
System boundaries, 189
System objectives, 185
System reliability, 208–209
  corrupted data, 208, 209
  lost data, 209–210
System specification, 191, 192, 193–203
  hardware, 193–195
  interface, 193, 194, 198–199
  software, 193, 195–198

Throughput (of data), 47, 112, 179, 186, 188, 195, 199, 207
  calculating, 189–190
  collecting data on throughput, 190
  data kernels, 189, 190, 191, 210
  definition, 189
Time and attendance, 18, 34, 124, 126–127, 144, 145, 193
  attendance reports, 127
  salaries, 127
  terminals, 121–129
  time event tracking, 127
  work premiums, 127, 128
Total quality management (TQM), 4, 5
Transponder (*see* RF tags)
Transportation, 169–172
  automatic toll collection, 171, 172
  automatic vehicle identification (AVI), 169, 171–172
  parking control, 169–171
  parking lot control, 171
  traffic monitoring, 171
  vehicle tracking, 171

Uniform Code Council (UCC), 99

Vehicle identification number (VIN), 148–149, 171, 223
Vision systems, 23, 36–38, 149, 222
   ambient light, 38
   camera multiplexer, 36
   CCD array and line camera, 36
   comparison to other auto-ID technologies, 36–37
   decoding, 37–38
   digitizer, 36
   feature extraction, 36
   for gauging, 36
   for guiding, 36
   for identification, 36
   for inspection, 36
   image buffer, 36
   item positioning, 38
   mark consistency, 38
   pixels, 37, 38
Voice recognition, 38–39, 151–152, 222, 223, 224, 227
   continuous recognition, 39
   digital voice template, 38
   echoing, 39
   speaker independent, 39
   voice unit, 38, 151

Wand:
   for bar codes, 86, 88, 89, 119
   for OCR, 23
   rules of use, 86
Warehouse management, 143, 153–156
   inventory, 154–156, 186, 189
   picking, 154
   putaway, 154
   storage fragmentation, 154
Watchdog, 105
Wave shaper, 84
Wedge, 41–42, 64, 85
   interface to bar code readers, 42
   interface to magnetic stripe readers, 42
   keyboard types, 42
   postamble, 41
   preamble, 41
Wizcon, 111–113
   compound gates, 112
   gates, 112
   pushblocks, 112
Work in progress, 143, 156
   definition, 143, 146
Working procedures, 180, 181, 197
   analysing 190, 191